Marriott

Marriott

The
J. Willard Marriott
Story

Robert O'Brien

Deseret Book Company
Salt Lake City, Utah
1977

Library of Congress Cataloging in Publication Data

O'Brien, Robert, journalist.
    Marriott : the J. Willard Marriott story.

    Includes index.
    1. Marriott, John Willard, 1900-   2. Hotels,
taverns, etc.—United States—Biography.   3. Food
service—United States—Biography.
TX910.5.M333027   642'.5'0924   [B]   77-17123
ISBN 0-87747-683-7
ISBN 0-87747-682-9 pbk.

Pictured on the back cover are some of the Marriott-owned enterprises. Clockwise, starting at upper right: the Marriott-owned cruise ship Solaris; *pavilion at the Great America theme park; a Hot Shoppe drive-in restaurant; employes of Farrell's Ice Cream Parlor; Marriott In-Flite food-service trucks delivering to airliners; Roy Rogers restaurant; Marriott hotel in Cairo, Egypt; Country Fair gate at the Great America park; one of the popular rides at the Great America park; the Marriott Corporation's headquarters in Washington, D.C.*

Foreword

By Mark Evans Austad

The definition of *friend* that I like best is: "One before whom one can think out loud." For that reason, this is a choice opportunity. You see, Bill Marriott is my best friend. I challenge any man to know another better than I know "Montana" Marriott. I saddled him with this nickname when we were horseback riding twenty years ago—in self-defense he calls me "Wyoming." What makes this ridiculous is that the roots of both of us sprang from a valley in the majestic Wasatch Mountains of northern Utah where our fathers once herded sheep.

Knowing "Montana's" faults as well as his virtues is both a help and a hindrance in writing objectively a foreword to this brilliant account of his productive life.

The late Bing Crosby once answered the question regarding his success, saying, "The average guy hears me sing and feels he can do as well." To know Bill Marriott and realize his immense success makes the average person feel he could have done as well under similar circumstances. The average person also relates to "Montana." For that reason I feel this book can achieve its purpose by inspiring the young and not so young to realize that they too can succeed by emulating the life and principles of this twentieth century Horatio Alger.

Evidencing that he is also very human, Bill is a bundle of contradictions—both gentle and tough; devoutly religious, and yet fun-loving; demanding, yet tolerant; half pessimistic, half optimistic; penurious, yet philanthropic. All he wants of family, employes, and friends is perfection. Though he is a worrier, he knows no fear. He has no use for laziness, dirtiness, dishonesty, social climbing, or wasting time.

In analyzing his eventful three quarters of a century

plus, one cannot but recognize that this is a lot of man, one who can charm male or female any time after the cradle or before the grave. His responsibilities as a youth caused him to mature early. The large family of which he was the kingpin always regarded him as the family leader.

Bill's unswerving devotion to his faith has dominated his life. He has worshiped more in deed, however, than in word, without inflicting his views on others. His true love of God, his Allie, his family, his fellow man, and his country has been the rudder of his life.

Much has been made of his uncanny business judgment accounting for his considerable economic success. In watching him close up, I have concluded that his judgment has often resulted from questioning, probing, challenging, and arguing the judgments of others whose opinions he values before he makes a decision. I don't think he has ever made an off-the-cuff, quick, or easy decision. He labors through them all, resolving most often in what others call his "uncanny" business judgment.

Bill's most ingratiating quality, the one most admired by friends old and new, is his God-given humility (to keep him humble, I often tell him he has much to be humble about). I sometimes feel he thinks his role with his considerable wealth is to act as its steward. I don't think Bill ever thinks of himself as wealthy. Neither do I. To me he is rich in spirit, rich in faith, rich in integrity, and last of all, rich in his pocketbook. A great Mormon leader, David O. McKay, once wisely observed, "No other success in life can compensate for failure in the home." Bill's true worth lies with the love he enjoys in receiving and giving to his devoted wife, his offspring, and even to an old buddy.

To spend countless hours with "Montana," some sad, mostly glad, is something I would have liked to have shared with everyone. Since that isn't possible, the alternative is to know that you and yours can read and enjoy the in-depth story of this uncommon man with the common touch.

To Allie

Chapter One

The weather was warm for a change—deep blue sky after raw, clammy days of Pacific ocean fog and temperatures in the lower sixties. Just yesterday guests who'd brought light summer clothes, anticipating Southern California heat, had shivered and complained. But today, the official opening day of the Los Angeles Marriott, a soft westerly off the sea carried only a fresh, tonic tang as it played among the palms. The morning seemed pleasantly filled with life, color, meetings and encounters, comings and goings of cars, planes, and people, and something else as well: a mounting excitement, a tingling suspense.

The immense inner patio, surrounded on three sides by five tiers of balconies and loomed over on the fourth by a high cliff of eighteen tiers, lay rich and indolent in sunshine and color. On the broad porte cochere of the Century Boulevard entrance workmen arranged the speaker's platform and spectators' chairs. Smooth-skinned, country-fresh girls in red and green uniforms held the front doors open to the welcome flood of sunshine and warmth. Limousines tooled up to be greeted by a Graustarkian doorman in white uniform, scarlet epaulettes, and scarlet-plumed shako. Bellmen trundled handcarts stacked high with Vuiton and Mark Cross luggage toward the elevators. Plaintive-gay music of violins and muted Mexican brass came from somewhere off behind the sunken lounge in the lobby.

Among the daily events for that Thursday, the bulletin board by the front desk listed meetings of the Congress on Evangelization, Southwestern Industries, Xerox Computer Service, Blue Cross of Southern California, IBM, E. F. Hutton & Co., and Sambo's Res-

1

taurants, but not Opening Day of the Los Angeles Marriott.

No matter. It was in the air. The program was all plotted, all programmed, to unveil the sophisticated, expensive, jet-age, last word in hotels of a corporation that had gotten off to a shaky start forty-six years before as young Bill Marriott's hole-in-the-wall root beer stand on Fourteenth Street, N.W., Washington, D.C.

In those days, having anything to do with a hotel like this was, of course, beyond his wildest dreams. Fresh from the open spaces of Utah's sheep and sugar-beet country, launching his venture with a borrowed $1500, another $1500 he had saved, and $3000 put up by a law student-friend, Bill thought he'd be lucky to make it through the summer. But now in 1973, here he was, chairman of the board. There were, to be sure, stockholders. But the corporation was literally his creation—his lifelong poem, his heart's blood masterpiece. His drive and later his dream, his philosophy, the effort he gave and the effort he demanded of others, his concern for people—for nearly half a century these had conditioned and vitalized every policy, every decision, every corporate move.

Ideas became an empire. In this year Marriott sales were up 27 percent, to well over $538 million (to well over $1 billion today); net income was up 22 percent; total number of operating hotels, restaurants, and other units had risen to 570; total number of employes, to 38,700.

On this very day, from San Francisco and Acapulco to the Isles of Greece, Marriott establishments—Hot Shoppes, Big Boy Coffee Shops, Roy Rogers restaurants, specialty and tollroad restaurants, hotel and motor inn restaurants, business, industrial, and institutional cafeterias—were serving meals to nearly half a million customers. In airliners high over five continents and several oceans Marriott's In-Flite feeding services, biggest in the world, were providing meals for another 185,000.

Before the day was over, some 10,000 customers would check into Marriott hotels in the United States, Mexico, and the Caribbean. Marriott's white-hulled Sun Line cruise ships, packed to the boat decks with vacationers and tourists, were cruising the Aegean, steering for Mykonos, Delos, and Rhodes.

And more than this: the company was expanding—exploding. At least $120 million in new construction was in progress. Tens of millions more was on the drawing boards. Top management's sights were trained on retail sales curves that rocketed off the charts and out of sight.

A remarkable story. Everyone who knew about it thought so. Bill himself thought so. Because it proved that something very fundamental about America was still true. Business *had* grown big and complicated. The government might very well *be* a self-inflating bureaucracy. People *were* filling up the country. Growth and technology *had* created a new order of problems that threatened the quality of life. Cynics and malcontents *did* scoff, deride, and tear down.

Nevertheless, the story said, America was still the Promised Land. Even now, with all frontiers gone, with all the odds piling up against the individual, it could be done. You had to believe in yourself. You had to be willing to work—morning, noon, and night, if need be. But you could make it. Bill Marriott did. So could you.

For this hotel, in this city, on this particular sunny Thursday in September 1973, a lot of planning, a lot of work, had gone before. It was all down in reports, minutes of meetings, and contracts in the books of the Marriott Corporation at 5161 River Road, Washington, D.C.

The tax and the real estate battles had been lost, or won, or compromised. Design, construction, and personnel problems had been met and solved. All the conferences were corporate history. The scale models of bedrooms, public rooms, and restaurants that architects and designers had fashioned, like sections of doll houses, in the River Road workshops of the Architecture and Construction Division, the scale model of the hotel it-self—all had been made to materialize life-size: a white, graceful, $52-million Mediterranean palace beside the endless traffic of eight-laned Century Boulevard, hard by the rubber-streaked runways of Los Angeles Interna-tional Airport.

This was the thirty-first in the continental chain of Marriott hotels, and Marriott people were proudly aware that it was their newest, their costliest, and their biggest. Most of them thought it was their best. The best airport hotel in the world, a complex and stunning expression of an extraordinary man and his lifelong passion for careful preparation, for work, for service, for painstaking atten-tion to detail—for perfection.

The way it evolved, from original idea to opening day, is typical of the Bill Marriott method and the refined sum of his nearly fifty years of experience in the restaurant and hotel business.

A full eight years before ground was broken, a Mar-riott-trained research team conducted an in-depth market study and concluded that there was, or would be, a de-mand for a hotel of quality and amenities near the Los Angeles airport, second busiest air terminal in the world. Business would be varied and excellent: eighty-five per-cent occupancy on weekends, seventy percent on week-days. Some would be "escape" business—people spending a weekend away from home in a luxury hotel. Some would be honeymoon business; some "fly-outs," travelers spending the night before enplaning the next day for New York or the Orient or across the Pole to Europe. Some would be tourists, there to visit nearby Hollywood Park, the beaches, the Los Angeles Forum, the fishing village and waterside restaurants of Marina del Rey (where a new Marriott hotel is now being built).

4

The land was high, $7.8 million for 14 acres, and on the site was an aircraft factory. Marriott representatives bought the land and sent in their own construction crews. They dismantled the factory and built the company a new plant in Irvine. Then, late in 1971, they started work on the hotel. When you get breaks from the weather and avoid delays over labor and contract disputes, you push right along. In June 1973, the construction crews moved out, three months ahead of schedule.

Back on River Road that summer, Jim Hazel, one of Marriott's top interior designers, had talked about the new hotel and the opening and how they embodied the Marriott approach: the seven restaurants and lounges; the 124 conference suites and parlors; the 13 spacious meeting and exhibit rooms, each named after a city in which a Marriott hotel is located; El Pequeno Ballroom, which sat 1200 diners, and, across the hall, the Grand Ballroom, which at the same time could seat and feed another 1300—both equipped with built-in audiovisual systems, special high-voltage power lines for movie and television stage sets, climate control, sound control, electrically driven divider walls that swiftly and silently divided each ballroom into six component rooms with separate seating capacities ranging from 130 to 430.

The flexibility, Hazel said, was incredible. You could hold a convention one day, a wedding reception the next, and at the same time handle a dozen meetings, trade exhibits, sales conferences, fashion shows, dog shows, or anything else people came together for.

That was why Marriott people called it "the convention hall with the hotel on top." But like all the others, it still had the distinctive Marriott touches: tables and table lamps in the lobby to give it a living-room look; decor keyed to the region; golds, reds, and oranges to evoke warmth and welcome; and carpets wall-to-wall everywhere. Public room ceilings were high, and corridors were one or two feet wider than almost anyone's. This, Hazel said, was "non-yield" space—space that would never earn a buck for the company.

"It's part of our business 'psych' that others can't understand," he said. "Some of our own people don't understand it. But it makes for a good feeling. It brings people back."

What else? Wall sconces, Italian chandeliers of Vernini glass—a quarter of a million in decorative lighting alone, three million in interior furniture. A touch of counterpoint that Mr. Marriott insisted on in all his hotels—a view, somewhere, of a kitchen; it was there in the Fairfield Inn, the family restaurant with the 24-hour service, and in the Mexican buffet of La Plaza. The front and side exteriors have a huge bed of various ground-covering flowers.

The L.A. Marriott, Hazel said, was, for Marriott, on the grand scale. It was an incredible palace. Had they topped out? Had they gone too far? The marketing people didn't think so. Time would tell.

"But we've gotten very good at this," he concluded. "We not only design, we document. We take pride in finishing not on time—*ahead* of time. Our opening dates are always set dates. We slide up to them and through them. No panics. No last-minute bunglings. Everything smooth, professional, on the ball, like the Oakland Raiders. That's design control. That's the way it'll be in L.A. on September 6th."

Some 700 guests of the Marriott family and more than 150 newspaper people and travel writers from everywhere in the United States had been flown in for the opening, and now at mid-morning were beginning to leave their rooms, balconies, and room-service breakfast trays for the bustling lobby and dazzling sun of the poolside chaise lounges.

None of this nonsense for the corporate brass. They

had been up for hours. They'd had breakfast, been on long-distance phones to the east coast, conferred about last-minute details of the day's busy schedule. Now, this morning of all mornings, there was something else to do. For the past six weeks the more than 900 employes of the hotel had been learning their jobs. Now trial-and-error time was over. The executives wanted a last word with them, a closed-door, locker-room session before the opening kick-off. The big game was about to start.

The meeting took place in one of the new ballrooms. Leaving skeleton crews on duty, the employes came streaming in from all floors, all departments—housekeepers, waitresses, laundry and kitchen workers, bellmen, maintenance men, office staff, all in uniform. They came to listen to the men from the home office back in Washington, D.C.: to Bud Ward, vice-president of organization and development; to Bud Grice, vice-president of marketing; but most of all to Mr. Marriott, "the Chairman," who had parlayed his root beer stand into the multi-, multi-, Marriott millions, a legend among his people from the Potomac west to the Wasatch and south from there to the Superstitions.

Ward, smiling and friendly, spoke as if they were all sitting together in his living room: "We don't have 'this Marriott' and 'that Marriott.' We're *all* Marriott. As you get to know our family, you're going to feel the same way.

"How're we going to put something in your pocket, and something in the corporate pocket? One little word: service. But you've gotta work together. You're part of a big family, and you've got people all over working for you. In our hotels all over the country, Marriott employes are wearing a big blue badge that says, 'The Los Angeles Marriott is Now Open.'

"Thirteen thousand people were interviewed to hire nine hundred and twenty-five. You are a bunch of beautiful people. Stick together. Work together. Have fun together. Marriott believes that the customer is great, but you come first. Mr. Marriott knows that if he takes care of his employes, they'll take care of the customers."

Grice outlined the day's program and introduced the hotel's bosses. He told about the guest reporters and columnists, about the movie stars who would add glitter to the opening banquet and ball. He told about the ribbon-cutting ceremonies. Beginning with Bob Hope, John Wayne, and Mayor Tom Bradley of Los Angeles, he ran down the list of notables who'd be there for the ribbon-cutting or the banquet and ball or both. Then, at last, to a fanfare of superlatives, he introduced the Chairman.

Stooping a little, Bill Marriott gripped the lectern and waited for the applause to die away. Lean and spare of build, just under six feet, thinning sandy hair, blue eyes that closed when he laughed, he was 11 days away from his 73rd birthday. He started off in a dry, folksy voice, in his characteristic country-western style. Then, for the next twenty minutes, he talked to the employes like a father, a brother, a wise and kindly uncle. He said plain, simple, astonishing things—astonishing not because they were so striking and new, but because they were so old and still so valid: affirmations of faith in God and country, in hard work and self-denial and strength of character. Many would consider them naive—cast-off Sunday school aphorisms totally out of touch with today's violent and materialistic world. But Bill Marriott left no doubts in the minds of his listeners about where he stood. These were the truths he lived by. These were the golden rules.

"Well, as I've often said, anybody—almost anybody can't run a hotel unless they have some great people to do it. I think one of the big problems in the hotel industry today, and in many other industries, too, is indifferent employes. You go up to a desk clerk and he growls at you, makes you feel like he's doing you a great service, a great

8

honor, to give you a room—you know? Not that good, old, friendly hospitality.

"So that's one of the problems we have in this business. About all I do now is visit our hotels and restaurants and see our people. But I'd rather do that than anything, because I'm not a desk man. I like to get out and say hello to people, see them smile. I was reared on a ranch, dragged up by the heels. I came up the hard way. I can remember when three of us slept in a bed. And we didn't have too much to eat. It was really rough. I know something about the problems of people who don't have a lot of money.

"Well, anyway, we do need a good attitude. That's what counts. I get a lot of letters from our customers. They don't tell us how beautiful our ballroom was, they tell us how wonderful our people were. They say, 'How'd you get such friendly people?' You know, if you're interested in your job you can do anything. You really can. I've never seen anybody who's interested in a job who couldn't do it well.

"A college education," he continued, "doesn't do much good unless a person gets out and works at something and learns how to do it. You don't need a college education in this business. All you need is just good common sense. We know that we've got to keep our floors clean. When you've got a greasy floor in the kitchen, you're apt to fall down and break a leg, or walk out of the kitchen and track up one of those $20,000 carpets. We have to keep our entire hotel clean, because cleanliness in a hotel, just like in your own home, is so important if we want the customer back. And we know that food has got to taste good, too. You don't want it to be just ordinary stuff, worse'n you get at home. You want it to be better. You've got to make your food pleasing and unusual, so people will say, 'Gosh, isn't this good!'"

Bill talked on, his manner informal yet serious. Faces

upturned, the audience listened attentively. He reminded them of the tough competition in the hotel and restaurant business. He said that like thousands of other Marriott employes, they'd own company stock some day. If they stayed with the company, they could retire well-off. But it was up to them to produce. Neither Marriott nor anyone else could afford to pay two people to do the job of one. Nobody could afford to waste labor any more than he could afford to waste food. And the price of both labor and food was going up. This meant that they'd all have to work a little harder, plan better, think more clearly, use common sense, do a better job.

He said he hoped they'd take good care of themselves. "Have good health. There's nothing like good health. And good health comes through plenty of rest, plenty of sleep, and good habits. If you feel good, you'll treat people right. You'll do a great job, and we'll have a great organization."

He paused for a moment and looked out over the audience, studying the serious faces. The big room was utterly still. There was a strange, palpable communion in the air.

"I'm going to close now," he continued. "We both have work to do. But just remember, I've tried a lot longer than you young people, and I know that sometimes things can get mighty discouraging. We all have worries. We all have sleepless nights, and pain and sorrow in our lives. But you know something? Adversity isn't all bad. It gives us opportunities to grow. And we usually get what we work for.

"While I was selling woolen goods in the lumber camps of northern California, I noticed that there were great tall trees, and right beside them, scrubby trees not worth cutting. It struck me that they were like people. Later, I found a poem that expressed this better than I could, and here's the way it goes:

The tree that never had to fight
For sun and sky and air and light,
But stood out in the open plain
And always got its share of rain,
Never became a forest king,
But lived and died a scrubby thing.

The man who never had to fight
To win his share of sun and sky and air and light
Never became a manly man,
But lived and died as he began.

Good timber does not grow in ease—
The stronger the wind, the tougher the trees.

"That, my young friends, about says it. If we have problems and overcome them, we grow tall in character, and in the qualities that bring success."

He stepped to one side of the lectern and raised his hand in a valedictory wave. "I wish this hotel success, and I wish all of you success. I hope and pray that you'll be the happiest group of people in all Los Angeles."

The young men and women in their work clothes and uniforms filled the big room with applause and smiles. On the platform, Bud Grice, Bud Ward, and the others pressed forward to shake the Chairman's hand.

Chapter Two

The day after the opening was a Friday. Bill and Allie were going to spend that day with Roy Rogers and Dale Evans, driving to their ranch in the San Fernando Valley. Then Allie was returning to Washington. Bill and I were traveling together to Salt Lake City, because if I was going to write anything about him, he said, I'd have to see that town and that valley and the Wasatch Mountains, where he and his Mormon folks came from.

Bill and I had aisle seats on the Air West plane to Salt Lake City. He was one row ahead of me, up against the forward bulkhead.

Bill is gregarious, always talking with strangers, asking questions, finding out something he didn't know before. Next to him was a man with a range-rider's weather-beaten face, probably in his sixties. Even before the "No Smoking" sign flicked off they were at it. They would be talking about either sheep or sugar beets. Bill knows more about both than most of us care to know.

The stewardesses came by with the drink cart. The rancher had a Jack Daniels "and branch." Bill nodded them off and turned to the New York *Times* he'd picked up in the terminal.

As he read on, turning the big pages, he gradually slipped off his loafers. His toes tapped the carpeted floor. The stewardesses came by again, picking up the plastic glasses and the napkins. We'd be there, the pilot said, in another 34 minutes. Like many men who travel a lot, Bill can catnap anytime, anywhere. He folded his paper, tilted his chair back, and closed his eyes. . . .

Slide shots flipped over in my mind. I thought of him in his office, the walnut-paneled office back at Marriott headquarters on River Road, where I'd met him one morning: the fieldstone fireplace and the polished set of longhorns above the mantel. The mounted rattlesnake skins, and the oil painting of a tall dog-tired cowboy holding a saddle by the horn, the painting of a Utah mountain scene in autumn, blue sky, yellow flaming aspen, grizzly bear on all fours, head raised, listening beside a fallen log. The curious miscellany on the mantel—the small bronze statue of Massasoit, the bronze cowboy boot, the bronze buffalo, the color photo, in a gilded frame, of Allie.

On the table beneath the oil painting, the family pictures of Allie and the boys and their wives. On the wall to the left of the fireplace the three copies of oils painted and given to Bill by President Dwight D. Eisenhower. A couple of ship models, the running "JM," Bill's brand, fashioned in the fireplace andirons. The American flag in the corner.

Bill's office is in a low complex of two- and three-story buildings, and I remembered that his windows look out upon a driveway circle, a flagpole flying an American flag, and, across River Road, a tall TV transmitting tower and a Junior Hot Shoppe. In the driveway circle that hot, hazy morning were two of his Washington cars: the long blue Fleetwood limousine with the telephone and television set, and the new apple-green Eldorado with the custom-crafted reclining front passenger seat so he could catnap while his driver chauffeured him to and from planes.

There must have been times, many times, when he was in his office and that gleaming Eldorado was out there, when he yearned to get his hat, say good-bye to Mervel Denton and his other secretaries, and go out and get behind the wheel and head west out U.S. 66, not to the Far West exactly, but to the far-enough west. Then, out on the highway, hat and coat off, tie pulled down, "Honolulu Smile" or "Little Grass Shack" on the tape player, heading west to his 4500 acres in the Blue Ridge foothills, singing along with the music, left hand on the wheel, heading west to the sheep, the cattle, the rolling meadows, the western horses and saddles of Fairfield Farm and Fiery Run Ranch, to the waiting Jeep with its windscreen folded forward and its steel-blue .222 Winchester slung across the dash. . . .

Without really seeing them, I had been gazing out the window of the 727 at the white, drifting cumuli. I felt the pressure changes as the seat belt and no-smoking signs flashed on. The plane hit some chop and bucked, then came out of it and began a slow, descending turn. In the distance lay the vast whitish glaze of Great Salt Lake.

Bill woke up, slipped on his loafers, said something with a smile to his seatmate. He turned back to me. "You know what Brigham Young said when he came in here for the first time, don't you? He said, 'This is the place.'"

The plane banked again and the rugged Wasatch peaks wheeled into view beyond the wingtip. We kept going down, and all at once the white runway markers flashed past and the runway rose to meet us.

About 30 miles north of the Salt Lake City airport, on the Ogden River delta flats between the mountains and the Great Salt Lake, in a vague collection of tomato, corn, and sugar beet fields, sun-bleached barns, sheds, and homes loosely held together by a grid of empty country roads, in a three-room farmhouse that burned to the ground years ago—that is to say, in Marriott Settlement, now known simply as Marriott—John Willard Marriott was born on September 17, 1900, the first son and second child of Hyrum Willard and Ellen Morris Marriott.

Strapping and easy-going, strong enough to pin a struggling sheep to the ground with his body and arm and one hand and to shear it faster than any other man in Weber County, Hyrum loved those flatlands and their rich loamy soil, and you could hear him crooning hymns to himself and his horses as he drove a wagonload of beets to the sugar factory across the field in the warm farmland gloaming. He loved the Wasatch Mountains too, a rugged wilderness wall and barrier for hundreds of miles from the Snake River plains in the north to the Painted Desert in the south. Up among those peaks ten and twelve thousand feet high, he knew, were mountain meadows lush with buffalo grass, good summer pasturelands for his nimble-footed sheep and his spooky, clannish, white-faced cattle. Summer them there, then drive them down the canyon west to the winter range in Nevada, then railroad them to Omaha or San Francisco, and hope the foot rot or the black bears don't get them and the price stays high, and they don't trample themselves to death in the cattle cars, and meanwhile, chop those sugar beets and mow the hay and hope you can keep Ellen and the boys in shoes, so they can help out too—that was Hyrum's life and he loved it.

Hyrum's father, John Marriott, Northamptonshire-born convert to Mormonism and founder of Marriott Settlement, was another man, another matter. Well over six feet tall, John had come to the valley in 1854 with the second wave of Mormons to flee the mobocrats and persecutors of Ohio and Illinois and Missouri. To him, as to the tens of thousands of others who had followed Brigham Young west, this valley and these mountains, the vast salt-rimmed lake and the vaster desert beyond, this was Zion, the Promised Land. "Zion," said Brigham Young, stocky, bewhiskered, blue-eyed Lion of the Lord, "is the pure in heart, and the Zion within is the kingdom of God in each man's heart." But there was also an earthly land of Zion, and it was here in the valley of the mountains.

Hounded from their farms and homes by the persecutors after the Prophet Joseph Smith and his brother Hyrum had been murdered in the Carthage Jail, they had made and broken 1200 miles of wilderness road, Brigham said, from Nauvoo on the banks of the Mississippi to this place on the western slopes of the Wasatch. Some of the time they followed Indian trails, some of the time they ran by the compass, and when they left the Missouri River they followed the Platt. They killed rattlesnakes by the cord in some places, and made roads and built bridges till their backs ached. Where they could not build bridges across rivers, they ferried their people across, until they arrived there, where they found a few naked Indians, a few wolves and rabbits, and any amount of crickets; but as for a green tree or a fruit tree, or any green field, they found nothing of the kind, only a few cottonwoods and willows by the edge of a creek. Some had blankets or shirts, some had not; a few had shoes, while most walked down into the valley on bare and blistered feet. "And here we are," said Brigham, "in the valleys of the mountains, where the Lord directed me to lead the people. We have faith, we live by faith; we came to these mountains by faith. . . . There is not another people on the earth that could have come here and lived. We prayed over the land and dedicated it and the water, air and everything pertaining to them unto the Lord and the smiles of heaven rested on the land and it became productive, and today yields us the best of grain, fruit, and vegetables."

But the story went farther back than that—to a luminous spring day in 1820, to a field and dusty country road in the Genesee country of western New York a few miles south of the backwoods village of Palmyra. Along that road, on that day, walked Joseph Smith Jr., 14-year-old farm boy, one of the eight children of Joseph and Lucy Mack Smith.

The spiritual quickening of those frontier years, nourished by circuit-riding preachers, riverside revivals, salvation jubilees, and summer-long camp meetings, had inflamed the whole countryside. For months the boy had struggled with tormenting questions of redemption and salvation, the mysteries of the Trinity, the doctrines and theology of Christianity. Conflicting answers came at him from all sides, from all sects. "In the midst of this war of words and tumult of opinions," he later recalled, "I often said to myself: What is to be done? Who of all these parties are right; or are they all wrong together? If any one of them be right, which is it, and how shall I know it?"

It was the Epistle of James that told him what to do. There it was, in chapter 1, verse 5: "If any of you lack wisdom, let him ask of God, that giveth to all men liberally, and upbraideth not; and it shall be given him."

On this spring day, with these words in his heart, he left the dusty road and crossed a field and entered a grove of young maples. He knelt on the ground in the glade and began to pray.

Almost instantly he felt himself seized by some dark satanic power. His tongue seemed to swell in his mouth. His prayer choked off. The grove reeled into darkness. For a moment he all but fainted. But then he rallied. "Deliver me, O my God," he cried.

At that moment, a pillar of light brighter than the sun appeared high in the air above his head. As he watched, the light descended, until it bathed him in its luminous glow. Two men appeared in the light, all brightness and glory. "One of them spake unto me, calling me by name, and said, pointing to the other, 'This is My beloved Son. Hear Him!'"

As the dazzlement left him, the words of James came back to the boy. So he asked the Lord which religious sect was the truthful one. Which one should he join?

"I was answered that I must join none of them, for they were all wrong, and the personage who addressed me said that . . . [the preachers] 'draw near to me with their lips, but their hearts are far from me; they teach for doctrine the commandments of men, having a form of godliness, but they deny the power thereof.' He again forbade me to join with any of them: and many other things did he say unto me which I cannot write at this time."

Joseph's mother and father and brothers and sisters received the news of the revelation with awe and total belief. They knew Joseph. Unless such a thing had happened, he would not tell them so. But the preachers and elders and ministers in the countryside round about laughed with derision. Didn't Joseph know that the days of signs and revelations were over—had been for 1800 years?

But the boy stood fast. "Nevertheless," he said, "I have seen a vision. I know it, and I know that God knows it, and I cannot deny it. I dare not deny it."

Four years passed, during which Joseph prayed for divine strength and further guidance. Then, on the night of September 21, 1823, a brilliant light flooded his bedroom. He awoke to behold a white-robed figure hovering in the air beside his bed. The figure spoke. "I am Moroni, and am come to you, Joseph, as a messenger from God."

This, as recalled by Joseph, was God's message:

God had work for him to do, work that would make him both reviled and loved around the world. First of all, there was buried on the side of a nearby hill a book of gold plates upon which was engraved the history of ancient peoples who had inhabited the Americas and "the fulness of the everlasting Gospel" as taught to these peoples by Jesus Christ, nearly 1900 years before. Buried with the plates were two "seer" stones set in silver bows and fastened to a breastplate. They would make possible the translation of the ancient writing on the plates. Moroni told Joseph where to find the plates.

What was his, Joseph's, mission? God had chosen him to translate the writing on the plates and to spread abroad the message of this new book of scripture. Thus he would be an instrument in the glorious restoration of the gospel and the Christian church as it had been established during the days of the apostles, before the falling-away from Christ and His holy teachings after the martyring of His disciples and their immediate followers.

The next day, after two more visits from this heavenly messenger, Joseph walked a few miles to the hill he had been told about, where, in the spot designated by Moroni, he came upon a large, rather flat rock, half-covered with earth. He found a pole and pried the rock loose. Underneath was a stone box, inside of which lay the breastplate, two bluish stones, strangely luminescent, set in silver, and a heavy book of thin gold plates that weighed, Joseph estimated later, at least 40 pounds. Each side of the plates was a mass of engraved hieroglyphic-like characters resembling ancient Egyptian.

As Joseph started to remove the objects from the box, Moroni appeared beside him and stayed his hand. "The time has not yet come," he told the youth. "But return here each year for four years, and I will teach you how and in what manner God's kingdom is to be conducted in the last days."

Joseph followed the angel's instructions, and on September 22, 1827, Moroni delivered the contents of the box to him, charging him to guard them to the death, if need be, until the work of translation was done, and until he, Moroni, came to take them back.

Sixteen years, nine months later, in the late afternoon of June 27, 1844, Joseph Smith moved to the brink of death—and immortality.

Now a tall, big-boned man of 38 with light brown hair and soft, steady blue eyes, he was prophet, seer, revelator, and president of The Church of Jesus Christ of Latter-day Saints, commonly called the Mormon Church after

Mormon, historian of the ancient tribes, who had entrusted the gold plates to his son Moroni. This was the same Moroni who sealed the plates, hid them, and then, many centuries later, revealed them to Joseph so that they might be brought forth from the earth "as the voice of a people speaking from the dust."

Now Joseph Smith was a candidate for the Presidency of the United States; mayor of beautiful Nauvoo on the Mississippi, whose 15,000 residents, most of them Mormons, made it the largest city in the state of Illinois; commander-in-chief of the 4,000 troops of the Nauvoo Legion; and spiritual leader of more than 30,000 Mormon men, women, and children ranging from the Missouri Indian country east to the Atlantic, from Canada to the Gulf of Mexico, across the seas to Britain, France, and Germany.

And if these had been years of building and growth and waxing strong, there were also years of persecution, of blood and tears. "By the rivers of Babylon we sat down and wept," the Mormons often sang. "We wept when we remembered Zion."

Hard-working, thrifty, nondrinkers and nonsmokers in a loose frontier society, keeping to themselves, inwardly convinced that the land was theirs by divine inheritance, they aroused resentment and mistrust and, among the intolerant, hatred, wherever they settled. Night-riding posses, masked or with faces painted, burned their houses, humiliated their women, drove off their cattle, dragged their men from their beds, tarred-and-feathered them or riddled their bodies with bullets and left them by the roadside. Wherever they went, they found no peace. Anti-Mormons, lusting to degrade and exterminate, hounded them from New York to Ohio, from Ohio across the Mississippi to Missouri, from Missouri back to Illinois.

And now, on this day, in the little town of Carthage, Illinois, Hancock County seat and some 20 miles southeast of Nauvoo, the last act was beginning. Evil and violence, wildfire rumors and vigilante madness charged the Carthage air.

An anti-Mormon newspaper in Nauvoo had been destroyed, its press smashed by Joseph Smith's city marshal, its type scattered in the street. Joseph had been arrested, tried, declared innocent, and released. Mobilizing for defense against an aroused and hostile countryside, he had alerted the Nauvoo Legion and placed the city under martial law, had found himself re-arrested, this time for treason. On the advice of Governor Thomas Ford, he had ridden his black horse to Carthage and surrendered. Despite the Governor's pledge for his personal safety, Joseph sensed the end. "I am going like a lamb to the slaughter," he told his people, "but I am calm as a summer's morning. I shall die innocent, and it shall yet be said of me, 'He was murdered in cold blood.' "

On June 27, 1844, at a little after five o'clock, Joseph and his brother Hyrum were killed when a mob broke into the Carthage Jail. One of their companions, John Taylor, was wounded; another, Dr. Willard Richards, was miraculously unharmed.

The next day Carthage was silent and deserted. Fearing a bloody reprisal from the Mormons, every last resident except the hotel keeper had packed up his family and fled. Twenty miles northwest in Nauvoo, Mormon elders, overwhelmed by the tragedy, pleaded with their people for forbearance, for submission to God's will. "Be still," they counseled, "and know this: *God reigns!*"

Dr. Richards, with the help of some of the Saints from Nauvoo, found a wagon for the wounded Taylor. Then they found two more, one for Joseph's body and one for Hyrum's. A little before noon, with a guard of eight mounted soldiers, they set out, single-file, along the dusty road to Nauvoo. The bodies were covered with young twigs and early green leaves, to protect them from the heat of the sun.

21

Chapter Three

"**Y**es sir," Bill said, with a shade of pride in his dry half-drawl, "this is where I come from—these mountains, these valleys."

It was early morning, and we were headed north toward Ogden on U.S. 91 to spend the morning at Marriott Settlement. That was where they all lived and died: Bill's paternal grandparents, John Marriott and Elizabeth Stewart, and his maternal grandparents, William Morris and Elizabeth Russell—Mormon converts from England and Scotland, refugees to Zion from the poverty and inhumanities of the Industrial Revolution; Bill's father, the good-natured Hyrum (named, of course, for the Prophet's martyred brother, as Bill himself was given his first name for his paternal grandfather and his middle name for Dr. Willard Richards, who was with the Prophet at Carthage Jail), and Bill's mother, Ellen Morris, who died in 1967 at the age of 99.

Bill drove easily, left hand on the wheel, right hand resting on his thigh. Though he had been to Salt Lake City and Ogden many times, it had been years since he'd been down the country road of his childhood in Marriott and Slaterville. Off the highway to the east stretched green fields of alfalfa and black-eyed Susans, butter-yellow and big enough to be sunflowers, facing the climbing sun.

Beyond them and the cornfields abruptly rose the Wasatch Mountains, the high, lonely, craggy rimrock shouldering the blue September sky, brooding up there in the silence above the long valley of the Saints, a wall, a conscience, an intimation of eternity. Up ahead where we were going, morning mist still choked Weber Canyon: a

22

boulder-strewn, chasm-like break in the mountain barrier down which the Mormon pioneers had toiled with their high-wheeled wagons and flimsy handcarts a hundred and twenty-odd years before, singing their hymns, coming home at last to their Zion in the Rockies as Joseph the Martyr had prophesied they would.

"Peaches and pears and cherries grow in this valley," Bill said. "This time of year, the peaches are great."

We passed the Pillsbury flour mill, and Bill for the first time motioned off to the west, where Marriott would be coming up soon. "There's the sugar beet factory—over there at the left—and there's the Ogden River. Goes right through our place. And there are the Southern Pacific tracks, running right by the settlement. We used to walk along those tracks and count the ties."

Bill was feeling wound up that morning, back in the mountain country, feeling good. He started a twangy chorus of "When It's Springtime in the Rockies," then broke off abruptly and said, "Look out there." An enormous diesel-powered tractor, trailing a light exhaust from its high vertical pipe, canvas sunshade rigged over the driver's seat, moved out over a couple of dirt tracks leading across a sugar beet field.

"It took man 7,000 years to invent one of those things," Bill said. "The Lord could have shown him how to do it 7,000 years ago. But He didn't. Why not? Because He wants us to work things out for ourselves. But He'll help us—if we ask Him to."

We turned off 91 at Slaterville, and there was really no way you could tell Slaterville and Marriott apart. They both consist of a broad grid of country roads, either dirt or two-lane hardtop, about half a mile apart, cutting the land into large squares with half-mile sides. Small farmhouses, barns, and outbuildings lay widely spaced along each side of the square. The big inner portion of each square is planted to sugar beets, corn, tomatoes, or

23

onions, or is open pastureland. We passed a small white schoolhouse with a sign, "Slaterville School."

Bill said, as we drove by slowly, "That's where I went to school—and there's the old road I used to come down to get there." We moved along to a grass-grown corner lot. "Right here used to be a small grocery and candy store."

We turned down a dirt road, stopped, and got out. We stood there in the silence under the now all-blue sky. The road stretched flat and straight between the fields, into the distance. Mountains to the left. Along the fields on the right an endless fence, and, one after another, forlorn, diminishing as they receded up ahead, telephone poles with single cross-trees at the top. Nothing moved anywhere, for miles around.

With a wave of his arm, Bill took in the broad field across a roadside irrigation ditch. "A corner of our farm. Sugar beets." Bill's father had bought the hundred acres from an Ogden racehorse breeder who used them for pasture. The land was now owned by Bill's sister Doris. She, in turn, rented it to Japanese sharecroppers, steady, hardworking farmers who knew their business.

He started off down the dirt road. I followed along, hurrying to keep up. Far down the road on the left, beside a homemade hay derrick that angled up toward an oak tree, sat a parked car. We walked toward it. A man in a straw hat and a denim work shirt sat behind the wheel. Off in the field to the left, a man and woman were picking tomatoes.

Bill and I stood in the middle of the road, looking at the driver. He appeared to be in his sixties. "Howdy, there," Bill said.

The driver looked hard at Bill. He slowly opened the car door and slid out, grinning. He came over, holding out his hand. "Hello there, Willard," he drawled.

Bill's face cracked into a smile. "Russell? Aren't you

24

Russell Morris?" Bill's mother's maiden name was Morris; his grandmother's maiden name had been Russell.

"That's right."

They stood in the middle of the road, shaking hands. Russell was retired and lived in Ogden. It was his brother Wallace's tomato field, and he'd driven some friends over to help themselves. There was a half-filled basket of large tomatoes in varying degrees of ripeness in the open trunk.

Attracted by the encounter, the woman came in off the field, carrying several large tomatoes. The gaunt, elderly man following her had a puzzled expression on his face. Russell introduced them, saying about the old man, " 'member him? He runs the Graycliff Lodge, up Ogden Canyon."

The old man squinted at Bill. "Marriott? You the feller that runs them cafes and hotels?"

"That's him, all right," the woman said. "That's him, right there."

Bill said, "I guess you're right."

But he wasn't for standing around talking about it. He told Russell to take care of these good folks here and meet us back at our car. We were going over to the iron bridge on Twelfth Street and would be back in an hour or so.

"See you later," we said, and struck off down a path alongside one of the broad irrigation ditches that line and divide the fields. The water in the ditch was clear, but dark, and not moving. . . .

In 1855 John Marriott, his first wife, Susanna, his second wife, Elizabeth, and their five children were the first settlers on this land. Like all the Mormons who had been driven out of Nauvoo and across the Mississippi, and the converts from across the sea, they had faith in God and in the Church established by Joseph Smith. They lived by that faith, and poor, sick, footsore, they came to this valley by that faith.

When the Marriotts first arrived to clear this land and plant it to wheat, they lived around here somewhere—Bill did not know exactly where—in a "wagon box," a covered wagon bed without its wheels, resting on the ground.

At first John and Susanna had gone to Kaysville, eight or ten miles north of the bustling frontier town Brigham had laid out in the Great Salt Lake Valley. There John met Elizabeth Stewart, his second wife, Bill's grandmother, whom he married in February 1854 in Salt Lake City.

Elizabeth, too, had come to the valley by faith. After a childhood of poverty and toil in her native Bedfordshire, she joined the Mormon Church in 1848, at the age of 19. She sold a dress and a shawl to raise money for her passage, sailed for America with her brother William, and arrived in St. Louis with one shilling to her name. William went west to Salt Lake in 1851, traveling there in the same wagon train as John and Susanna Marriott. In the summer of '53 Elizabeth joined an overland handcart company and walked the 1600 miles barefoot and carrying her shoes, because she wanted to have a pair to walk in when she reached the streets of Zion. Soon after her arrival she went to Kaysville to stay with William. That was where she first met John Marriott.

"One day while looking out the window I saw a man . . . galloping toward me on a horse, his beard blowing in the breeze, as rugged and unkempt as a man could look. The Spirit whispered to me, saying, 'This man is to be your husband.' A few days later he came again and asked me to be his wife. I was thoroughly convinced that this was the man the Lord wanted me to marry, and that polygamy was a true principle. . . . The same thing was revealed to my husband, and we were married February 26, 1854. . . ."

John and Elizabeth's first child was born the next year, and that was the year that John, his two wives (he was to have two more), and their children were asked by the church authorities to move farther north, near Ogden, to develop this land that Bill, his grandson, and I were moving across. In that summer of 1855, John built a one-room log house with a sod roof for his family, and dug the first irrigation ditch that carried precious Ogden River water to this rich, loamy soil.

We walked hard along the path for ten or fifteen minutes, alongside the still waters of the ditch. It was getting on toward 11 o'clock now, and the sun blazed down. Finally we came to the end of the cultivated fields and to a grove of oaks. It was a pleasant, spacious, shady grove. Sudden smell of fresh water, with dampness in it, and the odor of wet plants. Off to the right, glint of sunlight under the trees. "The Ogden River," Bill said. "The water's cold—right down out of the mountains."

We broke out of the grove to an open flat with a rail fence at its far side, and beyond that a two-lane highway stretching east and west, Ogden and the mountain barrier ten miles or so away at one end, the big lake ten miles or so away at the other.

We scaled the rail fence, climbed a steep, grassy bank on the highway. Empty both ways, as far as you could see. "Let's go down to the bridge," Bill said. I stepped along with him. The hard footing of the road felt good.

As we walked slowly toward the river, a pick-up truck bore swiftly down the highway, devouring the distance, flashing past, strung out the emptiness, dwindled fast toward Ogden. Silence.

Where the concrete highway bridge spanned the river, we leaned against the wall and looked down at the clear mountain water flowing lakeward. Bill pointed to a bend in the river. "Over there is where we used to go swimming. We'd come down here and watch the bridges. Sometimes, 'way over there in the farmhouse, I could lie in bed and hear the trains over here. Was there ever a sound like a train whistle at night, far away . . . lonesome . . . going somewhere. . . ?"

He turned away from the swimming hole and the iron bridges and the concrete wall. "Well," he said, "it's getting late. Let's get back to the car."

We swung off down the road, back the way we'd come.

There were three things, Bill said, that nearly everyone remembered about his grandfather Marriott. One was that he always wore a white shirt—everywhere, not only at church, but at home, at the breakfast table, in the fields, pitching hay, shoeing horses, repairing a wagon. Another was that he regretted bitterly his absolute refusal, as a boy, to go to school. "I was beaten for not going to school," he used to say. "Now I wish my father had beaten me harder." The third thing was his absolute intolerance of disorder or personal slovenliness. "He wouldn't let anyone eat," Bill said, "until everyone was clean—hair in place, hands and face scrubbed, and so on."

We were back in the car. Bill was driving. He had asked Russell to come along with us while we drove down the empty roads of Marriott.

We passed a small white farmhouse, freshly painted, well-trimmed lawn, then made a right-angle turn and started down a road just like the one we'd left. "Talk about my grandfather, though. He was strong. He had a temper. I remember my grandmother telling me that when my father was 14 years of age, he did something my grandfather didn't like. Grandfather chased him and tried to catch him and whip him. But my dad was too fast for him, and got away. My grandmother told my dad he'd better high-tail it out of there, and go down to Kaysville and stay with some of our relatives until grandfather cooled off. So he did. He went down to Kaysville and stayed there. Never came back."

28

Bill's father, Hyrum, also bore the middle name Willard. He was born December 6, 1863, twin brother to Esther Amelia, the only twins fathered by John, who probably did not miss Hyrum very much when he ran away, since by 1877, when Hyrum was 14, he already had 29 other children. Bill, who was born a year and three months after his grandfather's death, was one of 135 grandchildren.

John, according to the family memoirs, kept his household well in line, although, like most Mormons with plural wives, up to and including Brigham Young himself, he found a policy of dispersal the best way of getting along together. As time passed, he built one wife, Trezer, a house in Salt Creek, 15 or so miles to the west; he built another home in Marriott, in addition to the one he and Susanna occupied, for Elizabeth; and for his fourth wife, Margaret, he built a house in Ogden. There must, to be sure, have been arguments, disagreements, jealousies, heartaches, tears, slamming of doors. But there was always, in these people, the strengthening presence of the Lord, and the bonds of their common struggle to survive.

Many elements in the rest of the nation found it impossible to tolerate Mormon polygamy, even though The Church of Jesus Christ of Latter-day Saints regarded it as divinely sanctioned, and even though Utah was still a territory and was not to achieve statehood until 1896. Congress, in fact, outlawed it everywhere by passing the Edmunds Act in 1882, thus automatically disenfranchising some 12,000 polygamous Mormons and rendering them subject to three years in prison and $500 fines. John himself was arrested in 1887, pleaded guilty, and served six months in the Utah Penitentiary. In 1890, in compliance with the Federal ruling, the church withdrew its endorsement of plural marriages. Henceforth, any Mormon who took more than one wife, or one husband, would be excommunicated.

The last years of John's life were like his other years, filled with hard, dawn-to-dusk labor in the fields, service to his family and community, dedicated work for his Mormon ward, or parish. People say that his funeral, held at the settlement meetinghouse, was the biggest ever seen in Marriott.

We passed a lush field of alfalfa, then a front yard of high grass, half-concealing rusting mowers and reapers, symbols of neglect and irresponsibility.

"Tell 'im how you learned to ride, Willard," Russell said.

"Well, there's not much to tell. We had to walk a mile and a half to school, my cousin Thad and I. My mother reared Thad; both his parents had died. He had one brother, and my mother was raising both of them, and then the brother was kicked by a horse and killed. Thad was older than we were, but we used to walk to school together.

"Thad always liked excitement, so every few days he'd get me in a fight with one of the neighbor kids. He always wanted me to be able to take care of myself, and he used to teach me boxing. He got me in a fight with one of the Stanger boys one day, and the Stanger boy hit me over the head with his dinner pail and won the fight."

A pick-up came hurrying down the road. Bill and the driver waved to each other as it passed.

"Well," Bill said, "I finally convinced my father that I ought to have a horse to ride to school. He got me a beautiful pony named Feather. Somewhere, that little pony had learned how to handle kids. Every day he'd stop two or three times in the middle of the road and buck me off. But he must've got tired, 'cause after a while he stopped doing it, and we got along fine together."

We drove north to Slaterville to look at the schoolhouse where Bill had finished the eighth grade, but there

30

was nothing there. In its place a sandlot baseball diamond with a wire screen backstop. No benches. No bases. The old Slaterville meetinghouse was gone too.

Magpies, dark tail feathers trailing, white wing patches flashing, sailed over the fields. A couple of chestnut quarter horses grazed along a split rail fence. Beyond them, beyond the fields and beyond the homes and buildings of Ogden, loomed the Wasatch front—Malan Heights.

"Malan Heights," Bill said, "was named after a family of early settlers. Once, when I was going to Weber Academy, which was then the Mormon high school in Ogden, we had a school dance. We wanted to make sure everybody had a partner, so the girls wrote their names on slips of paper and put the slips in a hat. The boys drew the slips and took the girl whose name was on their slip. I drew the Malan girl.

"Well, I took her to the dance, and her boy friend didn't like it. He and about half a dozen of his friends jumped me while I was walking her home, only two blocks from the dance.

"Next day, I met him downtown. His friends were in the park, and he whistled them over. I went to the pool hall and got my friend Glenn Stanger, who'd hit me over the head with the dinner pail out in Marriott.

"Glenn was a farmer boy, big and tough. He stood watch while a big crowd gathered, and I took on the Malan girl's boy friend. He wore a ring made of a horseshoe nail that cut my ear so the lobe flopped down. But I gave him a good whipping anyway. I never had any trouble with him after that."

Fragments. Jigsaw puzzle pieces. Patchwork patches. Fragments of a lifescape.

"The first thing I remember?" Bill mused. "Well, I guess the farmhouse I was born in is no longer there. It was east of here a mile or so. Then we moved to the old

31

James' place, next to the railroad tracks. An irrigation canal ran past the house. It was contaminated. When I was a small boy, around three, we all got typhoid fever.

"I don't remember how sick I was. But I *do* remember this, and I guess it's the first thing. I was three or four years old. I started down the road one day, away from the house. I kept walking and winging rocks at fenceposts until I came to the lower fields, about a mile away.

"That afternoon my mother began looking for me. When she couldn't find me, she thought I'd fallen in the canal and drowned, so she roused up the whole neighborhood, and had them dragging the canal to find me.

"I guess I arrived at the lower field about five o'clock. My father was there plowing. When he saw me, he hitched up the horses and took me home. We got there about six. My mother was mad at me, but she was sure glad to see me safe and sound."

Russell slapped his knee. "Dog-gone," he said, "I bet your daddy was mad, too."

"He sure was. He locked me in a closet for two hours. Then he sent me to bed without any supper."

Bill turned down yet another road, one we'd already been on, and I began to see that we had traveled more or less irregularly in a large square, perhaps three or four miles to a side.

"The sugar beet fields here on the left—they were all part of our next farm, and that's where we're headed now. The house and the barns are there, but nobody's living there now. Yes, sir, we thought this was a grand country estate when we moved here—a hundred acres, all planted in grass."

There were box elders and young cottonwoods and maples, already turning to red and gold, and Bill came to the end of this road and brought the car slowly to a halt. There wasn't much to see—the silo in the field, the wooden barns. The roofs were sound and good, but the siding was gray, dried-out, warped, and weatherbeaten.

The house itself was similar to others we'd seen—four rooms downstairs, three upstairs when he'd lived in it, Bill said. Maybe four now. Behind a screen of tall grass and a tangle of wild rose, it stolidly faced the road.

Bill walked quickly around the old place, poking through the silent barns, noting the rusty pitchforks, the rust-frozen hay rake, the broken-down buckboard, the hay still in the hayloft, the dried-out doors sagging open. The house itself was locked.

Then we got in the car and turned around and started back to where Russell had left his car. Three or four houses were clustered together around a small general store. Plain City. We passed a vacant lot. "This is where the old ball park used to be," Bill said.

We made the last turn, into the road Bill and I had walked along, and there a quarter of a mile or so away, parked on the shoulder of the road, was Russell's car. The tomato-pickers were nowhere in sight. Someone came and got them and took them home, Russell said.

Bill pulled our car to a halt and looked out over the fields toward the white silo, miles off and lonelier than ever in the distance. "You know something, Russell? I'd like to fix the farm up real nice. Fix the barns and cut the grass and put white fences all around."

Russell seemed dubious. "Well, I don't know. Looks pretty good the way it is now. It's puttin' out a lot of produce. It's makin' money, just the way it is."

"I know it," Bill said. "But still—" Leaning over the wheel, looking out the window, easing the car slowly down the middle of the road, Bill left it at that.

Chapter Four

This, then, was where it began for Bill—this valley, this hard, lovely, treacherous land between the mountain ramparts and the inland salt sea. These roads, not much different, were the roads Bill walked along on his way to school, carrying his books and lunch pail. These fields were the fields he toiled in, even as a child. This was the land that tested him as it did all of them, a demanding, exacting, jealous land that bound them to it with furrows and crops, devouring blights of grasshoppers and crickets, blizzards and droughts, wind, rain, and snow and the wheel of seasons; the land that in the end would break them, as a wrangler breaks a colt.

These hundred acres were where Will Marriott, as Hyrum was called, raised his sugar beets and lettuce, his corn and alfalfa; and in the Ogden River, there under the iron railroad bridge, was where Bill and his brothers and sisters caught frogs in the evening and pan-fried the legs over a fire of cottonwood twigs. The house that we looked at that calm and hazy September morning had been rebuilt and enlarged somewhat after a fire, but it was pretty much the same as it had been in those far-off days. Bill, standing in the road and looking at it, must have heard voices from the past, must have seen children out in back—his older sister, Doris, and those who were younger than he: Helen, Eva, and Kay, and his kid brothers, Paul, Russell, and Woodrow. Certainly, vivid in his memories that day was Grandmother Marriott.

"Physically," he said, "she was a large woman—not fat, but she probably weighed a hundred and sixty or sixty-five pounds. She wore calico skirts and had a tanned complexion and a full, pleasant face.

34

"Her husband, my grandfather, died in 1899, the year before I was born, but even so her life was the farm, her children and grandchildren, and the church, which was only half a mile from where she lived.

"She was the kind of woman that kids like to be around. She wasn't preaching to you all the time. She was kind and gentle. But she had character. She told us how every year she used to walk 35 miles along the dirt road from Ogden to Salt Lake City to attend the general conference of the Church. Sometimes her shoes were worn out, but she'd go anyway. She'd wrap her feet in gunny sacks. When I grew older and things got tough, I'd think of her. And I'd work all the harder."

So these were childhood days and years of blazing summer sun, and January winds howling down off the mountains, barefoot days and years of schoolbooks and schoolyards, of catching frogs in the river by the railroad bridge, of trapping and skinning muskrats from the irrigation canal, and snaring rabbits along the sheep pasture fences—when the young mind and the young muscles were bent to hauling sugar pulp to feed to the sheep and cattle, to stacking wood and milking cows, to hoeing the corn and the lettuce rows, and thinning out the sugar beets.

But it wasn't all work. In the summer, after work on the farm was done, Will one day would shout, "Come on! It's time to go up the canyon!" And he'd pile Ellen and all the kids and provisions and sleeping bags in a wagon and hitch up a team of horses and off they'd go, leaving the farm behind for a couple of weeks—into Ogden and up the winding road between the canyon walls and towering crags of the Ogden River canyon. They'd keep climbing until they reached the headwaters of the river's south fork, where the country was wild and beautiful, and the streams were alive with firm-fleshed trout.

And in the wintertime, life there in the valley was, if

anything, even more direct and simple, and Ellen, the mother, rather than Will, who loved the out-of-doors so much, would be the one who would bring them even closer together and enrich the texture of their lives.

To be sure, harvesting was over, pantry shelves were sagging beneath rows of bottled fruits and vegetables, the sheep were safe on the winter range, and the cattle in the feed lot, and there were good times—fishing through the ice, skating on the cow pasture pond. Maybe on a Saturday evening Will would light pineknot torches and set them in the snow around the edges of the pond, and youngsters would come from as far away as Ogden to skate and play tag and crack the whip. Or Will would hitch up a pair of horses, pull on a long fur coat, fill a bobsleigh with children, his own and as many others as could crowd together into the sleigh, and take off down the hard-packed snow of the country roads, their songs carrying out over the white-blanketed fields.

Not only Bill, but all his brothers and sisters think back nostalgically to something else, something more special and of deeper meaning, and that is the winter dusks and the winter evenings snug and close and warm in the farmhouse, with Ellen always there, helping them with their homework, peeling apples for them, giving them exercises to improve their spelling and their handwriting.

Ellen was a rather small, quick, dark-haired woman with delicate features and a strengthening, sustaining faith in the church and in God. She worked hard for her family, and sometimes there were also her half-sister's two boys to take care of, and two or three hired hands as well. Cooking, washing, canning, making clothes, making ends meet, making a home, heating tubfuls of well water on the big wood stove on Saturday nights so her children would go to the Lord's house clean and neat the next day, never giving up or giving in on what she thought was right and righteous. "I'd rather have a stone tied around your

necks and have you cast into the ocean," she'd tell her
children, "than to have you forget your religion and not
live it every day of your lives."

She was a Morris, born there in Marriott Settlement
on December 14, 1868, in a four-room adobe house. Her
father, William Morris, was born in 1821 in Shropshire,
England. He and his first wife, Harriett, converts to Mormonism, immigrated to America in 1854 and settled in
Madison, Nebraska. There they had one child, a son. He
died soon after birth and was buried there. After a year in
Nebraska they struck out on foot for Zion with a handcart company, reaching Utah late in the summer of 1855
and making their home at Bingham Ford (now Five
Points), some three miles north of the center of Ogden.
After the birth of their third child they moved to Marriott, where four more children were born to them.

In December 1864, ten years after leaving England,
Harriett contracted diphtheria and died in a matter of
days. By the next February six of the seven surviving
children came down with the disease, and within the week
five of them were dead. William never really recovered
from the tragedy. For the rest of his life (he died in
December 1892, 28 years later) he seemed strangely mel-
ancholy.

But in the days and weeks immediately following his
crushing loss, William sought desperately for something,
or someone, to cling to. A friend said, "There is a woman
in Riverdale—Elizabeth Hamblin. Her husband was
killed a year or two back. She had a little girl. Maybe she
. . ." Riverdale was only three or four miles away across
the sugar beet fields. William rode over to see her. For-
tuitously enough, he found in Elizabeth a companion in
grief, and something more besides.

Her background, like his, was written in tragedy. Born
in 1836 in Clackmannan, Scotland, she was the oldest
child of John and Ellen Blackwood Russell, devout

members of the Church of Scotland. When in 1847 her
father broke from the national church and was baptized a
Mormon, the village doors closed in his face. To help support the family, Elizabeth, at the age of 11, worked as a
gleaner in the wheat fields. Stoned in the streets, taunted
day and night for their Mormonism, the Russells fled
Clackmannan for the more liberal community Boness.
There John was able to find work and preach his faith.

But Zion in the Valley of the Great Salt Lake was
where he wanted to be, and in 1862 he borrowed passage
money from the Mormon emigration fund and, with his
family, was soon bound for America. Six weeks at sea,
crowded, jolting, eight-day box-car ride to Florence,
Nebraska, then covered wagon train west. On the trail
one of the young, clear-eyed Mormon guides sent out
from Salt Lake asked Elizabeth if she'd like to ride his
horse. She smiled and said she would. His name was
Duane Hamblin; he was the son of the famous Mormon
missionary to the Indians, Jacob Hamblin. Not long after
the company arrived in Salt Lake City, they were married. For a while they lived in southern Utah with his
parents. But Duane and Elizabeth, soon to have a child of
their own, wanted a home of their own too, and Duane
began preparing the site for one not far from his parents'
cabin.

One morning on his way to work, he suddenly remembered that he'd left without kissing Elizabeth good-
bye. He turned back and found her and kissed her. Then
he waved good-bye again and rode off down the road. Less
than an hour later, as he dug away alone at his cabin
foundation, a towering sandbank loosened, slid down
upon him, buried him to the neck, and crushed him to
death. Calm and quiet in her grief, Elizabeth returned to
her family's home in Riverdale. There, several months
later, she gave birth to a daughter, whom she named
Duane in memory of her husband.

So that spring of '65, William called on Elizabeth at
her parents' home and asked her if she'd keep house for
him and the two children that were all he had left of his
family. They were married that very year, before the
spring planting.

As time passed, William proved a sturdy provider. He
built the first adobe house in Marriott, and its four comfortable rooms made it a settlement showplace for years.
As for Elizabeth, she bore William not only Ellen, but five
other children. She was a thrifty, hard-working, self-
improving wife and a loving, conscientious mother. Where
William hung back from the Church and church affairs,
she found or made the time to take an active role in the
Marriott Ward. She went to night school to learn to
write, and beyond all this did what most of the Mormon
wives did to help their husbands around farm and home.

When she was 15, Elizabeth and William's daughter
Liz contracted smallpox. Ellen, years later, remembered
that "when we discovered that Liz had the black
smallpox, the family moved to a vacant house where all of
us had to sleep on the floor. Liz was taken care of by a
man who previously had smallpox." Because of the fear of
contagion, William and Elizabeth and Ellen and the
others never saw Liz again. She died, and was buried in
the ward churchyard.

It was only a few weeks afterward that Lucy, one of
the two children William had brought to their marriage,
followed Liz to "that state of happiness which the Book
of Mormon said is called paradise," taken by a sudden
stroke.

These were good years, by and large, for the Mormons
and for the Territory of Utah, which the Mormons
themselves sometimes called the State of Deseret—the
word "Deseret" being adapted from the Book of Mormon
and interpreted to mean "honeybee."

They had taken this place, in their day, as Bancroft said, "as remote from civilization as the wilds of Senegambia." And there, within the space of less than forty years, in the name of the Lord, through unremitting, back-breaking work and frugality, they had established a thriving community, a springtime Eden in "the formerly unpeopled solitude, abandoned but a few decades ago to the savage, the coyote and the wolf."

Now the territory's population totaled close to 180,000, of whom some 25,000 lived within the corporate limits of Salt Lake City. Some thirty-five miles north, Ogden was now a bustling railroad and farmer's market town of 8,000 with a couple of first-rate hotels, a theater, three banks, and a spanking new $16,000 bridge across the Ogden River. Already it was one of the busiest division points of the transcontinental system, Central Pacific tracks gleaming northward around the lake, then southwest across the Great Salt Desert toward California, the Union Pacific rails stretching to the east toward Omaha, the Mississippi, and all that world the Mormons had left behind.

The lights, sights, and sounds of Ogden—this excitement, this power and growth and living vitality of Utah, the distant rumble and thunder of the trains, lonely wail of locomotive whistles in the night, the awareness of the bounty of the Lord pouring forth His plenty and peace at last in Zion—all this was in the air and the very life of the Mormon settlements clustered across the orchards and sugar beet and alfalfa fields north and west and south of Ogden: Harrisville and Huntsville, Slaterville and Plain City, Hooperville and Marriott Settlement—and it was no wonder that young, barefoot Mormon lads looked up from their hoes, their hay rakes and reapers, and followed trains with their eyes and hearts as they pulled out for San Francisco and Chicago and New Orleans.

But the settlement life, for the most part, was the day-in, day-out reality of the barnyard and schoolyard, the church (three times on Sundays), the picnics, the births, deaths, and marriages, the shearing of sheep, planting and reaping of crops, summering and wintering stock.

"When I was very young," Ellen once wrote about these days, "I walked to school. It was a mile and one-half to the Marriott school. The snow was so deep and packed so solid, I could walk right over the top of the fences."

She was at the head of her class, and in order to stay there she sat up late, by the kerosene lamp, to study her spelling. And there were always things to do at home.

"When I came home from school, I would chop all the wood needed for cooking purposes as well as that which was needed for keeping the house warm. I helped to feed the sheep and cattle."

There were youthful, light-hearted times too—skating on clear winter afternoons, church dances, summer vacation outings.

"The boys and girls would all get together and go to the mountains in covered wagons," Ellen wrote in her memoirs. " 'Will' Marriott, who later became my husband, would always catch more fish than anyone else. . . . The boys and girls went to dances at Huntsville and Plain City, and afterwards we went to the Marriott house for strawberries and cream."

The year Ellen was 19 and her sister, Kate, was 12, their mother took to her bed with rheumatism, and never really walked or worked again. Their father had been injured in a sheep-shearing accident when he was 65, fracturing his right hip. The doctor did not set it properly, and from then on, he walked slowly, with a heavy limp, supporting himself with a cane.

When Kate married at 17, the life of the country roads and the sugar beet fields bore down on Ellen. That year, just three days before Christmas, William died, and almost a year later to the day, he was followed in death by

Duane, Elizabeth's daughter by her first husband. Elizabeth lingered for three more years and then she, too, passed away.

Ellen was 27. She had no money nor means of earning any. She had promised Duane, as she lay on her deathbed, that she would take care of her sons, Danny and Thad. For a while she kept house for her brother Jim, but then he got married, and it was clear that she and the boys should move out. He found her a one-room adobe farmhouse near the church in Marriott Settlement.

One gray, overcast autumn day in 1897, Will Marriott's bay mare somehow broke out of the corral on the Marriott farm (or so he said), and he rode across the fields looking for her. He happened to pass Ellen's house, and thought he'd stop in and see how she was getting along.

She invited him in, fetched him some cakes, and poured him a glass of water. They chattered for a while of church affairs. In the yard behind the kitchen Danny, now eight, and Thad, five, played quietly with their cat and a little green wagon. Will could see how lonely she was, and how tired, and his heart turned over. They were married a few weeks later on the first day of December.

Chapter Five

Ellen's brother Jim took Dan, Duane Hamblin's older son, to live with him and his family, and Ellen kept Thad, who was now nearly ten. She, Will, and the boy lived with the Marriotts for about a year. When Doris, their first child, was born, they moved to Ogden for just a month or so, then bought a two-room house at Five Points for $400 and moved it down the road to Marriott Settlement, close to the church. This was where John Willard, or Bill, was born, September 17, 1900.

It was less than 50 years since covered-wagon days and only four since Utah Territory became the 45th state, and except that the population had grown a bit, and the gold and silver ledges were pretty well played out and the Indian wars were over, nothing much had changed. It was still the same, simple, almost Old Testament life, featured by the same fateful, fundamental things that if you grew up there were under your skin and in your blood—sun and sky, desert and mountain, tilling of soil and reaping of crop, lambing of ewes in the springtime, bitter winter cold and baking summer heat, teacher's drone in the plank-floored classrooms of the old brick schoolhouse, Sunday bells of the new brick Mormon church next door.

"I had all the housework and outside work to do," Ellen recalled later. "One day I went over to the Morris home to pick some apples. I was pregnant with Helen, but I climbed to the top of the tree and fell. I broke my leg and had to remain in bed for a long time while it knitted. I had no one to do the work, but friends would drop by and help with the housework and care for Doris and Willard. Helen was born shortly after this. Willard was two years old at the time, and he was a little man. He would come to my bed and ask me what I wanted. And then he would get it for me.

"A year later we moved to our little home on the corner and this was where Eva was born. That very same day, our cow had a calf and our cat had kittens."

Will, the father, was away from home a lot of the time these years, shearing sheep, riding herd on the cattle, and Ellen was there at home with her four children, Doris, Bill, Helen, and Eva. Thad was now a youngster nearing his teens, and many were the times Ellen wondered what she'd have done without him.

"I would get up early in the morning, hoe the garden and water the alfalfa while Thad was taking care of the children," she recalled.

When Bill was about five, Will bought the big Faye place, with its high white fences, beautiful bluegrass pasture, and 20-stalled barn, where rich people from Ogden and Salt Lake boarded the racehorses that ran on the Ogden track. This was the farm that Bill and I and Russell Morris drove to that September day in '73, and that Bill had a hankering to restore, but hasn't done so yet and maybe never will; and this was where the rest of the family was born and raised—Paul, Kathryn, Russell, and Woodrow. Will, the indulgent, the loving and lovable father, bought the children a billy goat and a goat cart, and the goat pulled them and the cart up and down the road in front of the house. But when they turned the goat loose it chased the youngsters and butted them into the stream that ran past the house and took to eating the drying clothes off Ellen's kitchen clothesline. One day, arms akimbo, eyes flashing, Ellen rebelled. The goat had to go. Sadly, Will took the goat to Ogden and sold it.

To the rhythm of the seasons, life moved on. Ellen, remembering—

"The children and I helped on the farm, thinning the sugar beets, hoeing their weeds, topping them in the fall.

44

We also cultivated the potatoes and plowed them up in the fall and sacked them. We had twenty acres of beets alone, so there was much work to be done. We always had a hired man living with us, and I had to cook for him as well as for the eleven of us. We used eight loaves of bread each day for the children's lunches and meals.

"But the sheep and cattle business was our main livelihood. Each spring I had to outfit a sheep wagon for the sheepherders to live in while they were up in the mountains on the summer range. I worked outside a lot and raised chickens to help along. Each year, with Doris's help, I put up eight hundred quarts of fresh fruit. I had to keep her out of school. She didn't get too much education."

For anyone who lives where the climate is dry and the water is scarce, the fear he lives with night and day is fear of fire; once it gets going, there's not much he can do about it but stand back and watch it burn. One summer evening when Bill was about eleven, Will and he were in Ogden with the horses and wagon, getting a load of hay. Ellen called the children to her. "It's milking time. Get your pails." They got their pails and trooped down the lane away to the cow pasture.

The irrigation canal gates were open and sections of the pasture were under several inches of water. Before they reached the cows Eva, now four, and Helen, little more than six, had playfully splashed and paddled about in the water until they were thoroughly drenched.

"Go back to the house and put on some dry clothes," Ellen said. "They're on the stairway."

It was dim on the stairway in the fading light. One of the girls found a kitchen match and struck it, so they could see where the clothes were. Somewhere nearby was a can of kerosene. Then all at once Eva and Helen were running toward the pasture screaming and Ellen, looking back toward them and the house, saw wisps of smoke rising from the eaves. She and the other children ran splashing back across the pasture with their buckets thinking that they could fill them with water from the pump and put the fire out. But the roof was burning by the time they got to the backyard outside the kitchen where the pump was, and it was too late.

Meanwhile, Will and the boy, homeward bound with their load of hay, riding their wagon down Twelfth Street toward Marriott and the valley flat, saw the column of smoke rising lazily in the still evening air. The boy held the reins.

"H-mm," Will said. "Look at that. Must be a house on fire."

"Can't be ours," the boy said. Nevertheless, he slapped the reins down on the bay rumps. The horses moved into a slow trot.

As they drew closer, they could see the flames flickering through the distant roadside trees. They could hear the ominous crackling, and men shouting orders.

"Dad! It *is* our house!" The boy stood up, gathered the reins in short, and swung the rein ends forward and brought them down hard on the horses' hindquarters. The wagon lurched forward.

At the end of the street where they lived, where the road bore sharply around the bend to the right, they saw the horses and wagons of their neighbors jamming the road and the bucket brigades of men, women, and children relaying water from the canal and wetting down the hay barn and stables and the blacksmith shop against the flying sparks and embers.

While the wagon was still moving, the boy leaped to the road and ran toward the burning house. "Mom! Mom!"

He found Ellen and his sisters and brothers huddled together in the front yard by the stone cellar, Ellen stunned and dry-eyed, the children sobbing. Will tried to

46

comfort them, then hurried out back to help. The boy and the rest of them stayed there and watched the flames destroy their home and everything they owned and cherished.

That night, neighbors gladly took them in, finding them places to sleep in their barns or homes. And then, before the ashes cooled, they helped Will pull the charred shell apart, haul new lumber, and start rebuilding. Six months later the family had a home again, better and roomier, even, than before.

School was just out for the summer, and the late June sun beat down on Marriott, on the orchards and alfalfa and sugar beet fields. Will Marriott looked out over his crops. He called young Bill from the house. "Son," he said, "those beets sure need thinning. You're old enough to take care of that, aren't you?" Then he hitched up one of the horses and drove off up the road to Ogden to buy some groceries.

Bill rounded up his brothers and sisters, Doris, Helen, and Kay, Paul and Woodie, Russell and Eva. "How'd you all like a nice bottle of soda pop—a whole bottle, all for yourself? You'd like that, wouldn't you? Well, all you got to do is a little thinning, out in the beet field. Clear out the rows so there's a foot between every plant. Now Paul, you take this row here . . ."

He gave them each a row to work.

"While you're doing that," he said, "I'll go get the soda pop." And off he went down the road, with a wagon, to the store. When he came back he carried the bag of bottles, seven for his workers and one for himself, to the irrigation ditch. He held up the bag, tantalizing the thirsty toilers. "Here it is!" he called. "Finish your rows and it's all yours." He put the bottles in the mountain water of the ditch to cool off. The youngsters worked faster and faster in the blazing sun.

Bill, their overseer, checked the scene with satisfaction. The rows they worked on looked fresh and cleared out, healthy and neat, the way he liked to see crops look. Dad would be pleased. He surveyed the remaining rows across the expanse of field. They'd thin those tomorrow.

"All afternoon," Doris remembered, "we'd hoe the beet rows, just dying for a drink of that cold soda pop. Bill sure got a lot of work out of us. He was a born organizer."

But it went deeper than that, didn't it? "When I was a little fellow," Bill said once, "my father always gave me the responsibility of a man. He would tell me what he wanted me to do, but he never told me much about how to do it, and he never sent anyone along with me to show me how. It was up to me to find out for myself." And he was finding out things there in the alfalfa and beet fields, in the mountains and on the range—things he'd never forget, things he valued because he knew they worked. The loaves and the fishes. He didn't know how the Lord had magnified or multiplied them, but he did know that if you had an idea, or if you could envision the end result you wanted to produce, and if it was too big for you to do yourself, it was possible to motivate others to do it for you.

That same summer Bill became aware of several acres of pasture that were lying unused because no horses had come down to Ogden or Salt Lake for grazing on them. One day he asked Will if he could have them for the rest of the summer. "You sure can," Will said. "But whatever you make off'n them, I'll take half." Bill said, "You can have it all."

For the next few days, Bill spent his spare time in and around Ogden produce markets checking supplies and demands. Before the week was up, he had his answer. Lettuce.

He plowed the land himself, borrowed money from Will, bought the lettuce plants and several cases of soda pop, again rounded up his young crew of farmhands, and went to work.

Six weeks or so later, when the plants had matured, he took samples to the Ogden markets. They were fresh and firm, large and crisp of leaf. He received a variety of offers, all good, and finally drove a bargain with a large produce dealer.

That night Bill came home with another case of soda pop. "We've got work to do tomorrow," he announced happily. For the next few days they worked steadily in the lettuce field and at the backyard packing tables, first picking the lettuce, then cutting and washing it and boxing it for market.

The 13-year-old boy came back from delivering the last wagonload to Ogden, shirt smudged with red, lettuce-field earth, arm-, back- and leg-weary from lifting lettuce crates—and aglow with pride at what he and his brothers and sisters had done. He held out a yellow rectangle of paper with writing on it. "Here, Dad. It's for you. It's all yours and Mom's."

It was a check for $2,000.

When the big sugar factory went up about a mile south of the farm, Will did the only intelligent thing: he turned his holding from a horse farm into what was largely a sugar beet and cattle-and-sheep operation. Of course, there was still acreage for hay and alfalfa and corn and produce, but most of it now was planted to sugar beets. Like a number of other farmers in these settlements north of Salt Lake City, he sold the beets to the factory for processing, then carted back to the farm the left-over beet pulp. Mixed with supplements of corn and hay, it made excellent winter feed for the cattle and sheep.

The other aspect to this was the summer and winter ranges. Will had about five hundred head of Hereford cattle and several thousand head of sheep—close, tightwooled Merinos, mostly—and toward the middle of June, he and other valley ranchers would drive their sheep and cattle up Weber or Ogden Canyon to the lush summer range east of the Wasatch ridge in the Big Basin, in what is now Snow Basin ski resort country. There they would turn the herds over to the clannish, brown-skinned, upland herders from the Basque country of Spain.

At summer's end the cattle were gathered in a wild, milling roundup that filled the air with clamor and choking clouds of dust. After two other ranchers with grazing land next to Will's cut out their feed cattle, Will and his Basques moved his animals down the canyon road and into the valley onto the farm. Then he drove the sheep down the same route. He kept the cattle, and sometimes some of the sheep, at the farm, feeding them there through the winter on silage and beet pulp. But usually, most of the sheep would be driven on out to the desolate, endless winter ranges in the western Utah and eastern Nevada deserts. They ranged on the desert until the time of the spring lambs, when the Basques would herd them back to the low hills at the north end of Salt Lake for lambing.

What with having to pitch in and help with the livestock, and keenly aware of his responsibilities as first and eldest son, the boy grew up, grew old, very fast in these first years of his teens.

He was learning that wrapped up in the sheep and cattle business were not only dawn-to-dusk hard work and the unpredictable hazards of bad weather and plunging markets, but also such other frustrating and uncontrollable elements as the foot-rot disease that attacked your sheep, forays by predator coyotes and bears, machinery breaking down, mowers, reapers, any piece of farm machinery and just when you needed it the most. Nor did you have someone standing around waiting to fix it for you. You had to get some baling wire and figure out how to fix it yourself; or if that didn't work, you could try to weld it—anything to keep it mowing or reaping and lasting for another year.

Stock-raising and farming were all that Bill knew, and he liked them all right, but—for the rest of his life? He never mentioned his doubts to Will, but gradually they came to be on his mind, in the evening, when he would work until after dark cutting the grass, or sweeping out the sheds, or touching up the fences with fresh white paint.

It wasn't that he hated this kind of work or considered it drudgery. Cleaning up, putting things in order, keeping yard and barns neat and clean, these to his brothers and sisters or even to his father might be hard work; to the boy, even at 13 or 14, it was a satisfying accomplishment. You made things orderly, the way the Lord intended them to be. You were serving the Lord. There weren't these two opposites, work and play, one bad and the other good. It was having a vision of the way things ought to be and then making them that way. To the boy, a line of white fence, standing out crisp and clean against the green of meadow, serving a purpose, useful and spare, was a thing of beauty, a work of art. It was his kind of poetry.

But he had to admit that what he liked most about his life were the summers on the range, up in the Big Basin country—living like a young cowpoke with the Basques in the sheep wagon that his mother outfitted each spring, or in tepees pitched on a flat beside a stream, under the mountain pines. Will sent him up there as the eldest son, to look after the Marriott sheep and Herefords, and it instilled in him a love of the western high country and the high country life that would never leave him—his own cow pony, heavy western saddle, lariat looped around the saddle horn, heavy chaps and high-heeled cowboy boots, flannel shirt and knotted red bandanna at the throat, dusty gray flat-crowned cowboy hat with upcurled brim,

.30-30 Winchester saddle gun in the holster at his knee, well-oiled, smooth-actioned Smith & Wesson .38 slung from the cartridge belt at his waist—at 14 the feeling of being a man among men, and among the men he admired the most, men who could ride and herd sheep and rope a steer, who could shoot fast and straight (more than once he'd seen them bring down with one pistol shot a pine hen on the wing), men who knew the lore of the range and the trail. He loved the high, bright, glittering western stars, and the distant night-yelping of coyotes up in the rimrock, the sharp, tonic, spruce-scented air, the tough, intelligent, loyal little sheep dogs, and the sheep themselves, running and bleating and flowing through the mountain draws before the Basques and the quick-footed dogs, or lying quietly across the meadow above the waterhole in the evening.

The pistol and the saddle gun were mostly for throwing potshots at pine hens or sage hens or jack rabbits, sometimes to shoot a coyote (if you could get close enough to him) that was killing the sheep. But they were handy to have around for self-protection, too.

He and the Basques kept the sheep and cattle moving; when one part of the range was grazed out, they'd move the herds to another section, perhaps every four or five days or so. One time—it must have been the summer the boy was 13—they pitched their tepees on a streamside campground on a mountain the Basques called Rattlesnake Mountain, up in the south fork of the Ogden River. Looking for strays in a canyon above the campsite, Bill felt his pony go skittery. It reared, tried to wheel away from the trail, and he heard the rattles buzzing, then saw the heavy, writhing snakes themselves weaving off the rock ledges beside the trail up ahead. He drew his pistol and let them have all six shots, but he couldn't find any that he might have hit. The frightened pony had been rearing back, and Bill either had missed completely or, if he had wounded one, it had got away. The pony was spooked now and balking, so he turned back toward the camp.

The Basques and the boy left the campfire early that night because of a sudden chill that drained down off the mountain peaks. The heavy woolen bedrolls felt good, and they were soon asleep.

The boy awoke early. He lay there for a few moments, letting his eyes and mind adjust to the new day. Then he rolled over on his stomach, raised up on his elbows, and pulled himself out of the bedroll. In the half-light of the tepee, he bent over the foot of the blankets and began to roll them up. Something beneath them stirred. Slowly he let go of the blankets and stood up and backed off to the sloping tepee wall and the pole from which, the night before, he'd hung his cartridge belt. The snake that had sensed the human warmth in the night unwound sluggishly toward the light that fell through the opening in the tepee wall. The boy saw the deadly triangular head, the thick body, the diamond markings down the back. His hand found the pistol butt; he unsheathed the pistol, lined the head with the barrel sight, and pulled the trigger three times. The snake flailed and twisted across the tepee floor and came to rest dead against the canvas to the right of the opening. The boy's tepeemates tumbled out of their bedrolls and crowded around him, thumping him on the back. He walked among them with a little swagger the rest of the summer. In his saddle bag he had, rolled up, the dried skin of the snake, five feet, eight and one-half inches long, to show to his Dad after the round-up, when he came up to help take the cattle and the sheep down below, to the Little Mountain range. He left the rattles on so the whole trophy would be intact upon the mounting board. There were fourteen of them, and even the oldest Basque said he hadn't seen a rattler that big in all the years that he could remember.

53

After that, Manuel and the others no longer treated Bill like a boy, a school kid up there on his vacation, but rather with a kind of mute, unspoken respect and as one of them. He had proved himself to them—perhaps had even saved a life—and they went out of their way to show this acceptance.

The next summer, for instance, they were all back again at Big Basin, and Manuel rode into camp late one afternoon with the mangled carcass of a lamb across his pony's withers. He dismounted and lifted the carcass and laid it on the ground in front of the sheepwagon. Four or five of the other riders and Bill as well drifted over. "Coyote?" Bill asked. Manuel shook his head. "Bear. They kill many lambs." Then Manuel looked at Bill, smiling. "You remember rattler. Tomorrow, you hunt again. This time, bear."

Manuel and Bill were up at sunrise the next day for breakfast and to saddle their horses. They both had saddle guns and Manuel bridled a packhorse. They rode back into the canyon where Manuel had come upon the dead lamb and where the fresh tracks had told him that the killer had been a bear—not a grizzly, although there were grizzlies in the Wasatch, but a smaller animal, most likely a brown bear.

The trail led them up the side of a canyon, along steep switchbacks that sometimes dropped off a sheer thousand feet or more to the canyon floor below. Manuel was sure the bear would be climbing here in search of single sheep or calves that had separated from the main herds and were up here lost, or browsing on the young leaves.

After a while, they stopped to dismount and rest their ponies. Manuel smoked a cigaret in silence. Bill checked his cartridge belt, his cartridge chamber, and the lever action of the Winchester, then checked them again.

The sun was well up—it must have been after eight o'clock—when they started on up the trail again. They had been moving only three or four minutes when the boy heard the crashing in the underbrush down the canyonside to his left. Manuel touched his arm and motioned for him to dismount. He unsheathed his gun and got down. Manuel gathered in the reins of the ponies and the packhorse. "You shoot," he whispered.

For an instant they stood stock still, Manuel holding the horses with a short tight rein, the boy holding the rifle. The blundering panicky movement through the underbrush came closer. The horses reared back. Manuel braced himself and gripped the reins tighter as a cub burst out of the brush onto the trail. It stopped for an instant at the sight of the men and plunging horses, then scrambled to a high red pine and started climbing, digging in its fore and hind claws the way a cat does, pulling itself up, scratching loose, and sending down showers of dried bark.

But the movement in the brush below them did not stop. An instant later they saw a full-grown brown bear, easily five feet high at the shoulders, plunge into a small rocky clearing fifty yards below them. Massive head swinging with each stride, tongue lolling, it lumbered toward a point up the trail from them, yet swiftly and with purpose.

"That's her," Manuel said. "The mother."

She kept coming. It took all Manuel's strength to hold the horses. Down below, where the mother bear had come from, they heard more crashing in the underbrush. "It's the father," Manuel said. "Shoot this one."

The mother burst out of the brush, wheeled toward them, reared up, and, before the boy could take aim, dropped to all fours. Teeth bared, a snarl in her throat, she charged. The boy fired once, then again. Both shots went home. The running bear's forelegs caved in and she slid forward, hind legs still pushing and thrusting, sending her skidding off the trail into the manzanita. She sprawled there and did not move.

The sounds of the other animal came nearer. "The cub," Manuel said. "You must shoot the cub, or the father will attack us."

The boy spotted the cub high in the red pine, at least a hundred feet up, the branches bending under its weight. Bill hated to have to kill it, but if he didn't, some day it would be grown, and grown bears slaughtered sheep.

He slipped two fresh cartridges into his rifle chamber, cocked the lever, got the cub in his sights, and fired. The branches moved but the cub did not drop. He fired a second shot, then a third and a fourth. The grip of the cub's claws loosened and the cub tumbled down several tiers of branches. The boy shot it again, hoping to dislodge it. The bullet went home, but the cub didn't move.

As the boy lowered the rifle, he was aware for the first time of the violent pounding of his heart. White-faced, he looked at Manuel. The sounds in the brush below receded. The other bear was going away.

The horses were calmer now. Manuel took a small bag of tobacco and some cigaret papers from his shirt pocket and rolled a cigaret. He flicked a wooden match alight with his thumbnail. Smoke curled around his sombrero. His face was serious, but a look that was a mixture of love and something else—admiration, perhaps—the look of a man toward a kid brother who is suddenly no longer a kid brother but a young man in his own right—a look of recognition like this lighted his warm brown eyes.

"Two bears in one morning," he said. *"Que hombre."*

He took the rope from his saddle and lined it through the bridles of the horses and tethered them to a tree. Then he went to his saddle bag and found a hunting knife.

"While you climb the tree for the cub," he said, "I will get the carcass ready so we can go back to camp."

Years and years later, people all over Weber County still remembered Bill as the lad who shot the two bears up above the narrows of the south fork of the Ogden River that summer, and they never saw him on the street or on the farm but what they remembered the two carcasses— the big one and the little one, wiry summer coats of gingerbread brown—hanging cleaned and spread-eagled in the window of the butcher shop on Washington Boulevard in Ogden; and the mounted clipping of the feature story in the Ogden *Standard,* and Bill's picture in his cow-poke chaps and flat-crowned hat, .30-30 in the crook of his elbow, also in the butcher's window with the bears.

Chapter Six

The years slipped by, the years of Bill's young manhood, each year much like the one before. But some things did change. As the farm prospered and Bill took hold with the cattle and sheep and the sugar beet crop, Will was free to spend more time on church affairs and politics. Well-liked and respected the length and breadth of the county, he was named as one of the two counselors of the bishopric of the Marriott Ward of the church. And, as an outstanding Weber County Republican, he was elected in 1912 to a two-year term in the Utah State House of Representatives in Salt Lake City.

Not only that, but Will memorably bought the first Buick in Marriott—a high-wheeled black touring car with mudguards, running boards, isinglass curtains, and a starting crank that could break your arm if you weren't careful. The first Sunday he took them all to church in it, they came out to where they'd parked it among the buggies and buckboards to find that while they'd been inside, awe-struck youngsters had scratched their initials all across its doors and hoods. Angry? Far from it. Will understood how they felt and was kind of proud of those initials; he never had them painted over.

In the spring of '14 they took their first family motor trip, piling with great excitement and eagerness into the Buick and striking out for Star Valley, Wyoming, where Will's twin sister lived. Their destination lay some 200 miles to the north, through baking high-country heat and along twisting mountain roads that were hardly more than cattle trails. Will let Bill drive most of the way there and back. Once the car stalled climbing a grade just

58

across one of the Snake River bridges, and would have slipped back down a couple of hundred feet into the river if they hadn't all piled out and jammed rocks behind the tires. Another time a protruding rock ledge in the crown of the road carried away a crankshaft oil line.

But from this trip on, there was no doubt about it: Bill was the official driver of the family, and with Will tied up more and more with politics and the Church, he was making almost daily trips into Ogden. One Saturday afternoon that fall, Bill parked the car on Washington Avenue and got out, and there was traffic patrolman "Peggy" Reese—called "Peggy" because he had a wooden leg—sitting right next to him in his red, two-wheeled pony cart. Off they went to the Ogden Police Station. For the next fifteen minutes the young man listened to a lecture from the desk sergeant on the evils of breaking the law, particularly the one about not driving a motor vehicle until he was 16. Long before Bill reached that age, "Peggy" got tired of running him in. He'd give Bill a friendly wave as he trotted past in the other direction, in his pony cart.

But not even the Buick meant freedom—freedom, that is, from the farm and the family. Since his attendance at school was constantly being interrupted by the necessity to herd sheep or feed cattle or harvest sugar beets, he spent much of his spare time studying his lessons and reading library books. He was hungry for knowledge, for word of the world beyond the desert to the west, beyond the mountains to the east. He devoured everything he could get his hands on, from Zane Grey and Gene Stratton-Porter to Hawthorne and Mark Twain. To find peace and quiet in the crowded farmhouse, he got up morning after morning at four or five o'clock and tiptoed downstairs to read and do his homework by the light of the big white-shaded kerosene lamp on the kitchen table.

Sometimes on these mornings—cool, quiet spring

dawns, dark winter daybreaks with the coal-stove fire warming the room and the snow swirling outside—Bill would be sitting there with the lamplight and his books, and all of a sudden he'd hear the muffled, far-off wail of a train whistle. He'd lift his head and listen.

One of the borders of the farm lay close to the main tracks of the Southern Pacific. From Ogden west they crossed the Great Salt Lake, then the desert, switchbacked over the Sierra Nevada, coasted into the Sacramento Valley and down the valley to Oakland and San Francisco Bay. At Ogden itself, in the sprawling railroad division yards, they connected with Union Pacific tracks that crossed the Wasatch into Wyoming and ran past Cheyenne and along the north bank of the Platte (like the old Mormon Trail) to Omaha, Nebraska, and all points east.

As far back as Bill could remember, his heart had turned over in some strange way as he watched the big transcontinental trains go driving by, steam laying straight out from their stacks and sending a rumble like thunder across the sugar beet fields, or when he heard the rolling click and clatter of the long freights crossing the river bridge.

A moment that he had never even dreamed of arrived in March of 1915. It had been a good winter for the farm, and Will and the lad were playing checkers one evening in the sitting room after supper.

Will, now about fifty, bent his huge frame over the board and pondered his next move. Ellen sat in a rocking chair reading the newspaper by the light of a kerosene lamp on the table beside her chair. There was a hint of spring in the air, and through the screened and open window drifted the cries of the other youngsters and their friends playing Hide and Seek in the valley dusk.

"Son," Will said, "there's something mighty big going on out in California. Have you heard anything about it?"

Bill thought he knew what his father meant, but he hesitated.

Ellen lowered her paper. " 'Course he has, haven't you, Bill? There's a story about it right here in the *Standard*."

"I reckon I know what you're talking about," the boy said. "They're having a big world's fair out there in San Francisco."

Will made his move, then leaned back in his chair. "That's right." He studied his son for a moment. "How'd you like to go out there for a few days—see the fair, and what some of the rest of the world looks like?"

Bill sat stunned. Sure, he'd been to Star Valley in the Buick and to Salt Lake City, and down to Provo once or twice—but San Francisco, where the trains went? The Pacific Ocean?

He swallowed hard. "Who—me?"

Ellen swung her paper aside. "Not if I have anything to say about it."

"That's right," Will said. "What I've been thinking is this. We've had a good spring with the sheep—two or close to three thousand of them ready for market. Now, out there in 'Frisco, they're running a big exposition all summer long to celebrate the opening of the Panama Canal. There'll be thousands of visitors every day. The restaurants will be needing lots of meat and vegetables and supplies, maybe double what they usually buy. Our lambs will bring a good price, better than in Salt Lake or even in Omaha."

The boy couldn't believe it. "And you—you want me to take them there—on the train?"

"Nothing to it," Will said. "We'll herd them up to Ogden, drive them on to the cattle cars, close the gates, and hook 'em up to a train going to 'Frisco."

Bill still couldn't believe it. "Where—where will I ride?"

His father laughed. "Where will you ride? In the caboose, with the crew. You'll be right up there where those little windows are, looking out over the countryside as you go by and learning something about this land of ours."

Ellen shook her head. "Will, that's downright irresponsible. It's putting much too big a load on the boy's shoulders—sending him off nearly a thousand miles to a strange city with thousands of sheep, when he's never been away from home before. What if he gets lost, or gets hurt—?"

The boy looked down at the board. His heart was pounding, and he never forgot what his father did next. The older man stood up, picked up his chair, and carried it over to Ellen's rocker. He sat down and took Ellen's small, work-worn hands in his big ones and looked into her eyes. "Ellen," he said, "Bill's not a boy anymore. He's a young man. For the past few years now, I've been busy with the Church and with politics and everything. Maybe I've neglected things around the farm here, and maybe there's a lot of things I should have done that I didn't do. But young Bill's stood in for me, and taken my place, just like a grown man. He's taken care of the barns and the beets. He's raised lettuce and made us a lot of money. He's taken care of the other children and you, while I've been away. He's ridden herd. Why, he's even shot a couple of bears. What other youngster in the whole valley has done that?"

He looked over at the boy with trust and confidence. "This'll be like rolling off a log for Bill. All we have to do is put those sheep on the cattle cars, and they're locked up. A couple of days on the road, and he's there. And all he has to do on the way is see that those sheep don't fall all over themselves when the train comes to a stop for water, or pulls off on a siding to let the express trains pass. I'll give him a long prod pole to take with him, so he can poke 'em up off the floor. That's all there is to it.

Ellen, I'd trust him with my life, and so would you. Sure as anything, we can trust him with a flock of sheep."

Together they looked across the room at 14-year-old Bill. His eyes were bright with excitement. He leaned forward in his chair, burning with pride at his father's words, yearning with all his heart to climb aboard one of those trains that he watched all those years, trailing west toward the desert.

Ellen's voice was soft, for the look on her son's face was unmistakable. "And would you come right back the same day?"

Will patted her hand. "Ellen, give the boy a chance. That's a big world's fair in San Francisco. Give him a chance to look it over for a few days. Then he'll come back."

"A few days," Ellen repeated. Bill would be the first of her children to go away from home into the outside world. It was hard for a mother to face.

Will kept patting her hand. "That's right, Ellen, just a few days. He won't be gone longer 'n a week before he'll be back home, right where he started from."

For the next few days, father and son worked hard. In small flocks, several hundred at a time, they and their horses and dogs herded the young sheep the six miles across the valley to the Ogden stockyards, corralling them in the cattle pens by the Southern Pacific tracks. Then the endless, back-breaking task of driving the sheep up the chutes into the long cars, more than two hundred animals to a car. Bill counted ten cars in all, long cars with horizontal slats, single-decked, with catwalks along the top.

It was late one evening in the second week of March that Bill and the sheep cars pulled out for San Francisco. The whole family stood beside the tracks in the freight yards to see him off. He shook hands with his father. "Be a good boy, son. Take care of the sheep."

63

He turned to Ellen. "Don't worry, mother. I'll be all right." He bent and kissed her cheek. His brothers and sisters crowded about him. "So long," he said.

A heavy, jarring jolt traveled down the length of the long freight as the engineer hooked up his cars. The caboose rolled back a few yards, then stopped. From far up front came a long-drawn whistle. Slowly the train began to move out of the yard. Bill, holding his straw suitcase, stood on the narrow rear platform of the caboose. An overalled brakeman with a lighted lantern swung up beside him. Bill waved good-bye. His family, upturned faces white in the gathering dusk, waved in return. The train picked up speed.

Mile after mile, hour after hour, the lad lay in the top bunk that had been assigned to him, looking out the narrow little window, rocking gently from side to side with the motion of the caboose, oblivious to the comings and goings of the train crew with whom he shared it, watching the night-dark land move past. It seemed filled with loneliness and mystery out there, under the western stars.

To this moment, some sixty years later, the memories of that fabulous trip stand out sharp and vivid, as though it had all happened yesterday—

Sitting on the rear platform of the caboose, eyes narrowed against the flying cinders, and listening to the steady, rhythmic clicking, watching the shining rails unreel from beneath the caboose, watching them seem to converge in the distance, then disappear into the motionless, mirage-like clouds far back, across the salt flats; feeling (as Will had told him he would) the train slowing down, braking for a water stop or approaching a freight point like Wells or Elko, the scramble up the iron ladder to the caboose roof, unlashing the prod pole that Will had given him, then the slow, careful run along the roofs of the freight cars, twenty or thirty of them, until he reached the cattle cars that held his sheep; then, as the train came to a stop and threw the sheep off balance and piled them up bleating and panic-stricken in the rear of their car, pushing the prod pole between the horizontal slats and poking it, swinging it into the tumbled mass of wool and bodies and hooves—anything to get the animals back on their feet so they wouldn't smother; repeating this in car after car until he was sure that all the sheep were out of danger. Sometimes the train would start with a jolt, and this, too, would jerk the floor out from under them, and Bill would have to prod them up again, starting with his lead car and poking up the others as best he could as they moved past. Then he would grab the iron ladder of the last one and pull himself up to the roof, so he could travel back down the tops of the freight cars (as they moved forward from under him) to the caboose.

There were the still snow-mantled Ruby Mountains, and the Humboldt River, and Truckee, where they took on another locomotive up front to help pull them over the Sierra divide; then west past the lake where the Donners starved to death back in '46, the year before the Mormons hit the trail to Zion; then snaking up the long hairpins to Donner Pass, marveling at the sight, out the caboose window, of the two engines working along the far side of the hairpin, drivers pounding, firebox doors open, firemen stoking, steam rolling from the tall stacks; suddenly the engines would disappear into the long wooden snowsheds, and as the caboose followed the cars into the snowshed or one of the tunnels, there was the shock of blackness, the ear-shattering blast of the exhaust hitting the ceiling.

Poppies flamed orange along the railroad tracks, wild lupin lay blue across the Mother Lode meadows, and already the Sierra foothills were beginning to be bleached tawny by the hot spring sun as they coasted down off the divide into the Sacramento Valley. There was the sweet scent of apple blossoms in the air, and the richness and languor of California all unfolded like a new Promised

Land to the wide-eyed, 14-year-old boy from Marriott, Utah. "So this," he thought, "is what the world is like."

The freight left the valley and at last reached the shore of the great bay. Freight-car ferries took him and his young sheep across the bay to San Francisco. A little switching engine pulled them to South San Francisco, the stockyards, and the waiting commission merchant to whom, before they left, Will had consigned the animals.

The week of his stay in that festival and bonny city passed in a dizzying whirl of hills and cable car bells, sea fogs rolling over Twin Peaks, the hustle and bustle of Market Street, the sandalwood-scented mysteries of Chinatown, names of exotic places he'd never heard of lettered on the windows of the shipping offices, white passenger steamers from the South Seas tied up at the Embarcadero piers next to battered rust-buckets flying strange flags of the Far East.

He stayed in a big rambling hotel on Market Street across from the new Civic Center, where workmen were putting the finishing touches to the magnificent new City Hall, whose dome, everyone boasted to him, was 16 feet higher than the dome of the Capitol in Washington, D.C. He ate in cafeterias in the side-hill streets off Union Square. Enticed by the lurid pitch of a Grant Avenue barker, he tagged along with a Chinatown tour, choked down a bowl of shark's fin soup served by pretty painted Chinese waitresses, marveled at the glazed ducks, lichee nuts, and dried sea horses in the shop windows, bought a souvenir sword made of Chinese coins (with square holes in them) for his mother, hung back, painfully ill at ease, fascinated yet repelled by the wax-complexioned and rag-clad "dope fiends" who lay on squalid bunks and pulled dreamily on their pipes in what their guide assured them was "the last authentic opium den in Chinatown, maybe in the entire United States."

He fell in with another youngster his age or a little

older, a lanky, tow-headed, blue-eyed Swedish kid named Jim Johannson. They went to the exposition together and strolled through the courts and along the palm-lined esplanades, and for the first time in his life Bill felt, personally, that he was different; he was set apart from most people. Why? He was a Mormon. Not that Jim was unkind; on the contrary, he was curious, a little in awe. They crossed the bay in a ferry to Sausalito and Jim took him to the white bungalow by the waterfront where he and his family lived. Jim introduced him as somewhat of a celebrity, with a note of pride in his voice: "Meet my friend Bill Marriott from Utah. He's a Mormon." Jim's young brothers and sisters crowded about. "Don't kid us!" one of them cried. "Where's his horns?" Another one clutched his arm. "How many wives have you got?" Bill shifted from one foot to the other. They made him smile. "Get away from him, you," Jim said. He winked at Bill. "He's got five wives, at least—haven't you, Bill?" Bill grinned. "I can't rightly say, Jim. Haven't counted 'em lately."

He remembered the blue morning glories of Sausalito and the warmth and friendliness of the Johannsons' little white cottage and Mrs. Johannson's home-cooking—he hadn't realized how much he missed his mother's—but most of all it was the big Panama-Pacific Exposition itself that opened his eyes and his mind and filled his head with dreams of travel and achievement and shining cities, world-makers and world-shakers who never had to hoe a row of sugar beets in the blazing Utah sun or ride herd on a flock of sheep through a choking white cloud of dust so thick that only your pony knew where you were going.

He marveled, wide-eyed, at everything he saw: the enormous sculptures in the sun-flooded courtyards; the stately terra cotta columns and the swan-haunted lagoon of the Palace of Fine Arts; the sea-green domes of the exhibit palaces, soft Mexican red of tile roofs, elaborately

67

formal sunken gardens, the flashing of crystal fountains; the picturesque foreign pavilions—the Turkish mosque and the Buddhist Temple, from Kyoto; the hawkers and barkers, bright lights and sideshow tents of the Fun Zone, the magic multicolored beam of the great searchlight that roved the night skies of the bay.

At an orange juice stand Bill struck up an acquaintance with a congenial businessman from Chicago. The lad liked the name of the company he owned—the Purrington Paving Brick Company of Chicago. It had, Bill thought, a kind of elegant ring to it. That afternoon—it was a warm, sunny Sunday and fair-goers were out by the tens of thousands—Bill and his new friend went down to the beach beside the bay, beyond the landing strip at the Fort Mason end of the exposition grounds, to watch Lincoln Beachey, the "flying fool," perform his breathtaking stunts in the little gossamer-winged, German-built Taube monoplane that he flew. As they stood in the crowd and watched with wonder that turned to horrified shock, the monoplane flew north toward the Marin side of the Bay, disappeared momentarily, then came back into view high over Alcatraz. Wings shining in the sun, the plane began the climb into a loop.

Before it reached the top, it fell off in a long, slipping spiral, then banked, at about a thousand feet, as if to return to the landing strip. But Beachey never made it. First one wing folded back and wrapped itself around the fuselage, then the other. The plane nosed over into a vertical dive and plunged into forty feet of water between two Fort Mason transport docks. As the crowds surged toward the docks, Bill and his friend turned away. "He's gone," Purrington said. Bill nodded. There was no doubt about it, and it was two hours and the sun was setting before a Navy diver from the battleship *Oregon* located the wreckage and a deck crew hoisted it aboard the transport *Crook* and they cut Beachey's body out of his seat belt and shoulder harness.

The next day, it was time to go. The ferry that would take him across the bay to Oakland and his eastbound train left the Ferry Building at the foot of Market Street at a little after three that afternoon. Bill was there an hour ahead of time, with his straw suitcase and wearing the new clothes he'd bought for himself at a men's clothing store on Market Street and that he'd proudly had his picture taken in at the exposition, new straw skimmer and new blue serge suit with long pants, the first he'd ever had.

Two evenings later, when he swung down from the long passenger train at the Ogden depot, Will and Ellen and his brothers and sisters greeted him as if he were Marco Polo returning triumphant from Cathay, or Peary coming back from the North Pole. In the midst of the tears and the laughter, the hugs and kisses, Ellen suddenly stood back and held him at arm's length and looked him up and down. "Why, Willard," she exclaimed. "I declare—you've got on long pants!"

Pleased, a little self-conscious, Bill held his arms out from his sides, then let them drop. "How do you like my new suit?" he asked. His brothers and sisters crowded in close to touch and admire it. He looked over their heads at his parents. The pride on their faces told him beyond words that they understood and approved. He really was grown up now.

He was so grown-up, in fact, that the next spring, Will put him in charge of another shipment of young sheep, only this time he took them east, to Omaha. At Cheyenne, less than four hundred miles from home, the conductor said that if he wasn't eighteen, he'd have to get off the freight; that was the Union Pacific rule—no riders under eighteen. Luckily, Will had sent him off with close to a hundred dollars in his pocket for traveling expenses.

He bought a coach ticket and rode a passenger train to Omaha, where he waited out the arrival of the slower freight, only to learn that his sheep weren't on it. Three days of telephone calls and telegrams finally revealed what had happened; they'd been taken off the train for feeding and watering back at a whistle-stop at Valley, Nebraska, and the freight had left without them. A few days later they turned up in Omaha safe and sound—and in a large stockyard pen with several thousand other head of sheep from someplace in Texas. To compound the problem, Will had put together his herd with sheep bought in the Ogden stockyards, so they bore mixed brands, all unfamiliar to Bill. He convinced the commission agent there was only one way to tell them apart: Utah sheep were raised on richer pastures than the sparse Texas range; his sheep, therefore, would be bigger and fatter than the other ones.

The agent cocked a skeptical eye at the 15-year-old from Ogden. "Maybe you're right, and maybe not," he said. "But since the Texas fellow isn't here to claim *his* sheep, and won't be for a day or two, I guess we'll have to do it your way. Go on out there and get on the cutting gate and pick the ones you want."

On the trip back home, Bill vowed that he'd had enough of sheep, and freight trains, and worry. Someone else could take them to market next year.

But when the next year came around and Will said, "Come on, son, let's put our lambs on the train and take them to Omaha," he couldn't resist the thought of lying up there beside the little window in the caboose, and looking out at the farms and the wheatfields, and hearing train whistles hooting in the night. So he went with Will to Omaha that year and the next. There was a restaurant by the stockyards whose specialty was fresh Missouri river catfish, grilled over an open fire and served with mountains of hot, buttered corn bread. Will loved the

70

taste and white flakiness of the catfish, and so did Bill. "This is the life," Will would say as the waiter set the steaming plates before them. They had some of the best times of their lives together, there in Omaha, after they had brought the sheep from Ogden.

Chapter Seven

Every worthy young Mormon generally spends eighteen months to two years "in the field" as a missionary. Some 25,000 of them are scattered all over the world, telling the Mormon story, making converts to The Church of Jesus Christ of Latter-day Saints, living on whatever they have saved or their families can spare.

Bill had taken it for granted that when the proper time came, he too would go wherever the Church wanted him to go. At the age of twelve he'd been ordained a deacon in the Marriott Ward, and ever since then had been helping with Sunday services. At fifteen he'd been ordained a church teacher, at seventeen a priest; and now at nineteen he had, with due ceremony, been ordained an elder in the Melchizedek Priesthood, whose special function, as is stated in the Church's Doctrine and Covenants, is "to administer in spiritual things." He should, it seemed to him, undertake his mission now.

But Will disagreed. "I need you here on the farm, son," he said. "Who's to help me with the sheep and the sugar beets? Besides, we've no money to give you. We've not only got nothing; we've got *less* than nothing."

The young elder countered with zeal and faith. If he went now, he would only be 21 when he got back—time enough to go to college. As for helping out, Paul, Woody, and Russell and even the girls were strong enough to pitch in; then when he came back and went back to school, he'd be there to help *them* through college. Getting by in the mission field was no problem at all. He was young and tough and could live on next to nothing. Finally, and simply, he gave his strongest reason for wanting to go: the Church and the Lord needed him.

In the end, Will could no longer resist. The family scraped together what money it could for train fare and clothes and something to live on until Will could somehow make enough to support him. He sold the Buick with the names scratched on it. Ellen sold her precious gold watch and chain. Once again, there was the tearful farewell at the Ogden station. Two years. That's all they could think of. True, it wasn't Japan or South Africa or any other romantic place that he'd been assigned to; it was only New England, Vermont and Connecticut, probably. Still, for Ellen those two years would be two lifetimes.

"God be with you," Ellen said, holding him close. "And don't forget—wear your sweater under your coat when it's cold."

"We're mighty proud of you, son," Will said.

Bill kissed them both, and his sisters, and shook hands with his young brothers—Bill, tall, gangling, strange-looking in his new, store-bought black woolen suit, the unaccustomed white shirt whose celluloid collar already chaffed his neck, his new black shoes, stiff and unbroken-in, his derby hat that the missionaries wore, which he said was too small and his brothers and sisters said was too big.

This time it was not the trampish, end-of-the-train caboose that he swung aboard, but one of the day coaches, in which he'd sit up all night. The conductor followed him on to the car with portable step. The metal cover slammed down over the steps. The bottom half of the door banged shut. Bill leaned out over it and waved. The station platform was crowded, but all he could see was his family, waving, in tears, he knew, growing smaller across the lengthening distance between them. He waved his arm slowly, rhythmically, like the pendulum of a clock, until the train curved toward the mountains, and they were out of sight.

There were twenty-five missionaries on the train bound for New York and the Eastern States Mission, of which George W. McCune was president. They came from nearly every state in the Rocky Mountain west. One of them Bill never forgot, a slender, sun-burnt young sheep-rancher from southern Utah. He swore it was the first train he'd ever seen, and Bill believed him. All the others wore their somber missionary clothes; he came aboard wearing a black suit, but with it a plaid shirt, curled-brim cowboy hat, and high-heeled cowboy boots. In New York, he refused to part with his hat or his boots. He would stutter and stumble through a street-corner meeting and finally give up in red-faced confusion.

A year later, Bill saw him preaching to a crowd on the New Haven Green. He wore white shirt, black tie, and celluloid collar, black suit and shoes, and in his right hand held a black derby. His face was paler, but he spoke confidently and forcefully. The crowd listened intently.

The transformation was amazing. "How'd you do it?" Bill asked after the meeting.

The sheepherder shrugged. "I just realized one day how raw I was, how poorly equipped to do the Lord's work. So I buckled down and changed my ways and my outlook, and studied hard, and began to do not what I wanted to do, but what the Lord asked me to do. I still have far to go. But I've started."

Later Bill said this proved to him for all time the tremendous change that true religion can have on the life of an individual who lives close to the Lord.

New York was a fantasy in iron, bricks, and concrete, dreamed out by futuristic madmen against the hot blue skies of Manhattan in September. All its marvels, the Flatiron Building, the skyscraping Woolworth Building, the Brooklyn Bridge, and the Hippodrome, the teeming streets, the opulent stores, the subterranean, heart-stopping plunge of the subways, the Statue of Liberty, the ferryboats, the ships from all over the world and their hooting whistles—for days these bedazzled Bill. He went around in a wide-eyed trance.

Between early morning study sessions at the mission home on Gates Avenue in Brooklyn and street-corner gospel meetings in the crooked canyons of the financial district, Bill saw the sights in style with the Bushnells, whom he looked up a day or so after his arrival. Laura Bushnell was a cousin of his from Ogden. Her husband was George Bushnell, who had started out west with the J.C. Penney Company and had impressively "made good." Now financial vice-president of the company, he lived in a huge apartment on upper West End Avenue. The Bushnells liked Bill, and with them and Laura's sister Ruby, who was about his age, he toured Central Park in the Bushnells' chauffeur-driven limousine and saw the *Ziegfeld Follies.*

After three brief weeks he was on a train again, bound this time for Burlington, Vermont, to preach the restored gospel across the valleys and forested ridges of the Green Mountains, beside the swift-rushing rivers, in the cool shade of village green elms, and later on in the small towns and the cities along the Connecticut shore.

Bill was met at Burlington by his assigned missionary companion, T.W. Tanner, ex-cow puncher, ex-sheriff from Snowflake, Arizona, a tiny Mormon outpost south of the Painted Desert. Sun-leathered face, permanently parched lips, calloused, flipperlike hands that could bulldog a steer faster than you could say "Longhorn." Tough? Sure—on the outside. Inside his heart was like lamb's wool.

They made a curious pair: the lanky, tow-headed nineteen-year-old and the old sheriff and cowhand (at least, in his forties, he seemed old to Bill), walking with a cowpoke slouch, talking with a cowpoke twang, uncomfortable in his somber preacher's clothes. But they were

75

earnest, eager to toil for the Lord in this back country vineyard where Joseph Smith and Brigham Young had been born more than a century before.

In the summer they walked the dusty roads with their suitcases, their Bibles, and their tracts, chopped wood for their meals, slept in bat-haunted barns and starlit haymows. Winter snows forced them indoors, into the cheapest of boarding houses; occasionally a Mormon farmer and his family would put them up for a day or two.

They would climb out of bed shivering in the 40-below-zero dawn and study the Book of Mormon and James E. Talmage's *Articles of Faith,* the prophecies of Joseph Smith, and the discourses of Brigham Young until breakfast time. After breakfast they would leave the house together and go "tracting" to people in homes, stores, and any warm place in the wintertime.

"What do you know about the Mormons, friend? We'd be glad to tell you about them, and then answer any questions you have about our religion."

Most of the time there was little interest. Nevertheless, there was something open and appealing about this ill-assorted pair; a twinkle of humor in their eyes, yet an earnestness. Now and then someone would reply, "Did you mention religion?"

"We're Mormons. Say, can we tell you something about Joseph Smith, about Mormonism?"

"Mormons?—no, thanks."

In the winter their favorite place was the railroad station. Here people were waiting for trains. As a rule, they found Vermonters ingrown, taciturn, suspicious of strangers, difficult to reach with their message of the restored gospel. But most people in a railroad station were ready to listen, just to pass the time of day, until their train came in.

They'd pick a man who looked relaxed and approachable, and sit down beside him. A few remarks about the weather—Burlington is sure a mighty nice little city, isn't it? they'd say. A lot different from where they came from.

Where's that?

Out west, Utah, Bill would say, Arizona, Elder Tanner would say.

The man would perk up his ears. How come you're 'way back here? Coupla drummers?

Yes, you might call us that—drummers. Not book peddlers or dry goods drummers. Nothing like that. We're drummers of the Gospel. Drummers for the living Lord.

When Bill said this, he'd think of the golden Angel Moroni high atop the temple spire in Salt Lake City, blowing his trumpet eastward across the mountains. That was his inspiration. He too—Bill Marriott—was a trumpeter of the Truth.

The "living" Lord? Humph. He died nineteen hundred years ago.

A shake of the head. Sorry, sir. That's just it. He *didn't* die. Jesus lives. He's as alive today as He was when He walked by the Sea of Galilee. Yes sir, He lives! A man in our time has seen Him—a man born right here in Vermont. Joseph Smith. Joseph Smith saw Him in a vision, saw Him in a maple grove—Him and His Father.

Joseph Smith? Don't know as I ever heard of the fella.

Just what T.W. and Bill had been waiting for, hoping for, even praying for. Well, now, here's a little leaflet that'll tell you all about him. Read it at home, when your day is over. But while we're sitting here waiting for the train, we'd like to tell you about the new religion that he started.

Now, what are people all over this great land of ours hungering for today? Why, it's kindness, isn't it? Yes sir, kindness, brotherhood, peace, love—something to believe in. The living Jesus wants and yearns to give us these things, to instill them in our hearts, if we'll let Him.

We know. Because it's happened to us, to our people. And it *works!* Why, mister, you ought to see what we've done out there in the desert in the last seventy years. Like Moses, we've brought forth water from the rock. We've made roses and peach trees bloom—!

It was hard for them to hold themselves back, there was so much they wanted to pour forth in the name and for the glory of the Lord.

Sure, Bill was homesick. He and T.W. both had moments when they felt forlorn and forgotten, when they covered page after page in letters to their families back home. And when one of them got a letter from home, he'd read it out loud to the other that night in their boardinghouse room.

One time in particular, home and family came back with a rush, and something that had happened there shortly before his departure came flooding back, to carry him through a crisis from which he emerged with more religious conviction than ever. One night, just as he was finishing a letter to his mother, the telephone rang downstairs in the boardinghouse hall, next to the parlor. Mrs. Bellow, the landlady, answered it. She put down the receiver. "Mr. Marriott. Telephone."

It was Richard Mather, a farmer who lived a few miles south of Burlington and was one of the dozen or so Mormons in northern Vermont. "It's my daughter Ruth, Brother Marriott. She's hurt. You're an elder of the Melchizedek Priesthood—the only one around —"

"Have you called a doctor?" Bill asked.

"He says it's bad. She slipped and fell off a cliff over near Lake Champlain. He says she's going to die."

Bill, receiver to his ear, eyes closed, remembered his brother Paul.

It had happened only a year ago. Paul had been deathly ill with spinal meningitis. After the doctor examined him, he slowly shook his head. "I'm afraid there's no hope," he said. Ellen remembered their baker. He called in his wagon twice a week. He was a Mormon and a member of the priesthood and had healed a Slaterville woman dying of diphtheria. The scene rolled through Bill's mind in an instant: the coming of the baker that hot summer night, a long-armed, heavyset man, moving silently and swiftly into the parlor. Will went with him, and the other family members followed. He asked them all to kneel down and have a prayer. The words of James, chapter 5, verses 14-15, came to them: "Is any sick among you? let him call for the elders of the church. . . . And the prayer of faith shall save the sick, and the Lord shall raise him up." After he led them in a prayer for Paul, the baker and Will went into Paul's room and closed the door. In a little while they came out. Their eyes and faces, Bill thought, seemed peaceful and reverent. The baker said solemnly, " 'According to your faith, be it unto you.' He will live."

Later, Paul couldn't remember much about the baker. "All I remember is, he and Dad put their hands on my head and commanded me in the name of Jesus Christ to be healed. Almost immediately my illness left me, and I raised up in my bed and asked for some bread and milk. I hadn't eaten for three days. My jaws were locked."

It was a half-hour drive to the farmer's house. On the way Bill asked about Ruth's injuries. Slipped and slid down this cliff, about 45 feet, the farmer said, and must have hit her head on the way down. No bones broken, but a cut on the right side of her head, across the temple. She had been unconscious while the doctor was there, and he couldn't revive her. But after he left, she seemed to come to. She began moaning and muttering. Neither he nor his wife could understand what she was trying to say.

His companion, Elder Tanner, had gone to a meeting, so Bill was alone. Always two elders go to administer to the sick, but he traveled to the home and met the family all alone because of the emergency. He went into Ruth's bedroom and shut the door. There, with an overwhelming sense of humility, he took her hand and asked for the Lord's healing presence to reveal itself in that room. He placed his hands gently upon her head and gave her a blessing by the power of the priesthood he held, and in the name of Jesus Christ.

The next thing he knew, there was a knock on the door. He had no idea how long he had been in the room. "Come in," he said. The door opened. The parents stood outside. "It's been more than half an hour," the farmer said. "We were afraid—"

Bill rose from his bedside chair. He knew that what he was going to say was the truth. "She'll be all right."

Even before he left, Ruth opened her eyes. "Mama," she whispered, "I'm very thirsty."

It was hard for Bill to understand Vermont and Vermonters. He and T.W. often discussed it, as they walked the country roads. "With all the change and uncertainty everywhere in the world today, you'd think people would be interested in listening to almost any religious message, wouldn't you?" Bill would say.

Both he and T.W. were convinced that they had a religion that could cure every ill in the world, if people would only listen and believe and live by it. What Bill loved to talk about more than anything else was The Church of Jesus Christ of Latter-day Saints as the "restored church"—restored, that is, to the true Christian church as it was in the days of Christ's apostles, restored by direct action of the Lord, in His revelations and those of many angels who appeared to Joseph Smith and his associates in the 1820s and 1830s.

And to Bill it was a source of endless fascination that of all places in the world, here he was in Vermont, trying to spread the truth about a religion—"The only religion of power and vitality," Emerson has said, "that has made its appearance for the last twelve hundred years"—and that this religion, incredibly, was founded by a native Vermonter, born in Sharon, in Windsor County, on the banks of the White River!

Some of his listeners were impressed; most were not. In fact, a Burlington newspaper printed an editorial warning its readers against the missionaries. "They're passing out Godless tracts, and holding their heathen revival meetings in our towns and villages. They remind us that the founder of Mormonism, and his brother, and some of their prophets and so-called apostles were Vermont-born. Well, those leaders, whoever they were, are enough Mormons to last Vermont forever. We don't want any more—not up here in the Green Mountain state. These missionaries should go—back to the Utah wastelands where they came from."

Then the terrible winter of frost and snow was over. It was spring again, warm and sunny. Bill and T.W., in their black suits and ties and derby hats, carrying their small black suitcases, struck out north from Burlington on the narrow winding road to Colechester Mountain. A couple of touring cars and a few teams and buckboards passed them, bound in the same direction. None stopped. Late that afternoon they rounded a bend in the road. A sign said, "Go Slow—Colechester."

They'd always remember Colechester. Backs against a towering elm, they rested for a while on the village green. Then they went from one to the other of the three small churches in the village, found the ministers, and asked each one in turn if they could conduct a religious service in his church that evening.

"Mormons? In my church? Most definitely not!" Slam of parsonage door—bang! And there they stood, alone on the parsonage steps. Finally they found a small town meeting hall with a stage and back door and platform. It was over the village drugstore. They got permission to use it for a night meeting. While T.W. went from house to house inviting families to the meeting, Bill got sheets of paper and thumbtacks from the druggist, wrote out meeting notices, and tacked them to telephone poles up and down the main street.

Thirty, perhaps forty, villagers gathered in the September dusk and climbed the outside steps to the meeting hall to hear about the Mormons. Promptly at seven-thirty, Bill opened the meeting. He thanked them for coming and led them in prayer. Faltering at first—it was difficult to warm up to it right away without accompaniment—but then full-throated and strong, they sang three verses of "We Thank Thee, O God, for a Prophet."

Then T.W. stood up and told them something about Mormon doctrine—how the Mormons believed it to have been divinely inspired, and how through The Church of Jesus Christ of Latter-day Saints it had restored the relationship of man and God to the simple, direct relationship that existed nearly two thousand years ago between Christ and His disciples. He told them about the visitation of the two "Personages" to Joseph Smith in the grove at Palmyra, and of the appearances of other heavenly beings, and of the establishment of the Church.

When T.W. had finished and they had sung the closing hymn, "God Be With You," Bill passed out Mormon tracts. Suddenly they heard angry noises in the streets below. T.W. went to a front window and looked out. He came back pale, but his voice was calm and even. "There must be two hundred out there. Let's talk to them."

Bill turned to the little congregation. "Brothers and sisters, you'd best stay right here. Brother Tanner and I'll draw these people away from here, then you can go home." They got their hats and suitcases. "Don't you worry about us," Bill said. "We can explain why we're here."

It was after nine o'clock and dark and cool outside. They moved swiftly and quietly out the rear door, and Bill could make out the dark forms of men milling around, some of them brandishing torches. In their flickering light he thought he saw one of the ministers. Above the commotion he heard a hoarse yell. "Get the Mormons!" The crowd shouted approval. "Run 'em out of town." The men waved their hats and shook their fists and cheered even louder. Rotten apples smashed against the side of the building. One thumped against Bill's suitcase, another struck him on the shoulder. It didn't hurt, but the smell sickened him.

Halfway down the steps the missionaries ducked under the platform, jumped to the ground, and broke for the lane that led to the street. Before they reached the street, the mob was after them.

As they ran and stumbled through the dark they heard the angry men behind them. A tomato hit Elder Tanner between the shoulder blades.

"Tar and feather 'em!" the crowd yelled. "Get the Mormon rascals!"

Bill and T.W. were young, in condition—and scared. When they felt the firm dirt road under their feet, they knew they could outrun the men behind them. They ran half a mile at full speed, then stopped, gasping. T.W. held up his suitcase. "This is getting heavy."

"Let's get off the road," Bill said.

They plunged into the roadside brush, splashed across a drainage ditch, and dropped to the ground. A moment later they heard the running footsteps of the men coming after them. As they pounded past, Bill saw random flashes and heard cracks, like a stick hitting leather. Rifle shots.

On hands and knees, feeling their way through the dark, they crawled to the end of the thicket, at the edge of a clearing. A few hundred yards beyond the clearing lay a dark line of trees. In a crouching run they moved into the clearing—a cow pasture—toward the trees.

In the blackness of the shelter of the pines they lay panting on the ground, and Bill could hardly believe it when he heard a crashing in the brush off to their right. Something else, a dark mass, moved closer on their left. T.W. said grimly, "I'll be darned if I'm going to run another step." He stood up, lurched toward an advancing shape, and kicked out as hard as he could. The shape bellowed and lumbered off through the undergrowth. There was the sound of more crashing and heavy hoof-beats, receding. T.W. collapsed on the ground beside Bill. "Cows. They must have smelled the rotten apples on our clothes, and came to have a bite." In a few minutes, when the woods were still again, they began to laugh, rolling on the hard ground and the pine needles. It wasn't funny, and yet it was. And they were safe.

As the weather grew colder, Bill and T.W. heard from New York that one Vermont winter was enough for any Mormon missionary, however dedicated. Bill was being reassigned to Connecticut, and T.W. to Virginia. So that winter of 1920-21, Bill spent most of his time in New Haven, a few blocks from the Yale University campus, and in nearby Norwalk and Stamford.

Now that he wasn't on the move so much, he took more pains with his diary. Every evening before going to bed, or sometimes the next morning if he got to bed too late or had sleepless spells during the night, he filled a page with the events of the day. He wrote, as he would all his life in similar diaries, in a modified Palmer-method script, using abbreviations and ellipses to save space.

The diary for that year presents a humdrum yet fascinating account, day by day, of the life of a young Mormon missionary, or, one would guess, of any kind of missionary, allowing for doctrinal variations.

84

Bill and his missionary companions spent their days tracting, ringing doorbells, getting rebuffed, getting invited in for gospel talks, explaining Mormon doctrine, selling the Book of Mormon or loaning it when the person wouldn't or couldn't buy it. They attended missionary meetings at the Whalley Avenue mission home in New Haven, preached on street corners, spent endless hours studying the life of Joseph Smith, the history of the Church, the Bible and the Book of Mormon. They were bitten by dogs, ordered out of houses by irate husbands, threatened with arrest as heathens and polygamists. They dickered with their landladies over the gas they consumed, cooked each other's breakfasts, slept together to save room rent, washed their own clothes, praised the Lord and at all times thanked Him for their manifest blessings.

As for Bill personally, he frequently wrote of feeling poorly, of an unhealthy diet, and of plain, simple fatigue. He dreamed of home a lot and worried for fear the terrible financial problems on the farm would force him to abandon his mission before two years were up. But, for all these troubling things, he was always able to write that the day was beautiful, the air off the Sound was fresh and clean, and surely there could be no more beautiful city in the world than Stamford, with all the trees in leaf and the shade cool and the park lawns green.

March, in particular, was a critical month. On the second, for instance: "Studied Gospel all morning. A beautiful day. Called on Mrs. Wilton this afternoon. Delivered a Book of Mormon, Pearl of Great Price and Doctrine and Covenants. She asked a few questions, but I was unable to answer them properly. I felt like I was in a stupor. Came home & prayed to the Lord for forgiveness of negligence & faults—because I do not feel in harmony with the Spirit. But now I feel better. Called on Mrs. Jerman and stayed an hour. Bed at 11."

On the 10th, things looked happier. "Up at 6:15. Studied, & out tracting at 8:30. A beautiful spring day. Sun diffusing its effulgent rays, warms everything & makes one feel like tracting. Stayed out this afternoon until 4:30."

But, on the 16th, bad news. "Received a letter from mother today, stating their condition was very bad. It would break my heart to be released. I am just beginning to really enjoy my work, & get the most out of it. I can study & remember now & am learning how to get the Gospel before the people more proficiently. Wrote to mother a long letter telling her of my sentiments. Makes me feel very bad. I hope & pray the Lord will open up the way for me to stay & finish. Called on Mrs. Barrett tonight. Wasn't home. Bed at 9:30."

On the 19th, he hitchhiked along the Post Road from Stamford to New Haven for a few days' work with the missionaries there. They conducted gospel meetings on the New Haven Green and on street corners in poorer sections of the city, sometimes running for the police to come help them with the drunks and hecklers who wanted to punch the missionaries in the nose. Two days later, they held an all-day missionary meeting conducted by President McCune from New York. He was Bill's only hope. "I told Pres. McCune of my condition at home so he is going to wire the folks. My, but that makes me feel bad. I could just set down & cry for an hour to think of it—to leave this splendid band of missionaries would be very sorrowful & esp. the good work. However, the Lord's will be done."

On the 26th he was in New York, attending a meeting at the Gates Avenue mission home in Brooklyn. He heard a fine talk by Congressman Don B. Colton from Vernal, Utah. Then, back in Stamford, on the 30th the world turned bright again. "Up at 6:20. Studied Old Testament all morning. A beautiful day. Received a letter from Pres.

McCune inclosing a telegram from home, saying for me to remain in the mission field. That was happy news to me. Received a letter from mother. I feel thankful for such good parents & to the Lord. He has opened up the way. Tracted 2 hours this afternoon."

Bill was released from his mission in New York on September 15. The Bushnells helped him celebrate that evening by taking him and Ruby to a Broadway musical.

Since he didn't know when he'd ever be back in the East, he had his heart set on returning home by way of Washington, D.C. Senator Reed Smoot of Utah was a mighty powerful man there in the nation's capital, and he had met Congressman Colton. These men frequently got government jobs in Washington for promising and ambitious young Mormons. Maybe some day—

He arrived at Union Station, Washington, on the Pennsylvania Railroad at 6:35 P.M. on September 17, his 21st birthday. He walked to a small hotel a few blocks from the station, checked in, and spent the rest of the evening studying timetables and trying to put together his train ride home.

Next morning, a Sunday, he walked back to the station, bought his passenger and Pullman tickets to St. Louis, then boarded a sightseeing bus for a tour of Washington. When this was over, he walked from Capitol Hill to the Washington Monument, toiled up the steps to the top, walked back down again, and strolled over to the Lincoln Memorial. Everywhere he went tourists and pedestrians sweltered and sweated in the sultry, humid air. On the way back to his hotel, he just stood there in the street watching the crowds. He couldn't get over it: a pushcart peddler would come along the street selling lemonade and soda pop and ice cream, and in minutes he'd be cleaned out and on his way to stock up with another cartload.

He left Washington Monday and on Tuesday night caught the Missouri Pacific sleeper out of St. Louis for Independence, Missouri, then traveled on to Kansas City. From there to Denver, a last change of trains, this time to the Denver and Rio Grande, and at 7 A.M. on the morning of the 23rd, he woke up in Utah and thanked the Lord for bringing him home safely.

Will and Ellen and his brother Paul met him at the Ogden station, and he rode home with them in a buggy. The others were at the farm waiting.

"Can't imagine I'm home again," he wrote that night in his diary. "Children here all grown so much. Girls especially. Had a good supper. Aunt Kate, Lucille, and Myrtle Parry and her husband came down to see me. Dad and I killed a calf tonight for my welcome home party. Had prayer and went to bed at 10:30."

Chapter Eight

Some things were the same after two years, but a lot were different and would never be the same again. And of those that were different, some of them had happened at home and some had happened to Bill.

For example, the mountains were the same, mighty and eternal, towering against the blue September sky—a presence that he had longed for on many New England nights and days—and they never looked so good to Bill as they did when he came home that year. And there were the green pastures and the corn and sugar beet fields stretching westward to the salt marshes and the lake, and the familiar, longed-for smell of sage.

Ogden, though struggling through the post-war depression that had collapsed cattle, sheep, and farm produce prices, looked pretty much the same, too. More "gas buggies" on the broad streets, perhaps, one or two more moving picture theaters, a few more radio antennae strung across the rooftops, but otherwise, it was the same town that he'd left two years before.

The farm and the life there were as Bill remembered them, and before he'd been home a week, Bill knew that this was the trouble. As a child, riding with the sheep-herders and hunting and fishing and packing a six-shooter had all been so much the kind of life he loved that it had never occurred to him to dream of anything different. But as he grew older, beginning, perhaps, with his visit to San Francisco, he began to see that there were worlds other than that of the farm and the cattle range.

And now, though Will himself had never told him, and though all his life the Marriotts had been better off than most of the farmers in the valley, it was evident that his father had gone broke in the sheep and cattle business. He had loved it; it was his life, and he was as good at it as any man in the West. He had good land and worked hard over his crops, but none of this mattered. Times were bad. Everyone was in trouble.

He'd never let on to Bill, when he sent the boy on his mission, that he was going under and needed help. But the letters from his mother had given it all away. No use pretending any more.

"Sure I had to borrow," he told Bill. "I was lucky our friends there at the Ogden State Bank would loan me any money at all. I know a couple of farmers they turned down."

"How much did you borrow?"

"Just after you left, we needed twenty thousand. And then I borrowed another twenty thousand, and another ten."

Bill was shocked. "We owe the bank fifty thousand dollars?"

Why sure, Will said, and if Bill wasn't such an impatient son of a gun, he'd see that everything was going to be all right. "Times're going to get better, son, and that's when we'll cash in. Why, right now we're runnin' twelve to fourteen thousand head of sheep, close to five hundred head of cattle. With the bank money, I paid twelve to fourteen dollars a head for the sheep. Today they're worth three, maybe five. Now I know it, Bill, and you know it: prices can't stay this low forever. They're going up. And when they do, we'll sell. We'll make it all back, and then some. This time next year, we won't owe a dime, I hope—"

As he listened, Bill's heart sank. He knew his dad wasn't the only one. Every farmer in the valley was in the same predicament. War in Europe and rising prices and good times; Armistice Day and peace, it's over over there, the boys come marching home—and unemployment, falling prices, strikes, and things have gone bad. Suddenly the bottom drops out of the livestock market, and you've mortgaged the farm, your stock, your future, your life. It was all a gamble, a crazy kind of roulette. The fine free frontier life was gone. The frontier itself was gone. There wasn't any West to go to any more; it was all staked out and fenced in. For better or worse, even Utah, Promised Land and New Zion, was a dependent part and parcel of America, as attuned to Pennsylvania Avenue, Wall Street, Michigan Boulevard, and Montgomery Street as any other state. Bill saw this now, and knew that for the rest of his days his father would be working for the bank.

He knew, too, sadly, because he loved his dad and his family and the West and all it stood for, and yet with a surge of excitement at the life that beckoned him back across the mountains—he knew that this farm, these problems, this struggle, this life, were not for him.

The way out, the lifting hold on his own bootstraps, was an education. He had to know more about everything. He had to know how to study, think, and act like an educated man, like those he'd seen riding up Fifth Avenue in their chauffeured limousines. He was willing to work; God knew he was willing to work his head off. But how could he compete in the marketplace without a college degree? It'd be like trying to rope a steer from a sawhorse.

An education demanded two things: money and, just as important, college credits. Hopelessly, he had neither. He'd come home from his mission with something like four dollars in his pocket. As for credits, he hadn't even finished high school. How could he, when every year he had to leave school to help on the farm or with the sheep and the cattle?

In the first days of his return he took his frustrations out on his family and tried feverishly to work it off in any way that presented itself.

When he caught Paul and Eva dumping spoonsful of sugar over their breakfast oatmeal, he curtly ordered them to stop. "Don't eat that stuff. It's bad for your teeth. And it's too expensive. We can't afford it." Somewhat sanctimoniously, he expressed shock at his sisters' lipstick. "Go upstairs and take it off." And he insisted that they lengthen their modishly revealing skirts.

Outside the house, he cleaned up the neglected yard, patched the siding of the barns, and mended the sagging pasture fences. Nearly every night after supper, he attended a church meeting in some ward of Weber County and spoke out about his mission—how he and his brother missionaries preached the gospel on busy street corners and in country railroad depots, on trains and in front parlors of anyone who'd let them inside the door, enduring with the Lord's love in their hearts the cold, the rain, the hecklers and belligerent drunks, the angry mob pelting them with rotten apples.

He stood before them at the ward chapel podiums, tall, gangling, rail-thin, tow-headed, squinting a little against the lights, speaking still with a sagebrush twang, and two things setting him apart: the New Haven-tailored, Yale-man suit that he was so proud of, and a kind of electric faith in God, the good life according to the Mormon Word of Wisdom, and the virtues of hard, unremitting work.

"You sure learn a lot in the mission field," he told them. "I learned a lot about self-reliance. I learned to meet people, to talk with them, to get along with them. I learned how to explain the gospel, and to tell the story of Joseph Smith and Mormonism.

"And another wonderful thing. We were living right every day, clean moral lives, almost as perfect a life as you can live on earth. We were trying to help people, trying to get them to accept a system that would help them lead better lives. The growth, the change in all of us, was unbelievable. Most of us had never made a speech, never been off the ranch, but prayer and hard work led to miracles in our personal development.

"And I could see the difference—the difference between people who lived clean like us and those who didn't. They were unkind and mean and unhappy. They knew very little about God and His relation to man. They couldn't understand that He's a real person, an Individual, a resurrected Being. They couldn't believe what we know is the truth—that God is a power, or a source of power, that could appear right here in this room, right now.

"But that's the greatest thrill of missionary work—to tell people about life and the spirit, to bring them the gospel truth and inspire them to leave their bad habits behind and walk hand in hand with the Lord."

One afternoon Bill went to see Aaron W. Tracy—and it was like finding a trail in the desert, a trail that would lead him out of the wasteland.

Tracy, a thin, nervous, red-haired man, had taught at the Slaterville School. A first-rate teacher and administrator, he was now a professor of English at Weber College in Ogden. This would be the school's first year as a co-educational junior college offering four years of high school and two of college. Until then, it had been Weber Academy and had provided only high school courses. Located in an imposing red brick building two blocks east of Washington Avenue, its enrollment this year would total about 500.

Aaron Tracy had always liked the Marriott boy and was the only one, aside from the boy's mother, who always called him Willard. He knew what a struggle it had been for the young man to get an education when he was needed at home to help with the cattle and the crops, and he knew, too, how important an education was if that young man were ever to escape to a better, broader life. He remembered that he'd already broken the rules with Willard. Back when Willard had been dropping in and out of his grade school classes, it didn't look as though he'd completed enough work to earn promotion from the sixth grade to the seventh. Yet Tracy believed—nay, knew—that the ability and the yearning were there. One day, just before summer vacation, he'd told the class to draw a map of the United States and to put in as many states and state capitals as they could. Bill's carefully drawn map had been more accurate, more complete than any of the others. "Willard," he'd said, "just for that, I'm going to promote you to the seventh grade."

And when, a few days later, they were saying good-bye for the summer, he'd put his arm around the boy's shoulders. "You're a good student, Willard. You've got a good mind. I have one parting word: never give up. You can accomplish anything in this world that you want to accomplish, if you will just work hard enough."

Now, once more, as he listened to Bill that September afternoon in his office at the college, he saw that once more he was a young man desperately in need of help. Of course he was twenty-one and didn't have the high school credits, but—what of it? As Bill talked on about his mission, about the sheep drive that had held him back, Tracy looked out his window at the mountain ridge. If someone had only helped him when he was twenty-one—

Bill could make up the back work as he went along. As for money, he could find Bill odd jobs around the college that would provide almost his full tuition. In fact, a couple of college projects really needed a young man with his ambition and hustle. He smiled and shook Bill's hand. "Don't worry, Willard," he said. "Come back next week, when classes begin. There'll be a place for you here."

Bill never knew days and nights, weeks and months, to go so fast. The mornings broke with the tinkling of his alarm at 4, the lighting of the oil burner to warm his room, and the kerosene lamp to see by. Then he dressed hastily while it was still dark outside, dashed cold water in his face, got himself a piece of toast and apple butter and a glass of cold milk for breakfast, and studied in his bedroom until time to leave for class. Then he hitched up a horse and buggy and piled in with Eva, 17, Paul, 15, and Kay, 13 (they were attending Weber, too, in the high school classes), and drove five miles east across the valley floor to the red brick building. After classes came the long afternoons trudging up one business block in Ogden and down another soliciting advertisements for the Weber *Herald,* the college's bimonthly newspaper, and the *Acorn,* the college yearbook. And when he'd done all of this he could, he'd return to the college bookstore to help out selling textbooks and stationery supplies and setting its stock and accounts in order. Sometimes he helped out with the editing of the *Herald.* To add to all this, he was also elected president of the student body.

But he made it. On a sunny morning in June, a few months away from his 23rd birthday, Bill became one of the fifty-odd young men and women to graduate in Weber Junior College's first class. Aaron Tracy, who had recently been named president of the college, shook his hand warmly as he handed Bill his diploma. "Forward, my boy, forward," he said. Tears came to Bill's eyes. The first stage of the journey, perhaps the hardest, was behind him.

The next three summers went fast, too. In a way, they were extensions of his mission years, providing opportunities to do things he was good at and liked, things that became more and more important to him as he grew older: traveling, meeting new people, making available to them goods and services that satisfied their needs. During these summers, it was woolen goods—rough, honest, warm woolens spun from the fleece of Utah and Nevada sheep in the mills of Utah and sold door to door in the lumber camps of the Sierra Nevada mountains north of Lake Tahoe and in the Pacific Northwest.

Bill, remembering:

"In the summer of '23, Ed Nelson, a classmate of mine at Weber, and I went to California to sell woolen goods— sweaters, dresses, long underwear both black and white from the Logan Woolen Mills, located about 45 miles north of Ogden. We also were selling men's suits and overcoats for the Marks Clothing Company of Chicago. All of our samples fit into big black sample cases about three feet long, two feet high and a foot wide. Somehow we scraped together a couple of hundred dollars for a second-hand Ford roadster with a canvas top, stacked our sample cases in the rumble seat, and took off for Nevada.

"Some first day. A hundred miles east of Winnemucca, in a spring snowstorm, we hit the ceiling of a low railroad underpass and tore off the car roof. We got to Winnemucca with 25 cents between us. We parked the car and Ed took one side of the street and I took the other, and we went from house to house. The way it worked was that we showed our samples to the husband and wife, if they were both at home, and gave them our sales pitch. If they ordered anything, we took their measurements and filled out an order blank, which we'd send back to the company the next day. Then we collected 25 percent down, which was ours to keep, as our commission. They paid the company the balance on receipt of the goods through the mail. When we finished our first round of sales, at about 11 o'clock that night, we had made $33, which meant $132 in sales. Most of it went to buy a new top."

After Winnemucca, they went on down Highway 40 to Reno, then north to the redwood country of northern California and the Douglas fir forests of southern Oregon.

"We worked from six in the morning until 11 at night,

showing our goods to the loggers at their mess halls and to their families at home. Business was good. Loggers were getting $20 a day. Many a day we'd end up with $100 in cash each, our commission on sales."

Bill sold about 12,000 dollars' worth of Logan sweaters and underwear and Marks suits and overcoats that summer and came home with almost $3,000 to help out on the farm and pay his way at the University of Utah, which he entered as a junior in September 1923. The next summer he hit the road again in the Ford, this time with Roland Parry of Ogden, one of his classmates at Utah, a Sigma Chi and the university's lightweight boxing champion. They were selling for the Baron Woolen Mills of Brigham City, about twenty miles north of Ogden.

"Roland brought along his ukelele, and we drove from one logging camp to another singing 'Lovely Hula Hands' and other Hawaiian tunes. The lumber camps were tough. It was during Prohibition, but in every one was a back-room bar, with gambling and girls who made their living in the camps. The men'd work all week, then drink and gamble on Saturday night, and some would lose every nickel, and have nothing left to take home to their family. That's why we'd always try to finish off our sales before Saturday night."

Their most popular item was the men's long underwear that was made of virgin wool with long staple fibers, protection against the cold wet climate of the Northwest, yet able to absorb the lumberjacks' sweat as they swung their long, double-handled rip saws. The underwear came in white or black and was indestructible, so strongly sewn that Bill and Roland would toss a pair to a couple of hulking loggers and say, "Go ahead, have a tug of war. Pull 'em apart." They'd each grab a sleeve, dig their heels into the sawdust, and strain away. Their mates would cheer them on. They'd pull until they got red in the face, but the wool never ripped or stretched, the seams never parted. After such a display of quality, Bill and Roland wrote out orders by the hour.

Again Bill cleared $3,000 for a summer of selling, and he came home to his family and the farm all eager to return to the University of Utah for his senior year and the completion, at last, of his education.

But the very first night back home, his father told Bill what he'd done. "Bill," he said, leaning forward, eyes alight, "just in the time you've been away, things've been changing. The Republicans back there in Washington are pulling us out of this slump. All over the country, people are talking about a boom. And with all this happening—people going back to work, people making more money, prices going up—well, the price of lamb has got to go up too. It's just got to."

Bill had seen his father this way before, like a prospector who knows that tomorrow he'll strike it rich. With a growing sense of foreboding, he waited for his father to continue.

"Now, Bill, you know I'm as good a sheepman as there ever was in the West. I can walk through a herd of sheep, feel their backs, look at their teeth, and buy 'em on the spot. Well," he said sitting up proudly, "that's just what I did."

Bill was stunned. "You bought another herd of sheep?"

"Yes, sir. With money I borrowed from the bank."

"When did this happen?"

"Two weeks ago, over in Elko, Nevada. They're beautiful, Bill—3,000 head, all Merinos. We'll lamb them next spring up at the lambing grounds at Tremonton, then drive them through Ogden Canyon up to South Fork Canyon to fatten up. Remember that country, Bill? Remember how you used to love it?"

Bill, exhausted by the summer's work, indeed by the work of twenty summers, sagged inside. Looking at his father's face, aglow with optimism, he knew that for all his hard work and high hopes, the farm, this herd of sheep, had trapped him again. It was going to be one man's job to bring the sheep home. His. As far as the university was concerned, a whole year lost. But there was no way out.

"The sheep," he remembers, "were delivered to me at Cherry Creek in White Pine County, eastern Nevada, maybe two hundred fifty miles southwest of Salt Lake City as the eagle flies, across the Great Salt Lake desert. My job was to get these sheep, as many of them as I could, from Cherry Creek to Tremonton, about thirty miles north of Ogden, starting in October and getting them there in May. The route I mapped out took us northeast to Wendover, then on to the pass between Pilot Mountain and the Grouse Creek range, then over toward Park Valley, and around the head of the Salt Lake to Tremonton. The plan was to feed one day, then make maybe four to five miles the next day."

Bill picked up equipment and working animals at Cherry Creek: a steel-tired sheep wagon with broad bunks built across the back and a wood-burning stove, a buckboard for supplies, a water barrel, a team of two strong, thick-coated blacks to pull the sheep wagon, some riding horses, and several sheep dogs. He hired two Basque herders, Ramon and Pablo, and stocked up on provisions: beans, bacon, dried beef, flour for flapjacks and heavy-crusted sourdough bread, canned vegetables, rice, potatoes, and dried fruit.

Getting away wasn't easy. The day before they were to move out, Bill took the sheep wagon into Cherry Creek for last-minute buys at the general store. He tied the blacks to the hitchrack and went inside. Next thing he knew, the Elko freight came high-balling down the tracks, whistle screaming like a banshee. The frightened horses reared, snapped their reins like store string, and took off.

Bill burst out to the wooden sidewalk in time to see the horses disappear at a full gallop around the corner, the wagon careening crazily behind them. They were headed up the mountainside back of town. He untied the next horse on the hitchrack and took off after them. Trails of dust rose over the sagebrush. A half-mile out of town, the runaway team came to a small ranch house. A Basque woman ran out of the ranch kitchen, fluttering her apron at them. They veered toward a corral fence, and a Basque ranch hand ran from the corral, seized the broken reins, and pulled them to a halt. That's where they were when Bill drew up, a moment later.

With the wagon repaired, the drive finally got under way. Christmas and New Year's found them struggling across the winter-struck desert range toward Utah, feeding where they could off the sparse, bitter sage, making three or four miles a day when they were on the move, trying somehow to keep this mass of 3,000 vulnerable, defenseless, and all but witless animals together, struggling to keep them somehow nourished in the barren desolation, prodding them on to the shelter of the lee side of the next hill or mountain ridge where they could feed and wouldn't freeze to death in the howling winds that blew down off the snowfields.

To keep up with his studies, Bill had brought with him a winter's supply of college literature textbooks—and found himself completely carried away by Emerson's *Essays*. One after another he devoured them, poring over them at night by the light of the kerosene lamp, studying them on horseback on quiet days when the sheep were browsing for the next push. Emerson both comforted and inspired him and seemed to have special meaning, just for him. What Emerson said on almost every page was that to grow strong and tall and self-reliant, you needed obstacles to overcome. You needed adversities to challenge you and bring out the best in you. And the bigger and tougher the obstacle, the stronger you grew in character and self-confidence and in the ability to succeed.

But there was one more thing, and it was important. You had to respect the obstacle. You had to realize that it might beat you the first time, or the second or the third. You had to realize that it had something to teach you about the world and life and yourself, and that you could learn from it the way he himself was learning from this winter drive on the desert—learning to be more resourceful, to prevail, learning that not this or anything else on earth, in the long run, was going to keep him from finishing at the university and crossing the mountains to the bright, busy, exciting world beyond. You had to face all this without fake courage or bravado, but with coolness and grace.

Mile by grueling mile, they pushed on. They were having difficulty finding forage for that many sheep, and they weren't sure of finding any at all up ahead. The sheep were growing thin. Some were weakening and lagging behind, and it was all the dogs could do to keep them moving. One night, as a fine, wind-borne, pellet-like snow came driving across the mountains, Bill and Ramon and Pablo talked quietly and seriously around the sheep-wagon stove. In the end they agreed: turning back was out of the question, and they couldn't stay where they were, or the sheep would starve to death. One of them had to ride ahead to determine where the forage lay and the best route for the drive to follow. Next morning Bill saddled his pony, filled his canteens, packed a saddle bag with a loaf of crusty sheepherder's bread and some dried lamb, tied on his blanket roll, and set out. He wore the heavy woolen underwear that he had sold to the lumbermen, heavy jeans and leather chaps, a short sheepskin coat, and woolen gloves. He carried a Winchester .30-30 in his saddle sheath. He took one of the tough, canny, heavy-coated little sheep dogs with him.

One hundred twenty-five desolate miles. Five days and five nights. Luckily it had stopped snowing before dawn, and what snow had fallen had been too fine and wind-driven to settle. There was just the endless desert and sage as far as the eye could see, and the leaden, foreboding sky, and a lifeless penetrating cold that brought tears to his eyes. Bill felt lonelier than he ever had on his mission, lonelier than he had ever felt in his life.

The dog kept him company, but in the afternoon of the third day a band of mustangs came pounding down out of a draw in single file and fanned east through the sage and brush. The dog yelped and bolted after them. Bill called him back, but he kept going. Bill followed the animals until they were miles away and out of sight. He never saw the dog again.

At about noon that day Bill passed another sheep camp. There were three Basque herders with 3,000 sheep wintering on the range. The temperature was dropping into the teens, and they pressed him to stay with them until the next day. Bill shook his head. He had to move along; there'd be another sheep camp farther on. But with the waning of daylight he hadn't found one, and he could feel himself growing numb and drowsy with the cold, which pressed upon him and his pony like chilled iron. Finally he turned back. The camp of the three Basques was his only hope.

Night came down and the icy stars glittered like diamonds. The vast desert was limitless and empty and still, and Bill and his horse seemed totally alone, the only creatures alive in the world except the howl of a few coyotes. The pony, more than Bill, sensed the way in the dim starlight. Fighting his drowsiness, Bill sang the songs of the islands that he and Roland had harmonized on together on warm summer nights in the big timber country. He knew he was lost. Was the pony lost, too? With a pervading euphoria Bill was beginning to feel that he didn't care. He and the pony'd just bed down together and keep each other warm and get some sleep. He felt himself swaying in the saddle, felt himself giving in, struggled desperately against it, then saw something that made him grab the pony's mane and the saddle horn and hold on: a pinpoint of firelight far in the distance. The three Basques welcomed him warmly and cooked him some supper. Then they all climbed into the big bunk, side by side. Minutes later they were all asleep.

With the pencilled-out map that Bill brought back to Ramon and Pablo, they took the sheep on the east side of the mountain where Bill saw the best feed. Toward the end of March a mountain lion attacked the herd an hour after sundown and tore open the throats of 22 sheep before Pablo shot him. Only a few miles farther on, 200 or more of the sheep broke away from the herd and moved off toward a small pond, gray with alkali. The two dogs streaked yelping across the sage to head them off, but the sheep got there first and plunged in until they were fetlock-deep, and began drinking. Bill never knew whether someone had poisoned the waterhole or whether they'd eaten some kind of toxic weed, but by noon the next they were all dead.

Nothing much happened after that. They drove the sheep uneventfully to Lucin and around the northern end of Great Salt Lake to Blue Creek, a few miles from Tremonton, where Will had rented the lambing grounds. Will joined them there. It was mid-April and for all the problems with the wagon and the forage, the luck of the drive—the good and the bad—had got them there only a few days late, and the dog-tooth violets blanketed the mountainside below the snowline with springtime yellow. Nevertheless, early spring cold snaps and a heavy snow killed many young lambs before anything could be done to save them.

Toward the end of May, when the lambs were five and six weeks old, Will and Bill and the two Basques packed up the sheep wagon and the buckboard, broke camp, and started the drive to the summer range in South Fork Canyon east of Ogden. It took the four men and two dogs a week of dawn-to-dusk riding and the very last ounce of patience, skill, endurance, and herding know-how at their command to get the herd up the canyon to the south fork of the Ogden River.

Their first camp there was on the old site at Rattlesnake Mountain, where Bill had shot the rattler in his tent twelve summers before. Just as they had been then, the swift-flashing trout streams tumbled down the canyonsides. So there were broiled trout and pea hen wings for supper, and they tasted good to Bill and the Basques after the winter on the high desert range.

Overall, the drive was a success, Will reckoned. Losses weren't too bad, and they'd manage to reach the summer range with close to 2500 lambs. Prices were up now, and that would mean several thousand dollars at least that he could turn over to the bank in Ogden.

Bill had done a lot of thinking back on the range. He knew that this was the way it would turn out—that the drive and all the work and all the weeks and months would be, in essence, work for the bank in Ogden, and he was glad that he'd done it for his father and for the family. But he was even happier, in a quiet, peaceful way, about something else. He knew now that he was leaving the farm forever. This sheep drive would be his last. This would be his last winter on the range. He knew the kind and quality of life he wanted, and no matter how much work it took, he was going to achieve it.

Chapter Nine

Bill was in a hurry after coming down off the Blue Creek sheep range. He wanted three things. The first, as always, was money—cash to keep on helping his family (his brothers would soon be called to their missions; they'd need assistance) and to finance the second thing he wanted: his senior year and his degree from the University of Utah. The third was a job, work, after he graduated—not just any job or work, but something that would take him away from ranching and farming, from ranching and farming communities, away, preferably, from Utah.

For those first three summer months, he'd gone back to work for the Baron Woolen Mills. His selling record for the previous summer had earned him promotion to the post of regional field supervisor for seven western states: his old territory of Nevada, California, Oregon, and Washington, plus Idaho, Wyoming, and Montana. Fanning out over this territory for the summer were 45 salesmen whom Bill had recruited on the University of Utah campus that spring and had trained by taking them along Salt Lake City residential streets and selling with them, door-to-door. Taking in 25 percent of all his own sales, plus 5 percent of all the sales his trainees made, he'd done well that summer. It was a Coolidge year and the country was booming, and by September and his reentry into the university as a senior with the Class of '26, he'd made almost $5,000.

He picked up here where he'd left off before the sheep drive, living on South Temple Street, a few blocks off campus at the Phi Delta Theta house, the fraternity he'd joined in his junior year. He continued with the history and political science courses that he was majoring in and devoted every spare minute to his job as campus representative for the White House Caterers, downtown, on First South Street. So-called because the pillared facade of its building reminded people of the White House in Washington, the company was run by Bill's friend, Franklin Richards, who had served in the Eastern States Mission with Bill (and who would, in 1935, be named head of the Federal Housing Administration). It sold baked goods, cakes, pastries, and cookies, and provided these as well as sandwiches, punch, and tea for parties and banquets. Bill's job was to drum up business on the campus and to organize and supervise the catering of campus parties, most of them fraternity and sorority parties.

He graduated in June and received his bachelor of arts degree all right, but commencement and all those frills were so mixed up in his mind with getting ready for another summer on the road for Baron Mills, and again organizing his field crew, that he could hardly remember them even less than a year later. He took his brother Paul with him this time. Traveling in Bill's battered black Ford coupe, they worked the ranching country of Montana, then made their way west to Coeur d'Alene, Idaho, and on to Spokane, Washington. When the summer was over, Baron had paid Bill a couple of thousand in cash but held on to close to the balance of $3,000 they owed him for his share of the field crew commissions: he'd have his money later, they said, when all the orders had been straightened out and they'd collected from the customers.

He had been in and out of school so often all his life, he couldn't have majored in anything that required a slow but constant accumulation of knowledge, such as engineering or some field of science, or law or medicine. He's just barely been able to get his degree in history and political science as it was. So now he was prepared for— what? He had proved that he could sell, and if he wanted them, there were jobs waiting for him at the telephone company and at several of the woolen mills in the state. But to be honest, he didn't like selling. No, he wanted something else—not these jobs that he was offered, and not farming. He was twenty-five, almost twenty-six. It was late, and time was rushing by. And there was Allie.

One February morning of his senior year he'd been going down the steps into the basement of the John R. Park Building, headed for the student cafeteria and soda fountain with a classmate and another friend from the Eastern States Mission, George Cushing. They'd reached the bottom of the steps and turned right into the long corridor and there she was, coming toward them, then passing them—small, slender, dark eyes, rich brown hair, cameo features touched with tenderness, dressed in something green, carrying an armload of books. She walked past without a glance. Bill stopped in his tracks. He turned around and watched her disappear up the steps.

"What's the matter?" Cushing asked.

Bill just stood there. "There's the kind of a girl I'd like to marry," he said. George pulled him on toward the cafeteria. "She's a junior—too young for you.

Bill was amazed. "You know her?"

"Alice Sheets. Her father was Bishop Sheets of the Thirty-third Ward here in Salt Lake, a lawyer. He died in 1919, in the flu epidemic."

"How long have you known her?"

"We were kids together." As they pushed into the crowded, noisy cafeteria, George grinned at Bill. "I have to tell you, Bill, there's a lot of competition. But if you want me to work on getting a date for you, I'll try."

Bill said, "The milk shakes are on me."

George saw Allie the very next day in the university library reading room. After they'd said hello, he went right to the point. "A friend of mine would like to take you out. Name's Bill Marriott."

Allie didn't have too much time for dating. She was eighteen, an honor student majoring in Spanish, a Chi Omega, active in campus affairs, and an officer of both the Spanish and French clubs. She practiced two hours on the piano every day, lived off campus with her mother and 23-year-old brother, Walter, and was seeing two or three young men fairly regularly. As for her future, secretly and in her own mind it was all settled: she was going to marry a doctor.

"Who's Bill Marriott?" she asked. "And where does he want to take me?"

"He's a senior. Good guy. Six of us are going to the Salt Lake Theatre to see *No, No, Nanette.* You and he could come along with us."

Bill and George and Mary Shettler picked Allie up at about eight at her house, a block or two from the campus, in Bill's rattletrap Ford coupe. Crammed into the front seat, Allie in the middle and George outside with Mary on his lap, they drove to the historic old Salt Lake Theatre, where Pavlova had danced and Maude Adams had played *Peter Pan.* They sat in dress circle seats, and drove right home after the theater, again four in the front seat, singing "Tea for Two."

When they got engaged that summer, Allie thought it was too soon. After all, she had her senior year ahead of her. Why tie herself to this tall, tow-haired, gangling, and somewhat self-conscious man of twenty-five whose idea of a fascinating evening was to show her snapshots of sheep, sheepherders, and sheepherding scenes, taken somewhere back in the mountains? But when she tried to put it off, Bill wouldn't hear of it. "Either we get engaged right now, or it's all off."

Allie believed him, and she didn't want to lose him, so he solemnly gave her his Phi Delta Theta pin and kissed her, and they were engaged.

Allie's mother, who wanted her to marry a medical

student she had been dating, couldn't understand it. "But why do you like *him* so much?"

Even for Allie herself, it was hard to explain. "I feel at home with him. I don't have to talk or try to make an impression. I just like him, that's all."

Mrs. Sheets persisted. "What do you know about his character, his family, his plans for the future?"

"Nothing, Mother, really—except that I like him."

That September, with some of the money he earned on the road selling woolen goods, Bill went to Daynes' Jewelry Store and bought her a diamond ring, and it was official.

But still he didn't have anything to do, anything to throw himself into with all his hard-won experience, all his pent-up drive and ambition, all his will to succeed. "I need you badly to help me out back here at Weber College," President Tracy had told him, even before he graduated. So that fall, a few days before his twenty-sixth birthday, he went back, and when he thought of all the things the president had him doing, even before Thanksgiving, it looked as though he really *was* needed. President Tracy made him secretary and treasurer of the college, and the two of them stumped the county trying to raise money to buy more campus land so Weber could grow from a two-year junior college to the full-fledged, four-year institution that Ogden really deserved. Not only this, but soon Bill found himself teaching theology and English, selling ads for the college yearbook, and again running the bookstore as he had done three years before. He also organized the "Little Theater," with the Weber Auditorium decorated like a theater, and the group put on a different play every week.

Bill never wanted just a job. He wanted to go out on his own. And the more he thought of it, the more he began to wonder about this A&W root beer. Funny thing to think about for a career—a soft drink—but there was an A&W stand downtown in Salt Lake City where you could drive up to the curb and a waitress would bring a mug of ice-cold root beer right out to your car. Bill thought it was a wonderful drink, and so did Allie. They went there a lot that summer in Bill's Ford, particularly on hot days. Five cents a mug. In the fall, when he was back working and teaching at Weber, he was telling his mother about this wonderful, refreshing summer drink.

She looked at him rather smugly. "Well, I know all about that. Your cousin Sherman Marriott's been writing home about it for months. He has the franchise for Fort Wayne, Indiana."

Writing to his cousin, talking with the people at the A&W stand in Salt Lake, Bill checked it out. It seemed that a Roy Allen and a man named Wright had started the business in Sacramento in 1923 or 1924. Though the formula was a secret, they put all kinds of things into their root beer: wintergreen leaves, wild cherry bark, angelica and althea and sarsaparilla and dandelion root, anise seed, sassafras, birch bark. It had to be absolutely ice-cold. No place in the world, it seemed, ever got hotter than the Sacramento Valley in July and August, so they invented a special refrigeration system built of 400 feet of aluminum tubing, perfected their own carbonating system, and sold the drink in frosted mugs for five cents a mug. And since more and more people were traveling in automobiles, they catered to them as well as to pedestrians by having waitresses who would take trays to cars parked at the curb or in the lot next to the root beer stand. All they sold was root beer.

A&W root beer had been an overnight hit in Sacramento. Soon Allen had bought out Wright's interest, had expanded to four new locations in addition to the original one, and in reaching for additional profits had quite possibly invented the franchise system. (Bill always thought he invented curb service as well.) The proposition

Allen advanced was this: for sums ranging from $500 to $2,000, he gave the purchaser the exclusive right to sell A&W root beer in a given city or area; the purchaser agreed to buy all his root beer concentrate, cooling equipment, and other supplies from Allen, and to sell nothing but A&W root beer.

The more Bill looked into it, the more intrigued he became. The Salt Lake City "store," as Allen called it, sold an average of 5,000 mugs of root beer every day during the summer months—$7,500 a month and almost no overhead! Franchise-holders in California were netting enough in four months of hot weather to take the rest of the year off and go fishing. Bill knew a place every bit as hot as Sacramento and Salt Lake City, and a lot bigger. Washington, D.C.

By the time March came around, he had an A&W franchise in his pocket for Washington, Baltimore, and Richmond, Virginia, he had a partner back in Washington, and he had found people to take over most of his jobs at Weber College.

Allie would be graduating in June. That gave him two months in which to open their root beer stand in Washington. Then he'd come back for her graduation, they'd get married, and for their honeymoon they'd drive back to Washington, and she could help him sell root beer. It wasn't exactly what Allie had had in mind for her first year, or perhaps first ten years, of married life. But Bill had it all planned. The only thing left to do was to kiss Allie good-bye and go.

When Bill left Utah, he had $3,000—$1500 that he'd saved from his woolen mill money and $1500 that he'd borrowed from Mr. Bigelow at the Ogden State Bank. This was being matched by his partner, Hugh Colton, Congressman Don B. Colton's brother. Hugh was about Bill's age and one of the promising young Mormons brought to Washington by Senator Smoot. He worked days as secretary to Ulysses S. Grant III, head of the Public Buildings Commission. Nights he attended classes at the George Washington University law school.

Their $6,000 was closely budgeted. The franchise itself had cost them $1,000. Another $2,000 would go to Allen for root beer concentrate and other supplies. The rest was to pay the store rent, make whatever alterations were necessary, advertise, and open for business. Bill, for the time being, would stay with Hugh and Marguerite Colton in their apartment, so housing was no problem. The partners decided that each one would draw $200 a month as salary to begin with, with the understanding that since Hugh already had his hands full with job and law school, most of the work would fall to Bill.

After he'd been in Washington for a few days, Bill received an envelope from Allie. It contained a photograph of the Lincoln Memorial, cut from a magazine. The caption said that several million sightseers visited the memorial each year. "This," said her note, "is where you should put your first root beer stand."

Bill and Hugh already had their location. Out on Fourteenth Street, N.W., a mile or two from downtown, in a residential shopping center heavily patronized by housewives and children from homes and apartment houses for many blocks around. They found a baker willing to rent them eight feet of his 33-foot frontage, depth enough for a counter and nine stools, and an equipment room in the back. The 400-foot aluminum cooling coil, carbonating machine, root beer concentrate, heavy glass mugs, and other paraphernalia were on their way. All Bill had to do was hire a carpenter to put up the counter, buy a barrel, paint it orange and letter it "A&W," and find a tiny electric motor to put underneath the barrel to make it revolve, and they were in business.

But—how high should the counter be? Where to put the barrel so it wouldn't take up too much space? What about the electrical wiring? In the space they had, where would they chill the mugs?

Obviously, they needed help. Bill called Allen long-distance and finally located him in Sacramento.

"Install all those things just the way we've done in every other store," Allen said.

"That's what I thought," Bill said, "but it's impossible."

"What do you mean, impossible?"

"Our place is too small."

What was the frontage, Allen asked. Eight feet, Bill said. There was a long pause.

"Well," Allen said dryly, "it'll be the first A&W root beer stand ever opened in a telephone booth. I'll have someone down there next week."

A brisk, cheerful, raw-boned Norwegian named Berntsen from the stand in Terre Haute, Indiana, arrived a few days later. Not only did he know first-hand the logistics of manufacturing, chilling, and distributing A&W root beer over the counter, he was also an able carpenter and electrician. He, Bill, and Bill's carpenter buckled down to work.

First they partitioned off a space at the back for the "kitchen." Here they installed equipment they'd received from Allen: a huge crockery vat and the carbonating machine that put the fizz into the root beer. The 400 feet of aluminum refrigeration coils they crammed into a casket-like box ten feet long, three feet wide, and three feet deep and lined with sheet metal, and fastened it all into place under the counter. Now, what about the mugs? Dirty ones could be washed in the kitchen, but the clean ones had to be under the counter too, within easy reach. And they had to be ice-cold. They looked everywhere for the kind of pan or receptacle they wanted, couldn't find one, and finally designed and built their own—four feet long, three feet wide, and six inches deep, lined with metal like the refrigeration box, and divided into four compartments to reduce the possibility of breakage. It fit lengthwise under the counter with only inches to spare. The operating procedure was this: The root beer syrup went into the vat and was mixed with sugar and tap water according to formula. It passed through the carbonating machine and picked up its fizz, then traveled through aluminum tubing to the refrigeration coils in the box under the counter. The coils were packed deep in chopped ice, and here the root beer was chilled. It was drawn from the coils with a big, beer-keg-style spigot mounted on the counter. The mugs were also stored—and chilled—in chopped ice in the adjoining, under-the-counter tray.

The rest of the task was simple. Under Berntsen's experienced eye they built the counter to the proper height, shaping it like an "L." Atop the short side, at the front of the store, they erected the orange barrel and placed the electric motor underneath the counter. They installed a foot rail along the bottom of the counter, sprinkled sawdust on the floor, and prepared to open for business. First, however, to stir up interest and let people know that something important was about to happen, Bill found a printer in the neighborhood and ordered a thousand tickets reading, "This Ticket Good for One Free A&W Root Beer. 3128 Fourteenth Street N.W. Grand Opening May 20." For several days before the opening, and on opening day itself, pretty high school girls hired by Hugh passed the tickets out lavishly to Fourteenth Street pedestrians and shoppers and to occupants of cars stopped at traffic lights in the District.

May 20, 1927, was a Friday, a beautiful spring day, fair and hot. Bill and Hugh arrived at the store at dawn and with Berntsen's help made their first vatful of root beer, carbonated it, chilled it, tested it, and vowed that of all the A&W root beer they had ever tasted, theirs was the premium best. They got their big glass mugs packed in ice and some tiny three-ounce ones for youngsters, whose drinks would be free. At 10 A.M. they removed the collapsible gate (there was no door) and hung it on the wall. At 10:02 on the dot, in walked their first customer—a man. Bill wished later he'd asked his name, just for the record, but he was so carried away by what was happening he didn't think of it. The man put his nickel on the counter. Bill was about to drop it into the cash register, then pushed it back. "It's on the house. You're our first customer."

The man raised his mug. "Here's luck."

Providentially, at that very moment Charles A. Lindbergh, at the controls of the *Spirit of St. Louis,* was two hours and ten minutes east of Long Island's Roosevelt Field, on man's first non-stop flight from New York to Paris.

As the day wore on and the heat waves shimmered over the sun-baked sidewalks, the customers crowded good-naturedly into the little store to quench their thirst. Bill and Hugh smiled, joked, broke into song, worked their heads off. Even Berntsen joined in and spelled them behind the counter. The cash register drawer filled with coins and bills.

Nearly everyone asked about Lindbergh. "Does anyone know about Lindy? How's he doin'?" Bill slipped out and was back in a few minutes with a small tabletop radio. He set it on the counter, plugged it in, tuned in a station carrying a running account of the flight, and turned it up loud. Except for when they closed the store at about midnight that night, it stayed that way until late the next afternoon, when Lindbergh touched down safely at Le Bourget.

Nearly 45 years later, Bill met Lindbergh at a White House reception.

"You don't know it, but you and I have something in common," Bill said.

"Are you a pilot?"

"No, it's not that. It's just that you and I went into business on the same day back there in May 1927."

Allie was due to graduate from the University of Utah on June 8. Bill had every right to be proud of her: she had earned nearly a straight A average for all four years and was graduating with the highest honors the university had to offer. He was determined to get back to Salt Lake in time to see her get her diploma. Then they could be married the very next day and start back to Washington in the Ford, now under a tarpaulin back at the farm.

Money? Well, he could draw enough from the business account for his ticket to Utah. He figured there was about $3,000 waiting for him at the Baron Mills, the balance owed him for the woolens he, Paul, and his crew had sold the previous summer. With this in hand he could bankroll their honeymoon and maybe have enough left over to pay back the $1500 he owed Mr. Bigelow.

He and Hugh had already found a location for their second store. It was downtown in Ninth Street, N.W., opposite the U.S. Patent Office, a busy district, crowded with government office workers. He thought of flying west, to give him more time to get the new store ready.

"Well," Hugh said, "I don't know. These planes are pretty small. They run into bad weather—thunderstorms—"

"You mean they don't always make it?"

"Seems to me I've read of some that didn't."

Bill decided against flying. He was going back home for his wedding. It was no time to take chances. The train got him there just in time for the graduation exercises.

Bill spent the night of the 8th with Will and his mother and brothers and sisters on the farm in Marriott. He slept in his old room—but not for long. Up at 5, six hours before he and Allie were due at the temple in Salt

Lake City for the wedding, he ate breakfast, packed, warmed up the Ford, kissed everybody good-bye, and was off at 7 for Brigham City and the headquarters of the Baron Mills.

He went directly to the general manager's office. "I wrote him," he said to the receptionist. "He should be expecting me." Would he wait? Yes, he would. He glanced nervously through a few pages of the morning paper. A secretary appeared. "Mr. Standart will see you now." He put the paper aside, rose, and followed her into the general manager's office.

Mr. Standart, a thin man with thinning gray hair and cold gray eyes behind steel-rimmed spectacles, looked at him bleakly. Bill sensed trouble.

Mr. Standart indicated the chair in front of his desk. "Sit down, young man. I received and read your letter about your work in the field with us last summer." He swiveled away, looked out his office window at the mill rooftops, and swiveled back. "Very interesting. However, with your claim in mind, our accountants have gone over our books very carefully. We find that we owe you nothing—not a penny."

Bill swallowed hard. "There must be some mistake, sir. It was all in my letter. I collected only $1500 for the whole summer. I figure that with my commissions and all, I've got another $3,000 coming. I've been counting on it—"

"Well, Mr. Marriott, we understand that." The general manager smiled palely. "But you've been away. We had a lot of kickbacks on the orders. A good portion of the goods couldn't be delivered because the people had moved away. Customers disappeared without paying their bills."

The electric clock on the wall said 8:30. Bill still couldn't believe it. "Sir, I'm supposed to be getting married in Salt Lake City in two and a half hours—"

117

"We owe you nothing, Mr. Marriott. I've explained to you why. That's it. There's nothing more to say."

Bill stood up and leaned over the desk at Mr. Standart. "If you don't pay me what's coming to me," he said tightly, "I'll get a lawyer and sue. I'll get an outside accountant and make you open your books. We'll see about those kickbacks and those undelivered orders and unpaid bills."

Mr. Standart swiveled away and looked out the window. Bill turned and strode out the door.

At a few minutes before 10, Bill was ushered into Mr. Bigelow's office at the Ogden State Bank. When the greetings were over, Bill, without further preliminary, said, "Mr. Bigelow, I know I owe you $1500 that I borrowed to open our root beer stand in Washington. Now I've got to ask you another favor." As evenly as he could, he told the banker about his failure to collect the money due him from Baron Mills. And he told him about his wedding to Alice Sheets, now less than an hour away. "What I'm leading up to, Mr. Bigelow, is, I need another $1500 now. I'll pay you back as soon as I can straighten out what's coming to me from Baron's."

Mr. Bigelow was sympathetic. But as he talked, Bill watched that blank, stonewall look come into his eyes— and knew that he was being turned down. Patiently Mr. Bigelow went over Bill's father's account; the bank had been carrying him and the ranch for years; there was still some $50,000-$60,000 outstanding on his notes. Moreover, he, Bill, still owed the bank $1500. Now—Mr. Bigelow cleared his throat—if he or the future Mrs. Marriott had some collateral the bank wasn't aware of—

There was the investment in the A&W equipment, Bill said.

Yes, Mr. Bigelow observed with a kindly smile, but it was thousands of miles away in Washington, D.C., and anyway, it wasn't enough.

Bill left Bigelow's office angry and humiliated. The only doors he knew of in Utah had slammed shut in his face. Brigham City, the mills, Ogden, the bank—places and institutions he'd known all his life, and which had known him all his life—were suddenly unfriendly. The wedding? The honeymoon? Ruined. With the money he had in his pocket they couldn't even get to Rock Springs, Wyoming, let alone Washington. Jaw set, more than ever determined to get out of the state, out of the cow and sheep country West—even here and now, this morning, the farm had dragged him down once more—he strode out of the bank. The street he'd known since childhood, the buildings, the ridge mountains themselves, looming to the east, seemed enemy territory.

By the time he got to his car it was almost 10 minutes to 11. Thirty-five minutes—at least, and that would be at racetrack speed—to Allie's place at the Cluff Apartments, where he was to change into his white wedding suit and pick up Allie and Mrs. Sheets for the drive to the temple. He called Allie on the parking lot pay phone. She was in tears. Bill told her where he was and tried to explain. "Mother said you'd changed your mind," Allie wailed. "She knew it all the time."

"But Allie—"

"You don't want to marry me—"

"Allie, listen to me—"

"You aren't coming."

"Allie"—slowly and patiently—"you don't understand. I've been trying to get the money for our honeymoon—I didn't get it—"

Silence. "Didn't get the money?—is that all?" There was the sound of something between a gulp and a sob. He heard the clatter of receiver against mouthpiece as she turned away. "Mother! It's all right!" She came back to the phone. "Oh, Bill—please hurry!" He'd never heard her sound so happy.

On the way from the apartment to the temple, almost an hour later, with Mrs. Sheets on the outside and Allie in her white wedding dress in the middle, he told them in detail what had happened that morning, why he was so late, why he, the bridegroom, was all but broke.

After he'd found a parking place near Temple Square, Mrs. Sheets leaned across Allie and laid her hand on his arm. "Please—don't get out just yet. There's something I want to say." She unsnapped her purse and took out four crisp $50 bills and a small white envelope. She folded the bills into the envelope and held it out to Bill.

"We don't have much money either, but this is what I'd saved for a little family party. I want you to take it.

Bill tried to push the envelope aside. "Mother Alice—"

"No, we can do without the party. Here—it will get you two back to Washington."

Allie buried her face on her mother's shoulder. And Bill himself, as he found himself holding the envelope, had to fight back the tears.

The beautiful marriage ceremony was performed by Bishop Joseph A. Christensen. In accordance with Mormon doctrine, the marriage sealed Bill and Allie not only for this life, but for life eternal.

Bill already had his bags in the trunk of the Ford. For a few moments he and Allie stood in the early afternoon sunlight on the temple steps, like all the other newlyweds who ever were or would be married there, while Doris and Helen, Bill's sisters, took pictures with their box cameras. They chatted with Will, at ease, comfortable, and almost urbane in his city clothes, and Ellen, dressed in white and dabbing at her eyes with a pink handkerchief.

The moment the good-byes were over, they drove back to the Sheets' apartment. They changed into traveling clothes and had a wedding luncheon of egg salad sandwiches, cookies, and cranberry juice. Bill carried

120

down Allie's luggage and somehow squeezed it into the trunk with his. By three o'clock, they were headed for Wyoming.

The highway was a two-lane gravel road. Chugging along at a steady 35, they made almost 90 miles that afternoon. Bill, knowing the Ford, had lashed a three-gallon tin of water to the running board. It came in handy. On every upgrade the Ford boiled over. He'd stop, set the emergency brake, loosen the hot radiator cap with a pair of pliers, let the engine cool off, pour in fresh water from the tin.

A little before dusk they reached Evanston, Wyoming, which looked to Bill like a cowtown set for a William S. Hart movie. It had been a long day. Why go on? There was one sagging, weather-beaten hotel on the unpaved main street. Bill got their traveling suitcase out of the trunk and parked and locked the Ford. With a smile at Allie and a man-of-the-world air he signed the guest register, "Mr. and Mrs. J. Willard Marriott. Washington, D.C."

They followed the room clerk up the stairs to the second floor. Rolling a toothpick to a corner of his mouth, he swung back the door to a front room. He preceded them in, reached up, and snapped on the unshaded bulb that hung from the low ceiling. Secondhand store dresser, rocking chair, and table. No rug, and a bed with an iron bedstead, V-shaped mattress, exposed bedsprings, but—surprisingly—clean white linen that looked like new, and a colorful blue and white patchwork quilt for a bedspread.

From the other side of the bedroom wall came the rumbling thump, roll, and clatter of scattered pins from the bowling alley next door. Through the floor rose the sound of men's voices and laughter, the click of ivory, from the first-floor poolroom. One narrow window opened on the street. Of course there was no air conditioner. It was terribly hot and there was not even a fan.

121

It was far different from the way they'd pictured it. So much for romance. So much for the storybook wedding night.

Thump—r-r-r-r-o-o-l-l-l—*crash!* Another ball rumbled down the alley and hit. Pins flying, the set-up exploded. It must have been after midnight before they fell asleep.

They thought Wyoming would go on forever—five nights. But it was never as bad again as it had been in Evanston. By the time they crossed the Mississippi, they were singing their way through the cornfields, across the greening heartland, and Washington and their happy future were only four days and another thousand miles away.

Chapter Ten

There was quite a group of Utahns in Washington, perhaps as many as thirty or forty young people whom Bill and Allie had known in Salt Lake City and at the university. Thanks to Senators Smoot and King and Congressmen Colton and Cannon, most of them had minor government jobs, and most of the young men, like Hugh, Bill's partner, were putting themselves through George Washington law school.

Washington was growing fast in those days, and builders of large apartment houses attracted tenants by extending them two or three months of residence rent-free. Bill's and Allie's friends, all of whom were counting their pennies, took advantage of these offers, moving every year or so from one new apartment house to another as the opportunities became available.

In the late spring of 1927, most of them were living in the eight-story Boulevard Apartments at 2121 York Avenue, N.W. There, a floor above the Coltons', Bill and Allie set up housekeeping. Sheets, blankets, and basic kitchen utensils they'd brought with them; that was all. The Murphy bed that pulled down from the wall had springs, no mattress. There was no other furniture. They figured they could spend $60. The day after they arrived, they found a side-street furniture store and before their money ran out bought a mattress, a small secondhand bookcase, a card table, one unfinished kitchen table, and four unfinished kitchen chairs. Bill dug down deeper and somehow came up with enough for a can of red paint and a brush.

"She was a city girl and had never done anything like this," Bill recalls. "But while I was working and taking care of the shop and getting ready to open our second stand on Ninth Street, she painted the furniture, and when I came home she'd have more paint on the floor and on her dress than on the tables and chairs. But at least we had an electric ice box and a stove and a sink. And we had this new red furniture and a place to sleep. We had a home."

Within a few weeks after their arrival, and with the same fanfare and free tickets that had made the opening of the first stand so successful, Bill and Hugh opened their second stand at 606 Ninth Street, N.W., between F and G streets. The location, admittedly, was a compromise. Rentals on F and G streets, two of the busiest streets in the city, were much too high for them; Ninth Street, in between, was next best. True, there were "tenderloin" overtones to the streets, second-rate movie houses and burlesque theaters that worried them. But to offset this, government workers swarmed through the area every day; and they'd found a vacant store with a luxurious 30-foot frontage and 40 feet of depth and a big bay window for the A&W barrel.

"We got so busy running the stores we didn't have time to worry about how we were doing," Bill reminisces. "We'd start at 8:30 or 9 in the morning cleaning up and work right through till we closed, around midnight. We'd get home at 1 in the morning, sometimes later. So we didn't even have much time to sleep, and this went on seven days a week.

"Before we got married, Allie said, 'You don't expect me to go back there to Washington with you and sell root beer, do you?' And I said, 'Of course not. I wouldn't think of having you do a thing like that.'

"Well, she didn't really sell root beer, but she took charge of the money, and did everything I asked her to. She wasn't too proud to pitch in and help. We couldn't have made it without her."

As the Washington summer days grew hotter and muggier and sales at both stands soared, it was thrilling to watch the young business get bigger—and more complicated.

"Business became so good at Ninth Street that we hired two counter girls; small, fast, cheerful, and popular with the customers. The skill they developed in handling those big, ten-ounce mugs was amazing. They could pick up five mugs in their left hand, shake them clear of the ice and ice water in which they'd been chilled, hold them under the spigot, pull the handle with their right hand, fill all five mugs without stopping, shut off the spigot, turn around, and have the mugs on the counter in front of the customers before they could wink an eye.

"Trouble was, it didn't take long for the girls to learn to put the nickels in their pockets instead of in the till. We got them uniforms without pockets, but then they'd just lay the nickels on top of the register without ringing them up. When they'd accumulated a half-dozen or so, they'd slide them off, take them into the dressing room, and slip them into their purses. We suspected this for weeks before we could prove it. We hated to spy on them, but it was the only way. We cut a hole high up in the door to the back room. Allie sat on a high stool and watched through this hole. When we were sure that's what they were doing, we had to let them go."

That September Bill and Allie moved into Hilltop Manor, a new apartment house only two blocks from the Fourteenth Street shop. They were able to afford somewhat larger quarters—a living room, a large dinette, a kitchen, and two bedrooms, one of which they converted into an office. For the most part, Allie worked close to home at "Number One"; Bill worked downtown at "Number Two." At the close of business, Bill would lock up the Ninth Street shop, get in the Ford, and drive home with the cash receipts, most of it in nickels. Allie would lock up the Fourteenth Street shop, stuff her receipts in a brown paper bag, and walk home. There she counted the money. Next day, she deposited it in the Park Savings Bank at Fourteenth and Kenyon streets.

Their bookkeeping was simplicity itself. All Bill knew about it to begin with was that to stay in business you had to take in more money than you spent, and you kept books to make sure this was the way you were operating. One of the first things he did on arriving in Washington with Allie was to go to the little stationery store on Fourteenth Street and ask for a bookkeeping book.

"Any particular kind?" asked the clerk.

"Simplest you've got."

The clerk returned with a small red-bound ledger with lines and vertical columns. Bill bought it and took it home and Allie wrote "Date" at the head of one column, "Receipts" at the head on another, and over the next two, "Expenditures" and "Balance." And that was it.

"As long as we were taking in more than we spent and kept up with our taxes—they weren't much in those days—I knew we were doing all right. Allie would count the money and check it against the register slips. If she was two dollars over, she'd put it in her pocket; if she was short two dollars, or whatever, she added that much, to make things come out even. She wasn't much for bookkeeping, but at least she knew how much we took in and how much we spent. Our system was very simple. It was all on one page. I wish we had it today."

As cooler weather approached, Bill and Hugh proceeded with plans to shut down Number Two for the winter. But it was unthinkable to close down Number One as well. Bill had no desire to leave Washington for the winter, nor did Allie—nor could they have afforded it after one summer's business. They still had furniture to buy, the Ogden State Bank loan to pay off, and Bill's family and the farm to help support.

Endlessly they debated what to do. To keep on selling root beer only was out of the question. Come the first cold snap and Washingtonians would forget about ice-cold drinks until next Easter. Food was obviously the answer. Hamburgers? Hot dogs? Bill wanted something novel, something different. Inevitably, as he always did, he went to his own experience, his own inner logic, for the answer. A regional specialty in the restaurants and roadside stands of the West and Southwest was Mexican food and barbecued beef, the hotter, the more highly spiced, the better. He loved them both; so did Hugh.

"How's this, Allie? In the hot weather we served cold drinks; now in cold weather we'll serve hot food—hot Mexican food: chili, hot tamales, barbecued beef sandwiches and hot dogs. And we'll serve it in short fast orders that people can eat at the counter. We'll still sell root beer, but add coffee, and maybe milk shakes. When warm weather comes again, we can go back to root beer full-time."

Allie, the realist, said, "You're forgetting something. The A&W franchise says we can't sell food."

Bill brushed this aside. "If we're going to stay in business, we've got to. We can't get by on winter root beer sales. They wouldn't even pay our rent."

Bill had already learned something about the way things are sometimes done in Washington. If you can't accomplish your objectives under the existing rules, don't give up; get the rules changed. Two days later he was on the plane flying west for a talk with Roy Allen. He came back with Allen's authorization, granted to him alone as a special case, to sell food at A&W stands in his territory.

No sooner had they cleared this hurdle than they came up against another. "Where," Allie had asked, "are we going to get our chef?"

Bill: "Chef? What chef? We can't afford one."

"Well, I never saw you cook a hot tamale."

"I never *said* I could cook one. Can't you?"

"No, and I can't make chili con carne, either."

That afternoon Bill put on his hat, left the stand, walked down Fourteenth Street a block or two, turned left, and walked a few more blocks to a mansard-roofed mansion behind an iron fence. Just as he remembered: from a portico flagpole hung a Mexican flag. The Mexican Embassy.

That afternoon they went back together and rang the doorbell. For Allie, the Spanish major, it was no trouble at all. An hour later they were on their way back to the root beer stand, a sheaf of recipes, carefully written out by the accommodating embassy chef, in Allie's handbag. Then came a fruitless search in Washington grocery stores for the true Mexican beans, peppers, and other ingredients that the recipes called for. They were nowhere to be found. Back at the embassy, the chef, enchanted by Allie's Spanish and her interest in the food of his country, gave them a name and an address. Soon the items they needed were on their way from a Mexican food supply house in San Antonio, Texas.

Next problem, the conversion itself. In Bill's view, it had to be instant. "If we close to make the change, even for a couple of days, we'll lose customers," he told Colton. "They'll think we've shut down for the winter and won't come back."

Determined to close as a root beer stand one day and open as a restaurant the next, he and Hugh began drawing plans, buying cutlery, dishes, pots, pans, cups, and saucers. They conferred with Mr. Hutzler, their carpenter, ordered millwork, a plate-glass window, and a griddle.

One brisk September morning, while they were waiting for the millwork and the shipment from San Antonio, a young friend dropped in for a root beer: Jack Cannon of Salt Lake City, Congressman Cannon's young brother and another Smoot protegé. He sipped his root beer, surveyed the two or three shivering customers, leaned on the counter, and said, "Hey, Bill, when're you and Allie going to open this hot shop I've been hearing about?"

Bill's hand, on its way to the cash register with Jack's nickel, stopped in mid-air. " 'Hot shop'?"

"Hugh said you were going to specialize in Mexican food, real hot, like we get back home in Vernal."

Bill grinned. Why not? They'd argued for days about what to call it. What was wrong with "Hot Shop"?

That night they had Hugh and Marguerite over for dinner. Afterwards, Bill sprung it on them. "It's too plain," Allie said. Neither Hugh nor Marguerite thought much of it either. "People will think it means that it's hot inside."

"All right," Bill said, "we'll give it some class. We'll add another 'p' and an 'e' and spell it the way they do in England: 'Hot Shoppe'."

'That's so bad it's good," Allie said.

A few nights later Bill, Hugh, and Allie closed the stand at eight o'clock. Mr. Hutzler and his helpers arrived with the milled facade, the big plate glass window, and their tool boxes. Bill had already trucked a small steam table for the barbecue and a hot dog grill to the store. They got out their pencilled sketches and went to work.

Out of the front window came the orange A&W root beer barrel, in went the prefabricated store front, the new door, and the new window. They installed the steam table behind the counter, drove hooks into the wall for the pots and pans.

It was a long, tiresome task of a thousand and one details, and the sun was coming up as Bill put the packages of beans and peppers and cans of chili powder on the shelves. (For two days running, Allie had been practicing the embassy chef's recipes in their Hilltop Manor kitchenette.) Hugh checked the mug sterilizer and the hot water heater to make sure they'd survived the conversion, then helped Bill put a coat of fresh paint on their eight-foot store front.

By midmorning the carpenters were sweeping up and getting ready to leave. Bill climbed down from a stepladder on the sidewalk and stepped back to survey the sign that had just been written in script, in bright orange paint, across the plate glass window. "The Hot Shoppe," it read, in an optimistic upward slant. The same sign had already been lettered on the woodwork across the top of the door and the window. A sign on the wooden frame below the window said, "Bar-B-Q."

It was just a few minutes before noon when Bill took a last look around the little restaurant. It was spic-and-span. Fresh sawdust on the floor. Nickel napkin holders and sugarbowl tops gleaming on the counter. Rich, spicy odors filling the air from the pots on Allie's gas range. Bill smiled at Allie. "Ready?"

"Ready as I'll ever be," Allie said.

Bill turned the key in the spring lock and opened the door. The first customer, a man in a topcoat with a rolled newspaper under his arm, stood waiting.

"Come in, friend," Bill said. " 'The Hot Shoppe' is open for business."

Thus he opened the door to their first customer—and the rest of his life.

Chapter Eleven

In practically every state in the Union, restaurant glasses could be washed and sterilized in chlorine, then rinsed in cold running water. Not so in the District of Columbia. Here a district law dating back to the 1890s said that all restaurant glasses had to be washed, then sterilized for five minutes in boiling water.

The mugs Bill used were clear crystal mugs that sparkled—expensive, 25 cents each. There wasn't room to store very many of these mugs, and on a hot busy day, when they sold hundreds of root beers an hour, and every one in a frosted mug, they had to chill hot mugs very fast, and they had to plunge trayfuls of relatively cool mugs into a compartment of boiling water. Both procedures tended to crack even a heavy A&W mug. At least several times a week a counterman or even Bill himself misjudged the temperature of a trayful of mugs and dropped it into the boiling water too soon, with a sudden cracking of glass that sounded like the Yukon River ice pack breaking up in the springtime. Passers-by all the way across Fourteenth Street would grin at each other and say, "Well, there goes another tray of mugs."

But to the Marriotts and their partner, Hugh, sterilization was a critical problem, frequently causing both broken glassware behind the counter and serious rush-hour delays. Sometimes customers could not wait and walked out. So the law as it stood meant lost time, money, equipment, and customers. They set about to get the law changed.

Meanwhile, in spite of the troublesome mug problem, the first winter of the Hot Shoppes went pretty well. Both stores had a steam table behind the counter, a grill for hot dogs in the window, some stools. At the larger Ninth Street store they set up a revolving spit in the window and hired an expert carver from New York to stand there and fashion sandwiches. He was such a showman and the aroma drifting out the ventilator so tantalizing, passersby couldn't resist going inside for something to eat. Of course, in winter weather, this arrangement created still another thermal problem: heat from the spit inside and the cold outside combined about once every other week to crack the big plate glass window.

For a while they had all the business they could handle. Every noon, government workers from the District wanted a quick noon meal—fast, hot, and good. Nothing could have been more satisfying than a Hot Shoppe barbecued sandwich or a bowl of Mexican chili.

In May of '28, when they closed the little ledger on their first year, it showed gross receipts of $16,000. The business had paid Bill $200 a month; Hugh, because of his government job, generously declined to draw his $200 a month, but added it to their profit for expansion costs.

Nevertheless, in spite of this encouraging performance, the partners found themselves at a crossroads. In the spring elections, without so much as a hint from him that he was a candidate, Hugh had been voted into office as city attorney of Vernal, Utah, his hometown in the Indian country up under the Wyoming line, 180 miles from the nearest railroad. The people there had known him all his life; they'd sent his brother, Don, to Congress for a couple of terms, and Hugh was graduating from George Washington law school in the spring. What better graduation present could they offer?

Bill tried to get Hugh to stay. "We'll make money here, Hugh," he'd say. "We'll lick the mug problem, and keep opening stores, and it'll work out fine."

Hugh wasn't so sure. There were too many headaches. Not only the mug problem, but problems with getting, training, and keeping help, dealing with wholesalers, keeping customers satisfied. And the hours! Bill and Allie both put in full sixteen-hour days, with little or no time off, month in and month out. Deeper than all this, Hugh was homesick for the West.

He and Bill agreed that $5,000 would be a fair price for his half of the business. Bill didn't have that much money. He walked across Fourteenth Street to the Park Savings Bank and told Mr. Stunz, the manager, that he needed a loan to buy out his partner. Mr. Stunz was different from most bankers Bill had run into: very friendly, relaxed, optimistic, a frequent root beer patron who had watched the Hot Shoppes' progress with friendly interest. He chuckled at Bill's request. "Striking out all by your lonesome, eh, young fella? Well, now, that's the spirit. Independence. Self-confidence. That's what we like to see in this community."

That night, Bill handed Hugh and Marguerite a check for $5,000. For better or worse, the Marriotts were sole owners of The Hot Shoppes of Washington, D.C.

In the early summer, always pushing for expansion, Bill and Allie found the location they'd been looking for all spring—a corner lot at Georgia Avenue and Gallatin Street, N.W., farther from downtown, closer to the suburban ring, in a growing neighborhood shopping district yet with enough homes in the area to insure a steady family trade. The owner had intended to build stores on the property, but Bill saw that it would be ideal for a Hot Shoppe with adjacent parking space for drive-in service, like the A&W stand in Salt Lake. He'd even introduce that newfangled tray some Texan had invented. Roy Allen was already using it out west, a tray with a fold-up bracket underneath that you could fasten to the top of a closed car door. If the door had a window, you just rolled the window all the way down.

No sooner had he talked the owner into giving him a lease than he found himself in the kind of crisis that had made Hugh head west for Vernal. District building officials balked at granting him a permit for the simple structure that he and Allie had designed at night on their kitchen table—rectangular, open on all sides, central work area surrounded by counters, and a roof with a prominent overhang. This would be supported by pillars that would accommodate a collapsible iron grille for after-hours security in warm weather and windowed wall panels in wintertime. It wasn't so much the structure itself the officials objected to; it was their lurid, Sunday-supplement concept of drive-in restaurants: young folks in cars after dark? Petting parties, hootch, raucous laughter, sin—right there in the nation's capital? Who wanted to open the door to that?

With the help of influential friends, Bill finally convinced the officials that his drive-in would tolerate neither rumble-seat sex nor the drinking of hip-flask Prohibition gin or white lightning down from the Blue Ridge moonshine stills, and the contractors moved in with graders, lumber, fixtures, and Hot Shoppe restaurant equipment.

A week later, when the shop was half-finished, Bill called Allie from a Georgia Avenue drug store. "Guess what," he said cheerfully. "Another problem."

Allie knew that problems didn't really bother Bill. In fact, he welcomed them. He often said life was an obstacle course. And that's how you got ahead—by meeting and overcoming obstacles. In fact, he was having cards printed for distribution to every employe, to get them thinking his way. Each card carried four questions: "1. What is the problem? 2. What is the reason for the problem? 3. What is the solution to the problem? 4. What is *your* solution to the problem?"

"What is it this time?" Allie asked.

"We're in real trouble now. The District building people won't let us cut a driveway into the parking lot."

A stone curbing extended along the front of the lot that Bill intended to use for parked cars and drive-in service. It was much too high for cars to drive over. But again, no precedent—and no permit. Day after day, Bill haunted the waiting rooms of the District office. Persistence, logic, and, again, influential friends, finally won out. Reluctantly, zoning officials agreed that if it was all right for drive-in filling stations to cut away curbings, it was all right for a drive-in restaurant.

From the day that it opened, Hot Shoppe Number Three was a tremendous success. Bigger, more efficient, more attractive than Numbers One and Two, it incorporated improvements that would serve as a model for later Hot Shoppes for years to come. It featured the by-now familiar "barbecue machine," the expert carver and sandwich-maker in the tall, white chef's cap, with the flashing, machete-like carving knife, the revolving A&W root beer barrel on the counter.

The menu offered standard Hot Shoppe fare, simple, fast, cheap—and good enough to make you ask for more: Mexican chili con carne, hot tamales, hot dogs, and the real house specialty, sandwiches made of either minced ham or beef, flavored with Allie's western barbecue sauce, topped with chopped cole slaw and served on a steaming, square, white bun. The sandwiches cost 15 cents, the other items 10 cents. Drinks—ice cold root beer, hot coffee, and milk—were 5 cents each. The building was painted stand-out orange and black, to catch the attention of people driving by in cars. To wait on cars in the parking lot, Bill took on a dozen or so lads eager to hustle trays from counter to car for tips alone. In time they'd be replaced by girls, but in those early days newspaper stories about the new Hot Shoppe seized upon the "running boys" as a distinguishing feature of this novel opportunity to sit in your car and have someone dash out with sandwiches and drinks for you and your friends. Bill had an artist devise a Hot Shoppe logotype showing a "running boy" in uniform, bearing a drive-in trayful of food. Curbers wore it as a patch on their jackets, and for many years it was the symbol of the Hot Shoppes.

The Georgia Avenue shop, in a quiet enough neighborhood between Rock Creek Park and Rock Creek Cemetery, was not long in developing a character all its own. Martin Buxbaum, who wrote lovingly of the early days for the company magazine, collected these impressions: the yellow jackets attracted by the swarm to the sweet-smelling root beer spills, the curbers chanting the "Volga Boat Song" as they pulled a heavy auto frame back and forth across the unsurfaced parking lot after heavy rains had turned it into a vast mud puddle; curbers washing windows every day, 18 panes to each window; the night the ex-Navy boxer Bill hired to keep order leaped over the counter, took on three trouble-makers at once, and sent then howling into Gallatin Street; the day the coffee urn sprang a leak and Bill rushed across the street to the Chesapeake and Potomac Telephone Company maintenance department to borrow a soldering iron and some solder to repair it. "No use buying these things," he said. "It may never leak again." (They told this story on Bill 20 years later, when he was elected to a C. & P. directorship.)

The important thing emerging, though, was the Marriotts' attitude toward the business. They didn't care about running a restaurant, *per se*. They weren't cooks, didn't want to cook. They were in the restaurant *business*—to turn out a product of quality, to serve the public, to keep prices low and still show a profit, to grow naturally and logically, from the inside out.

When Bill wanted something done, he was past doing it himself. Instead he hired an expert: a carpenter, a chef, a ham-and-beef buyer, a nutritionist, a bookkeeper. His role had become that of overseer, seeking new locations, poking into new methods, introducing more efficient operations. One of the first innovations after the opening of the Georgia Avenue store, for instance, was the renting of a two-story store next to the drive-in. He converted the first floor into a simple commissary for preparing pies, pastries, and other baked goods for all three shops. Into the second floor he moved the bookkeeping and accounting department, getting it once and for all, to Allie's delight, out of their guest bedroom.

Not that Bill lost sight of the value of the personal touch. He was always promoting good will with the help and with the customers. He made a point of visiting each shop every day, going through it from front to back, shaking hands with employes, smiling, cracking jokes, making them feel part of the Marriott family. But at the same time, he gave a white-glove inspection to every shelf, top side and under side, to every pot and pan, closet, inch of floor space. "Big Tamale," the employes called him. When his car drove up to the store, the word would pass from cashier to cook to curber, "Here comes Big Tamale." When his brother Paul showed up, they'd whisper, "Little Tamale on the lot." Either way, they stood a little straighter, moved a little faster. Frequently, after checking the stores, Bill would go out front, introduce himself to the customers, ask them what they liked or didn't like, make them feel at home and appreciated.

When the stock market crash came, in October 1929, the three Hot Shoppes, open 24 hours a day, employed about 80, not counting Bill and Allie. Their total income averaged $1400 a day. Out of this, they met a payroll of about 20 percent, or $280 a day. This was divided among all the help except curbers, who kept what they made in tips. Week after week, Bill and Allie waited for business to go into a spin. But it never did. In fact, holiday trade at the Hot Shoppes, surprisingly, was better than ever.

But as the depression worsened that winter, Bill had his hands full at Ninth Street. From a kind of tenderloin boom street of the Twenties, thronged with government workers, sidewalk vendors, and pushcart peddlers, and dominated by Jimmy Lake's Gaiety burlesque house, it rapidly deteriorated into a skidrow haven for down-and-outers.

Soon the enticing aroma of the barbecue machine wafting down the block on the January air drew as many panhandlers and tattered strays as paying customers. The manager couldn't let them in; they'd order, eat, and sidle out without paying, and because of legal loopholes, no cop would or could arrest them. For a few days Bill tried to fend them off from the store front by giving them a free sandwich and root beer and asking them to leave. Next day, they were all back again, accompanied by a small army of hungry friends. "We're not running a restaurant," growled Bill. "We're running a mission."

The city settled deeper into the depression. The arcades and fun shows along Ninth Street were the first to feel it, and understanding landlords began lowering the rent in the block between F and G streets—People's Drug Store on the corner, the candy store next door, even the Gaiety. Bill's property was held in a trust account in a downtown Washington bank. His request for a reduction in rent was refused. "Sorry," said the trust officer, "the terms of the trust are unbreakable." In spite of the volume of business at the Ninth Street store—with all its problems it took in $600 a day, as much as the Georgia Avenue drive-in—this was the final straw. Bill found a restaurant man eager for a busy downtown location. Sure, he said, he'd take over Bill's lease; it was just the spot he'd been waiting for. Bill had his Hot Shoppe signs down the next day, and a week later had moved out.

But it wasn't that easy. The buyer lowered the quality of his food, hired low-cost help, skimmed off all the profits

138

into his own pocket, and went under in three months. When he couldn't keep up with his rent payments, the bank said they were Bill's responsibility. Bill said no, they weren't. The bank sued, and Bill won. He had a release—in writing. He had learned the hard way, but he had learned.

Ninth Street drove home what always haunted him: nothing fails more often than restaurants. "If five restaurants open today, only one will be in business five years from now." How often had he heard it? A million times, it seemed. Yet it was true. Industry figures proved it. And it was probably worse now. Even banks were going broke.

He was never—ever—going to be at the mercy of his help, of the all-important sandwich-maker who turned out to be a drinker, of the key hostess who eloped without warning, of the temperamental chef who quit without notice to start his own restaurant. He wanted no more of that, and he wanted no more of having to advertise for and interview critical replacements; he wanted an available pool of his own people, Marriott-indoctrinated, Marriott-trained Hot Shoppe believers that he could draw on in an emergency. There was only one way to develop this pool: more Hot Shoppes.

Ninth Street also confirmed something else he'd known all along. What E. M. Statler said about success in the hotel business was dead-center correct about restaurants, too. "Here is the secret in three words: Location, location, location." From now on, it had to be right, right for now, right for ten years from now.

Robert Willey, now a management consultant in Washington, remembers working for Bill in those years. He was 11 or 12, and Bill hired him and a number of other lads as well to work after school as traffic counters. Every afternoon Bill would drive him to an intersection that he was checking out as a possible location for a new Hot Shoppe. He would park his Ford, lift a heavy milk-bottle crate out of the trunk, and up-end it on the curbing for the boy to sit on. He would hand him a push-lever counter and drive away. For one hour the boy would click off the cars passing in one direction. Then for another hour he would count the cars passing in the opposite direction. Then Bill would pick him up and leave him at another intersection, in another part of town, to count cars there. Bill always left with him a stack of free root beer tickets to hand out in case he had some spare time before Bill's return.

Sometimes, when checking prospective drive-in locations, Bill and Allie would team up. They'd park and count the cars that went by during the lunch hour, then from five to eight in the evening, for the dinner trade possibilities, then from 10 to midnight, for the after-theater business. Wherever they checked, they would end up knowing which side of the street was better, which corner they wanted, where cars turned off, which end of the bridge drivers slowed down for, which street, or even side of the street, had more men than women drivers, and vice versa.

They narrowed their choices to two locations and decided to go with both. The first, Hot Shoppe Number Four, opened late in 1929 in the 1700 block of Rhode Island Avenue, N.E., a busy, urbanized strip of U.S. Highway 1 between Washington and Baltimore. The second, Number Five, opened July 2 of the next year at 4340 Connecticut Avenue. If a chain of restaurants can be said to have a flagship, this instantly became the flagship of the Hot Shoppes.

To an exceptional and self-reliant breed of Americans the depression was no time for dismay and despair; it was, rather, a time that tested one's mettle, a time of opportunity. Bill was one of these. He sank just about

140

everything he and Allie had left into the Connecticut Avenue property. Located far out toward the Chevy Chase line, toward where it was banked with sycamores and tulip trees, it had a frontage of 150 feet along the street. It extended back 200 feet to the National Bureau of Standards Building, and at one end adjoined a large wooded lot. He paid $4 a square foot for the land, to him and Allie all the money in the world.

When they opened Number Five July 2, 1930, to the music of a brass band and showers of free root beer tickets, they started out with 50 smartly uniformed curbers, 40 girls and 10 boys. Soon they added 50 more, and still they were short-handed. Not only did the shop do an instant and thriving drive-in business with high school and college youngsters, particularly after movies and dances on Friday and Saturday nights, but it did a turnaway trade at the regular, sit-down restaurant inside. Nobody knows quite how it happened, but it suddenly became the chic place to go, *the* place to see and meet your friends. Bill rented the adjoining lot, cleared away the woods, took over more land from the Bureau of Standards, graded and graveled it down, and had what everyone said was the biggest drive-in in the whole United States.

Allie thought he was working too hard, and told him so. "Just slow down a little, Bill. We can afford to hire people to shoulder some of the load." That's right, Allie, he agreed. Let's do that, and he began to think of upgrading one or two of his shop managers. But before the Rock Creek maples turned red and gold that fall, he took Allie for a ride out Rhode Island Avenue. "I want to show you something," he said. A house with a yard? A new car? A fur coat for Christmas, in some shop window? Allie, sitting beside him, smiled. Just like a little boy, she thought, with a secret treasure.

It was early evening. Cars streamed in both directions

along the bustling thoroughfare. They came to a busy intersection, where Florida Avenue angled across Rhode Island. Bill turned right into Florida, went half a block or so, and came to the Fourth Street intersection. He found an empty space at the curbing and pulled in and turned off the motor.

"This is it," he said.

"This is what?"

"The perfect spot for our next Hot Shoppe." He fished in his jacket pocket and found two counters. He handed her one. "Here, you count the cars going past our way. I'll count them going the other way."

Allie took the counter. Bill was already leaning out his window and counting, totally rapt in the passing traffic. She sighed quietly.

"I might have known," she said to herself.

While all this was going on, something quite fascinating had happened to enchant and delight not only Bill and Allie, but the city of Washington and many elements of the nation at large. This was the late-in-life romance of United States Senator Smoot, whose first wife had died a few years previously, and Alice Taylor Sheets, Allie's widowed mother—a romance that, as the society page writers said, "blossomed charmingly with the cherry trees along the Potomac."

Smoot had been a member of the U.S. Senate since 1903. He was chairman of the Senate Finance Committee and the powerful Senate Public Lands Committee, head of the Senate Committee on Printing, chairman of the Public Building Commission of the District of Columbia, an outspoken member of the Senate Appropriations Committee, and a member and patron of a host of additional Congressional and civic commissions, committees, and agencies.

In his home state of Utah, he'd made a small fortune

in banking, mining, woolen goods, and other enterprises even before his election to the Senate. His standing in the Mormon Church had grown over the years to the point where he was one of its twelve apostles and second in line for its highest office, that of the presidency.

Early in the spring of 1930 Mrs. Sheets traveled to Washington from Salt Lake City to visit Allie and Bill, then living in the Cavalier Apartments, 3500 Fourteenth Street, N.W. She was youthful for her 54 years—stylish, outgoing, vivacious, with dark eyes and dark hair, and was prominent in her own right in Salt Lake City.

The couple met, inevitably, on a warm and gentle April Sunday after morning church services, then held at the Washington Auditorium. From that moment until Mrs. Sheets and Allie left for Salt Lake City in the middle of May, the Senator and she were constant companions at social and church affairs and took spring walks in Rock Creek Park together. They went out to the movies almost every night, traveling all over the District to find one they hadn't seen.

"Do you suppose they talk about politics all the time?" Bill asked Allie.

"No, they don't," Allie replied. "They hold hands."

The romance injected an intriguing and welcome note into that springtime. The appealing and dignified couple soon had the Washington press corps hard on their heels everywhere they went. Always the question was the same: "Senator, are you and Mrs. Sheets making marriage plans? And if so, when will it take place?" And always the Senator would good-naturedly shake his head. "There is no truth to that whatever. Mrs. Sheets and I are just good friends. She likes movies, and so do I."

But a month after Mrs. Sheets left for Salt Lake, taking Allie with her for a visit, Senator Smoot himself boarded the Overland Limited West. On June 30 he called reporters to his Salt Lake City office. His statement was characteristically brief. "Gentlemen, thank you for coming. I have an announcement which you may or may not find interesting to your readers. Last night, I asked Mrs. Alice Taylor Sheets to become my wife, and she did me the honor to accept." They would be married shortly, he said, and would leave on July 19 for a honeymoon in Hawaii.

Nothing short of a Capital crisis could have interrupted the stately flow of the Senator's nuptial arrangements. And that's exactly what happened. The day after his press conference, President Hoover called a special session of Congress to ratify the London Naval Treaty. Smoot's presence and support were essential.

The Senator and Mrs. Sheets were married the next day, July 2, at the Mormon temple in Salt Lake City. They left immediately after the ceremony for the Senator's home in Provo. On July 7, the following Monday, Bill and Allie received a telegram from Salt Lake City: "Leaving for Washington tonight to spend honeymoon at White House with President and Mrs. Hoover. Arrive Washington Thursday. (Signed) Mrs. Reed Smoot."

For Bill and Allie the next two weeks were a Potomac fairy tale, particularly that first, never-to-be-forgotten July morning: the drive to Union Station in the bright warm sunshine, in their new red Nash convertible; greeting the smiling honeymooners as they advanced down the platform beside the long Pullman cars; the bouquets of flowers, the news photographers, the crisply uniformed White House chauffeur; then following the Smoots in the Presidential limousine along Pennsylvania Avenue, sweeping through the White House gates, waved on by the White House guards, and there, under the portico, President Hoover in white linen suit, Lou Henry Hoover, fresh and lovely in light blue; breakfast in the fresh, cool shade of the White House porch, vases of freshly cut flowers, soft gleam of polished sterling. The breakfast, filling but Quaker-plain and Mormon-simple: melon, bacon and eggs, whole wheat muffins, toast, No tea. No coffee.

At the head of the table the Chief held aloft a stemmed crystal goblet, cracked ice tinkling musically. "A toast to the bride and bridegroom," he said. Allie and Bill and the others raised their glasses. The Senator and his bride beamed. "May every hour, of every day, of every year, bring you health and happiness."

The guests murmured, "Hear, hear," and drank. The Chief lowered his glass to the table and studied it, twisting the graceful stem between his thumb and forefinger. "A good glass of water," he said. "The greatest stimulant in the world."

Bill, four places down, watched the turning goblet send tiny cutglass rainbows wheeling across the rich, white-linen table cloth. He knew he would travel long and he would travel far, but he wondered if he would ever be farther from where he started that he was at that moment.

It was instantly evident that for as long as they remained the house guests of the Hoovers, the Smoots would be the central figures on the Washington social scene. Their improbable yet somehow touching romance had captivated Washingtonians, had immeasurably brightened what had started out to be another dreary and deadly Washington summer, and the press loved every minute of it.

There were dinner parties at the White House in honor of the Senator and his bride, intimate weekends with the Hoovers and their friends at the President's summer camp on the Rapidan River in Virginia. The papers made much of how the Smoots had selflessly forgone plans "to honeymoon in the soft Hawaiian nights" in order to answer the President's call for help with ratification of the London Naval Treaty. But the compensations were sweet. Headlined the New York *Evening Graphic,*

"Romance Turns White House into Cozy Love Nest." The feature story regaled *Graphic* readers with details of the accommodations Mrs. Hoover had provided for them: the Rose Suite, furnished in rose satin damask, overflowing with an endless supply of fresh pink roses, grandly and invitingly dominated by the bed of Andrew Jackson.

Most charming of all was Allie's mother's simple wonder at the miracle that had taken place in her life, as she and the Senator shuttled from White House breakfast to luncheons at the Mayflower, to teas at the Embassy, then back to the White House for dinner, and perhaps an after-dinner musicale.

"Can you imagine any little girl," she wrote back home to Utah, "coming across the ocean and almost the width of the United States as a little emigrant, dreaming that she would ever become the wife of a Senator of the United States, a man who has for years distinguished himself in both nation and church? Is it not beyond the realm of imagination for such a girl to see herself, with her distinguished husband, the honored guest of the head of the United States government?"

Toward the middle of July, with the powerful support of Senator Arthur S. Vandenburg and other Republican leaders, the London Naval Treaty was ratified by Congress. The need for the Senator's presence in Washington was over. He and Mrs. Smoot said good-bye to the Hoovers, to Allie and Bill, and left for the dark sands and blue skies of Waikiki and their second honeymoon.

A month back, Washington political and society reporters would not have dreamed it possible that they would ever miss the presence in their town of the dry, teetotaling, nose-to-the grindstone Reed Smoot. But as the statesman-honeymooner, with his refreshing and vivacious bride from Salt Lake City, he was quite another person—human, appealing, almost boyish. Together, they and their romance made Washington forget for a moment the lengthening breadlines, the bank failures, the nation's apparently irreversible slide to economic disaster. Not only for Allie and Bill, but for the city at large, Washington, without them, was suddenly a duller place.

Chapter Twelve

The city of Washington, then, as now, was a community—at once small town and world capital—that lived in considerable awe, for the most part, of the office of the Presidency, if not of the President himself. For Bill and Allie Marriott, an obscure young Mormon couple from Utah, to have breakfasted and dined at the White House; for them to be waved through the White House gates whenever they felt like it—for this to happen within the space of a few short weeks in the early summer of 1930 dissolved as if by magic all kinds of social, economic, and political barriers.

Before the month was out Allie was invited to become a member of the National Woman's Country Club, and accepted. Bill took up golf and hacked around the public course in East Potomac Park, on the island in the river below the Tidal Basin, playing with Isaac Stewart, Senator Smoot's executive secretary; Roland Parry, who was there studying music; Bonesy Jones, the University of Utah football star; Milton Hansen, another Mormon law student; bright, on-the-ball George Romney; David Kennedy, a young bank examiner who would one day become Secretary of the Treasury, and others of the Mormon colony. Bill, begrudging the time away from work, played so fast he invariably holed out before his companions reached the green. Even later, when he joined the Congressional Country Club, and, after that, Burning Tree, he walked faster than anyone he played with except for George Romney and Senator Smoot, a golfing eccentric who always drove first, no matter who had won the previous hole, then strode down the fairway before his companions had a chance to tee up. Moreover, he often played the first ball he came to on the fairway, whether his or not, and left his companions to pacify the irate golfer whose ball he'd played. By this time, however, the Senator would be far down the fairway, blithely hitting the wrong ball up to the green.

The Smoots had returned to Washington after Labor Day for the fall session of Congress, reopening after the summer the Senator's handsome seven-bedroom French Provincial mansion at 4500 Garfield Street, in Wesley Heights, a woodsy, fashionable corner of the western city in the angle formed by the Potomac River and the Maryland line, less than a ten-minute drive from Georgetown.

With their return and as the fall social season gathered pace, Bill and Allie took up where they had left off in July. To the dry and heavy tone of the Senator's intimates, they brought a note of youth, ingenuousness, and optimism that was indeed refreshing in these months of breadlines and bank failures.

Allie's picture, in cloche hat and fox neckpiece, began appearing on the society pages. "In Congressional Set," the overline would read, and the caption, "Charming Young Matron, Daughter of Mrs. Reed Smoot, living at 4100 Cathedral Avenue."

They barely had time for Christmas that year. First, there was a White House evening musicale, following a dinner given by the President and Mrs. Hoover for Cabinet members and their wives. A few days later they were in Philadelphia with the Smoots, cheering their heads off for Navy at the annual Army-Navy football game. Then, on the night before the New Year's Eve, they were back at the White House for a holiday dance given by the Hoovers for their handsome young son Allan. The White House Christmas decorations were still up. There was a jazz band imported from New York, and Allan gracefully led off the dancing with his partner of the evening, Miss Fanny Homans, great-great-great-granddaughter of John Adams, first President to occupy the White House.

The real New Year's Eve, when it came the next night, was for the first time in their lives an anticlimax.

Bill was learning, and Allie was learning. They had solved the cracking-mug problem, by pioneer persistence and much precious time at health department hearings, through a change in the District ruling that permitted chlorine sterilization instead of five minutes in boiling water. And they'd solved the driveway problem the same way: a change in regulations permitting the cutting of curbings for commercial drive-in purposes. Both changes were timely accommodations to emerging new factors in public service—the beginnings of modern, fast-food merchandising and the increasing role of the automobile in the life of just about everybody.

But then there was this. Bill had leased the Georgia Avenue property for three years, and on it had built Hot Shoppe Number Three. The owner was a real estate investor who held much of the run-down property along Ninth Street. "I expect to stay there longer than three years," Bill had said. The real estate man shrugged. "No problem. I'll renew your lease for another three years."

Now the time had come to enlarge the shop. Again the owner dismissed the matter. "Fine, my boy, go right ahead. I'll renew your lease on the same terms, this time for five years."

The warning voice that should have said, "Remember Ninth Street—get it in writing!" was for some reason silent. Bill ordered 3,000 dollars' worth of expansion. When it was finished, he drew the money out of their savings account in the Park Savings Bank and paid it. The owner was out of town. Bill called the owner's lawyer. "I need my new lease," Bill said.

The lawyer coughed, cleared his throat. "That, I'm afraid, Mr. Marriott, is out of the question. My client has changed his mind. He's not going to give you a new lease."

Bill couldn't believe it. "What do you mean he's not? He gave me his word."

"Sorry, Mr. Marriott. We're in a depression. Money is tight. You don't have any agreement on paper anywhere."

"I've spent a lot of money on that property. I'll have to take it to court."

"Go ahead. Waste some more money," the lawyer said, and hung up.

Bill found a lawyer, sued—and lost.

A month or two before the original lease was up, the owner telephoned Bill. Good-naturedly he asked about Allie, about the business, said he loved the Connecticut Avenue shop and that he and his wife ate there all the time. Then the point: He'd hate to see Bill lose his investment in the Georgia Avenue property—the shop seemed to be doing well and was an asset to the neighborhood—so he had second thoughts about the whole thing. Bill deserved a new, five-year lease, and he, the owner, would be happy to draw one up for him.

"How much?"

"Double what you've been paying."

What Bill was thinking, if spoken, would have fused the telephone wires in the mouthpiece—but he accepted. He had confidence in the location; he knew that the expansion would draw more customers, make more money, and more than compensate for the higher rent. But before he had hung up, he had made up his mind: he wanted and needed the best business lawyer in Washington. Everyone told him it was Roger Whiteford—expensive, but the best. Whiteford represented the Marriott family until his death in 1972. Bill never lost another suit.

And there was this. Both Bill and Allie liked Mr.

Stunz, the friendly, outgoing manager of the Park Savings Bank. He had loaned them the $5,000 with which to buy Hugh Colton's share of the business. They had banked with him ever since. He was thin, of medium height, dressed quietly, and wore glasses. He was always cheerful, infallibly conservative in money matters, always praising Bill for working hard and putting his money into a savings account, instead of flinging it away on some get-rich-quick investment scheme.

By this time, the country was about to hit the bottom of the depression: some 12 million unemployed, close to 5,000 banks (nearly one of every four) out of business, farm prices at their lowest in history; the national income down to $40 billion, half of what it had been in 1929. "Bill," said Senator Smoot over the dinner table one evening, "I think you'd better get your money out of that bank. More banks are going under. Yours may be one of them."

A word of wisdom—from the chairman of the Senate Finance Committee. A few days later Bill called on Mr. Stunz. He and Allie had $15,000 in their account. After their heavy investment in the Connecticut Avenue shop, it represented their total savings and working Hot Shoppes capital. He told Mr. Stunz that he wanted to withdraw the entire amount. Nothing personal, he wanted his friend to understand; but the Park Savings was a relatively small bank; it didn't have the resources to stand the pressures that might develop if things got worse.

To Bill's amazement, Mr. Stunz turned pale. His hand fluttered to his collar. "Please," he said hoarsely. "Don't close out your account. Your money is safe here. I guarantee it."

Bill hesistated. He liked Mr. Stunz. The banker had been a good friend, had loaned him and Allie money on practically nothing but sheer good faith.

152

"I know things don't look too good," Mr. Stunz went on. "But I have every confidence that we'll survive. If there's the slightest danger of closing, I'll call you, and you can get your money out."

Against his better judgment, Bill withdrew $5,000 but left the remaining $10,000 in the account. Two months after that, Park Savings closed its doors. Mr. Stunz did not call. The next day, he shot himself. Auditors discovered that it wasn't just hard times: over the years Mr. Stunz had appropriated some $250,000 in bank funds and had lost it all gambling, mostly on the horses.

Ultimately, they and other depositors were paid back, at 20 cents on the dollar.

Banks were all right, but this only confirmed Bill's inner feeling about them. He'd seen his father borrow money from the bank and go broke in spite of the loan, and the bank had moved in and foreclosed, and now it was in Bill's mind to buy his family a house in Ogden and rescue them at last from the drudgery of farming, and somehow buy back the farm from the bank.

The only sheep men he knew of in Utah who didn't go broke were the ones who didn't owe any money. He'd never forgotten that. He never had and never would borrow money for personal reasons; in fact, he never borrowed personally again at all after Mr. Stunz's original $5,000 loan. But a heavy corporate expansion program came after the war and made it mandatory for the corporation to finance new buildings. Even then it worried him, and he saw to it that the corporation borrowed no short-time money from banks, but borrowed from insurance companies on long-term loans.

Charge accounts he regarded as another form of borrowing. It wasn't until just before World War II, after the Hot Shoppes were grossing millions of dollars a year, that Bill permitted Allie to open a charge account at Garfinckel's, the first she'd ever had. Not that he didn't trust her. Not at all. She'd been the one who'd watched the cash register, collected the money and taken it to the apartment at midnight in a paper bag, after a long day's work, and counted it. No one knew better than she the value of a dollar, a dime, a penny. But if they didn't have the money to buy something—clothes, furniture, or a new radio to listen to Amos 'n' Andy or Jack Benny with— well, they just weren't going to buy it.

Same with lending. Now that he was moving around and moving up in Washington, men he did business with and who were getting hit hard by the depression were asking him to endorse bank loans for them or, in some instances, to loan them money himself. Bill would shake his head. "Friend, people are after me all the time to sign notes for them, but I never sign a note for anybody. If I wanted to help them, and if I could, I'd sooner give them the money and forget it. Start signing notes and most times, you lose your money, and you lose your friend too."

The more Bill saw what was happening all around him, the more deeply he knew that he was right. Lean on the Lord and count on yourself—your own two hands, your own hard work.

Mr. Whiteford was worried about Bill. Bill had asked him to close the deal for a good piece of property on Florida Avenue for Hot Shoppe Number Six (actually, it would be one of five in operation, since the Ninth Street shop no longer existed). Mr. Whiteford had looked pained, and said, "I'll do it if you insist, but my advice to you, young man, is to get out of this restaurant business. Quick. Right now. I've got a lot of clients in this business, and they're all going broke."

"So you think I can't make a go of it," Bill replied.

"Your trouble is, you want to expand. I can tell. Expand. Get bigger. That's what's driving you. And that's your weakness. But you'll never get anywhere by expand-

ing, because then you can't control it. You can't control
the root beer in eight or ten different shops at the same
time. You can't control all those people who make your
sandwiches, and be sure that they're all up to your standards. The bigger you get, the less control you have. I've
seen it happen a hundred times in your business. When
quantity goes up, quality goes down. It'll happen to you.
You'll go broke, just like the rest of them. Get out while
you can, and get into something more substantial."

Bill didn't agree. All over the country chain-store merchandising was proving to be one of the few success stories
of the depression. The Great Atlantic and Pacific Tea
Company, for example. Woolworth's Five-and Ten-Cent
stores, Piggley Wiggley. Because they sold so much, they
could keep their prices down. Same with his Hot Shoppes.
Sure, Mr. Whiteford was right about control. It *was*
essential. But Bill was convinced he could maintain it.
How? By centralization. One man to do all the purchasing. All food possible prepared in one efficient, closely
supervised commissary, according to tested, standardized
recipes. Tight, roving, white-glove supervision by Big
Tamale himself or Allie or one of Bill's brothers, possible
at any time of day or night. Finally, and perhaps most important, indoctrination into the help, from managers to
curbers to busboys, of feelings of loyalty, pride in quality
and cleanliness and service, and faith in the company
that, if they did things right, lived right, and worked hard,
they would be richly rewarded—right here on earth.

Bill listened to Whiteford, appreciated what he was
saying, and probably did proceed more conservatively
than he otherwise would have, because of it. But he
wasn't about to sell out. Instead, he pushed ahead with
plans for the Florida Avenue shop and opened it in midsummer, 1931, with curb-girl fanfare and flurries of free
root beer tickets all over town. It was a typical Marriott
location—on a main thoroughfare with heavy traffic in

155

both directions, close to a prosperous, semi-suburban shopping district, and surrounded by what Bill called "a big bedroom area," which meant, of course, heavy family patronage the year around.

Allie, to their joy and yet deepening sense of responsibility, was now pregnant. Not for very much longer could she and Bill cruise around checking on the stores together until two or three in the morning, taking off their shoes when they reached the apartment house so they wouldn't wake up tenants on the floor below. Nor would she be able to keep up the classes in interior design that she'd been attending six hours a week in order to help with the constant redecoration of the five shops.

Their Westchester apartment had two bedrooms, one of which they'd converted into a bookkeeping office for Allie. Their office had to be moved to a basement to make room for a nursery. Bill rented it, and into it moved the company headquarters. Incredible as it seemed to both Bill and Allie, the Hot Shoppes' annual gross business was beginning to crowd the $1,000,000 mark. No sooner had they hired a girl to replace Allie and double as secretary-bookkeeper than it became obvious that this wouldn't do; they needed a secretary *and* a bookkeeper. John S. Daniels resigned from Pat McDermott's construction company to take the job. One of the first of many Marriott employes to "ascend and increase," Daniels became a vice-president in 1941. It was only a matter of a year or two before the company outgrew the Westchester offices and moved to larger quarters in the commissary building adjoining the Georgia Avenue shop.

So Bill wasted no time in branching out. To Mr. Whiteford's horror, he optimistically extended the chain to the north, out of the District for the first time, establishing, with his brother Paul's help, their first Hot Shoppe in Baltimore, and negotiating, still farther north, for the A&W root beer franchise in Philadelphia.

Ike Stewart, Senator Smoot's secretary and administrative assistant, and his wife, June, lived at the Alban Towers, two blocks along Cathedral Avenue from the Marriotts. June, like Allie, was pregnant. They went to the same obstetrician, Dr. E. W. Titus. Dr. Titus estimated that they would have their babies on the same day, April 5, 1932. He booked adjoining rooms for them in Columbia Hospital. Early in the morning of March 25, Ike and June, taken by surprise, threw some things in a suitcase. As swiftly as they could manage it, what with June in preliminary labor, they descended to the street, got in their car, and roared down Wisconsin Avenue toward the hospital. Meanwhile, the same crisis had overtaken Allie. She and Bill filled an overnight bag, got in the Nash, and were driving down the street when a familiar car flashed past.

"Ike and June!" cried Allie.

"Well, what d'ya know," Bill chuckled, and floored the accelerator.

Three hours later, with Dr. Titus's help, Allie gave birth to a seven-pound boy. Two hours after that, June had a nine-pound boy. Out in the expectant fathers' waiting room, strain over, suspense lifted, Bill and Ike laughed happily, shook hands, clapped each other on the back. Perfect timing. No trouble at all. Only next time, no more Mack Sennett chase scenes. They'd all go in one car.

A little more than seven months later, on a rainy night in early November, Bill and Allie sat in the living room of the house in Garfield Street with Senator and Alice Sheets Smoot, listening with deepening gloom as Democratic candidates, led by the ebullient Franklin Delano Roosevelt, steam-rollered across the nation. The Senator kept score on sheets of ruled paper. He knew that even President Hoover did not expect to win, but his own was a special case. Of the 36 years that Utah had been represented in Congress, he had served as senator for 30. Utah had gone Democratic only once since the election of 1896, and that was in 1914, when it gave its four electoral votes to Woodrow Wilson. But he, Senator Smoot, up for reelection, had survived, had been sent back to the Senate in spite of the Wilson victory. Down through his 30 years in Washington, he had served his church, his state, and his country well and with honor. His opponent, Dr. Elbert D. Thomas, a political science professor at the University of Utah, of no practical experience, was nothing to worry about. Everyone in that room knew it would happen again.

But incredibly, crushingly, it didn't. When the votes began to trickle in from Utah, where polls closed two hours later than in the East, it became ever more evident that Utah was going for Roosevelt and the entire Democratic ticket, all the way. The margin of victory began to pile up. At a little after 11 o'clock, the Senator laid his pencil and paper aside, removed his glasses, folded them carefully, and placed them, as he always did, in his upper left vest pocket. He rose from his chair and extended a hand to his wife. "Come on, Alice," he said, "it's past our bedtime." He smiled, a little sadly, at Bill and Allie. "When you're ready to go, would you turn out the lights?" Slowly, he and his wife climbed the wide, curving staircase, up to the solace of their bedroom, and of sleep.

F.D.R. was inaugurated and went to work with speed and authority that to most Republicans was nothing short of insulting. He and his Cabinet pushed through Congress legislation that took the nation off the gold standard, started the Civilian Conservation Corps, and established the Tennessee Valley Authority. They drafted and saw enacted the Federal Emergency–Relief Act, the Agricultural Adjustment and Emergency Farm Mortgage Acts, the Home Owners' Loan Act, and the famous National Industrial Recovery Act. By this time the President had been in office a little more than three months. Enough for a while, he said, and went sailing off the coast of New England.

Meanwhile, with only a passing twinge of a feeling of disloyalty, Bill could not help noting that the Democratic victory had not hurt Hot Shoppe business at all. In fact, it was better than ever. He had added hamburgers and chicken pie to the menus, had opened coffee-shop restaurants at all the stores, and at Number Five had even started to offer full-course dinners. From noon until one and two in the morning, they had all the business they could handle. Bill could tell already that they were on their way to their first year of a million gross.

The cherry blossoms came and went. Allie, these days, was busy at home with the baby, whom they had named J. Willard Jr., or Billy. Bill's brother Paul was looking after the new Baltimore store and was negotiating for an interest in several A&W root beer stands in Philadelphia. Bill visited the shops, keeping the kitchen crews and the curbers and waitresses on their toes, chatting with the customers, scouting out new locations for when the country really turned the corner, and he could branch out in earnest.

Just as all this was building up and he could hardly wait for it to happen, he began to be aware of something that he tried for weeks, and then for a couple of months, to overlook: strange little lumps, the size of robins' eggs, under his arms. Then one formed at the back of his neck. He was waking up in the morning listless and weak, totally unlike himself.

A positive thinker and an optimist, a believer that keepers of the Word of Wisdom were rewarded with good health, vigor, and longevity, Bill had always resisted the notion of illness in himself. But the nodes grew larger. The listlessness attacked him more often. Eventually, in the early spring of 1934, he gave in to Allie's urging and had a physical examination. The doctor noted that he showed signs of overwork. His heart and blood pressure were satisfactory, but something was apparently acting up in his lymphatic system. He took tissue from several of the larger nodes for a biopsy.

There were fruitless, never-ending visits to Garfield Hospital, to the Hunter Laboratories, to the Grover Christie X-ray laboratories for radiation therapy, then, finally, one bright May afternoon, to a small Garfield Hospital conference room for a conference with five specialists, all of whom had studied the case. Their diagnosis: Hodgkins disease, malignant neoplasm of the lymphatic system, or, in everyday terms, cancer of the lymph glands.

"Can you cure it?" Bill asked.

The spokesman's voice was gentle. "We want to be as kind as we can, and perhaps some day it will be different, but we must tell you that today, Hodgkins disease is regarded as incurable. In a word, terminal. The nodes have not responded to radiation. Surgery would be ineffective. There is nothing else we can do."

The room fell silent.

Then the doctor continued. "We have not indicated the seriousness of your illness until we were absolutely certain. Now, I'm afraid there is no doubt." He looked at each of the other doctors in turn. "We all agree. The case, we're afraid, is hopeless."

Bill, only half-listening, was thinking of Allie, of the little boy, of the things he'd hoped to do, of the years he'd hoped to live.

"How much time do I have, doctor?"

"Six months? A year at the most."

Bill called Paul down from Baltimore, and the two of them and Allie sat up late for nights in the big house in Garfield Street that the Smoots had left behind and where Bill and Allie were living until they could find a buyer for it. They turned the business over to Paul and made arrangements with him and Mr. Whiteford to handle it for the next three months. Then they packed up the Nash and drove to Virginia Beach. It was so hot there that after a few days they left and drove slowly north through New Jersey and New York City, along the Connecticut shore and through Stamford and Norwalk and New Haven, where Bill had been on his mission. Whenever Bill got tired, they stopped for the night.

They drove on up into the Maine wilderness, to Moosehead Lake, to a remote fishing and hunting camp at the north end of the lake. The nearest house was miles away. There were capable but taciturn French-Canadian guides to take them fishing in canoes. The water was ice-cold, too cold for swimming. Offshore from their camp was a little island; they'd paddle out to it and cook something over a campfire. Bill had brought a portable wind-up Victrola and some records. They listened to it a lot—"Drifting and Dreaming," "Stardust," "Dancing in the Dark," "Moonlight Bay," "Home on the Range," Stephen Foster songs that Bill liked.

Ironically, it was their first vacation, and it was fun to do these simple things together for the first time, but what the doctor said haunted them day and night. Bill would wake up in the middle of the night and feel the nodes under his arms to see if they'd grown smaller. But they seemed larger than ever.

Time and again the words of James came back to him, as they had at the girl's bedside in the upstairs room in the farmer's house in Vermont: "Is there any sick among you? Let him call for the elders of the church. . . ." And didn't Matthew say, "They shall lay hands on the sick, and they shall recover."

Bill, as a Mormon, believed this—had, indeed, acted upon it. He believed that the authority in the church now was the same as it was when the Savior was on earth.

Through Joseph Smith He had restored that authority. Those who came after Joseph Smith and who now held priesthood in the church had the same authority to heal the sick as He had.

On the long drive back to Washington Bill made up his mind, and the day after they arrived home he telephoned Edgar B. Brossard, chairman of the U.S. Tariff Commission during the Hoover years, still a member of the commission and an elder of the Mormon Church in the District. The next evening Brossard and another elder, Federal Judge Gustave Iverson, came to 4500 Garfield Street. They gathered in the living room and without preliminary they anointed Bill's head with consecrated oil and laid their hands on his head and blessed him:

"As elders of the church, we promise you in the name of the Lord that you will be healed. We rebuke this disease. We believe, and we ask you to believe with us, in your mission of service to your fellow man and to your church, and we promise you that you will live to perform this mission. . . .

"Again, we ask our Father to rebuke the disease which is taking your life, and we do this by the authority of the Holy Priesthood and in the name of Jesus Christ. Amen."

Bill went to bed that night and slept the night through, without dreams, without waking, without night thoughts, night fears. The next day he seemed relieved of a heavy burden.

From that time on, the lymphatic swellings decreased in size. In a few weeks, they had vanished altogether. None of his doctors, not one of the five, could find a trace of Hodgkins disease. By Christmastime he was back at work, sixteen hours a day.

Chapter Thirteen

Days blending into weeks, into months, were all the same to Bill. Clocks, calendars, didn't matter. What you could do between waking in the morning and dropping exhausted into bed at night—that's what counted. In these years he tracked success the way, back in the mountains, he tracked a deer or a bear.

He and Allie and little Billy were living now in Senator Smoot's mansion in Wesley Heights. As late as the 1920s this had been a region of rolling acres, dirt roads, farms, and footpaths between the western fringes of the city and the Potomac River. But now it was where the upper middle ranks of government were building and moving, out along Foxhall Road, into Tudor, Georgian, and sometimes white-pillared, neo-antebellum homes— clipped green lawns, azaleas electric pink and dogwoods drifting snow white in the springtime, sweet smell of honeysuckle, Packard phaetons, top down, in the curving drives, collegians in Oxford bags or short skirts and rolled stockings, home for Easter from Yale and Smith and UVA.

Bill and Allie had not wanted to live there. Less than a mile away, at the Westchester, they had a nice apartment. But now the Senator and Mrs. Smoot had to leave Washington and go back to Salt Lake City, where he would resume his duties with the Church.

"Times are so bad, we can't sell the house," the Senator said to Bill. "You and Allie move in with Billy and live there until times are better. Then you can sell it."

So there they were, in the big house, with five extra bedrooms, the wide circular staircase in the foyer, the elegant dining room whose chairs were fitted (as they are to this day) with the needlepoint seat covers Allie's mother made in the first years of her marriage.

It was fine for the family. After his farewell party in Ogden, Bill's brother Woody dropped in for a few days of golf on the way to his mission assignment in England. Bill and Allie gave him another party, agreed to help with expenses, and sent him on his way. And that Thanksgiving, they filled it with autumn foliage and yellow chrysanthemums for the wedding of Bill's sister Kay to Ferdinand Kaufholz, a government lawyer, of Baltimore. (Eva, Bill's older sister, had been married to Harold A. Candland, also a government lawyer, the year before, in Alexandria, Virginia.)

But to Bill and Allie the house, for all its elegance, seemed at that time extravagance that bordered on the irresponsible. Bill drove himself harder than ever. He was beginning to see now that he'd been right all along about the automobile. From the days of his father's first, shiny, black Buick, he had believed in cars. Not even when he and Allie were struggling across the pot-holed roads of Wyoming and Nebraska in his rattletrap Model T did he lose faith in that car, or any car. He'd seen them packing the parking lot of the A&W root beer stand in Salt Lake. He knew what they meant to people like him and his mother and father, who'd never been able to go any farther, any faster, or any more dependably than a horse and wagon could take them. And in Washington, he and Allie saw more cars on Pennsylvania Avenue in a day than they'd seen in Salt Lake City in a week, cars with plates from states all over the East.

During the 1920s, the number of cars on the road rose from eight million to more than 23 million, and even now, during the Depression, they were increasing at the rate of half a million a year. Paved-road mileages were increasing even more rapidly. Added to this was another social force neither Bill nor anyone else could have foreseen: talking pictures. Nearly one hundred million Americans saw them every week. Not only was there a new public, there was a new America: predominantly urban, more and more on wheels, on the move, downtown, driving to work, driving home from work, going shopping, driving to the beach, taking dates for a ride, going to the movies, eating out, stopping for something after the movies.

The Hot Shoppes couldn't miss. Of course, it wasn't all that simple. For one thing, you couldn't just set one down anywhere. The location had to be right, or you'd never get a chance to serve this new public on wheels; it'd just drive on by.

"It's got to be an important, busy street. It's got to be an important corner," Bill said over and over again to Allie, to Paul, to John Daniels, their treasurer. "Suburbs are better than downtown. Land's cheaper, more parking space for the dollar. And we can build up a solid base of customers right in the neighborhood around us."

As Congress cranked out one remedial New Deal measure after another, the number of government workers in the District increased, spread north into Maryland, west across the river into Virginia. They were relatively well paid. Many were working women in no mood to cook dinner after a day at the office. They could afford cars. They had a need for readily available, modestly priced, dependable restaurants of quality. And Bill and the Hot Shoppes were there to fill that need.

Morning, noon, and night, he made his life and work an article of faith. Even as he and Allie, and Paul, too, scouted new locations, even as they planned for expansion and wondered where the capital was coming from, they kept their prices down: nickel root beer, ten-cent hot dog, fifteen-cent barbecue sandwich, fifteen-cent bowl of chili, fifteen-cent milk shake. And when they extended the menu, it was a plate luncheon: vegetable, potato, meat, and drink, thirty-five cents.

Personnel was a problem. Waitresses and curbers for the most part were inexperienced, as were the managers and assistant mangers. Drive-in restaurants were new. The Marriotts themselves were making up the rules as they went along. From nine in the morning until midnight or later, they toured the five Hot Shoppes in Washington, seeing that the food was prepared and served right, that the root beer was well carbonated and cold, that the windows sparkled, that the floors were spotless and polished, that parking-lot litter was picked up. Paul enforced the same rules and standards at the two locations in Philadelphia and the one in Baltimore.

Bill, indeed, was fanatic about appearances and cleanliness. He insisted that every window in every Hot Shoppe be washed every day if need be, inside and out. Each store was painted inside and out at least once a year. As soon as the business could afford one—they were by no means cheap—he bought a silverware burnishing machine, a long, revolving metal cylinder partially filled with small steel balls, and installed it in the Connecticut Avenue kitchen. There the silverware was burnished every day. At least once a week managers of other stores brought their silverware over for burnishing. Ultimately, each store had its own machine and used it daily.

His managers never knew what time of day or night he'd show up at the kitchen door and go bird-dogging almost at a half-run through the kitchen, the pantries, the storage rooms, the refrigerators, the restaurant itself, running a finger over the shelves to check for dust, checking under tables and in cutlery drawers, checking the ranges, the storage rooms, the trays about to be served, sampling the root beer, and raising hell if everything wasn't spotless, neat, clean, bright, polished, done efficiently, done well.

Another thing he preached was frugality. "Always remember," he'd tell his managers, "a penny saved is a penny more of profit." Not just for the Marriotts, he meant, but for them, too. They were all in business together. The more the business earned, the more they all earned. He started giving managers bonuses based on the performance of each shop: the more the profit, the higher the bonus. Some of them would rise in the company and retire millionaires. One inspired manager learned how to read gas and electric meters. He checked them every week. If there was a significant increase in consumption over the preceding week, he ferreted out the reason. He either eliminated the cause or demanded a corresponding increase in business from his help. At the end of the first year, he got the biggest bonus. The next year, *every* manager checked the meters every week. Power bills went down. Profits—and bonuses—went up. The difference from this one procedure was not huge, naturally. But Bill was certain that the attitude—the attention to detail, the initiative in cutting waste—was right.

In many respects, Bill was pioneering. A drive-in restaurant was a new, peculiarly American product of the automobile, migration to the cities, and an easier, looser, younger way of life that developed in the Twenties and Thirties. He had found out very early that he could not buy the kind of kitchen he needed; he had to design it himself and have it made to order. So he hired a carpenter and designer who did nothing but work on Hot Shoppe kitchens. It became the same with his buildings, which had to handle a drive-in trade and thus had to be oriented properly to the surrounding parking spaces, to the shape and location of the property itself. The staff of one kitchen carpenter grew to include an architect, more carpenters, a small crew of heating, plumbing, and electrical engineers. Searching for just the right interior for his biggest and most popular store, the one on Connecticut Avenue, he hired expensive professional decorators to redecorate it. Meanwhile, with time out to have

Billy, Allie took a course in interior decoration. Then she took charge of Hot Shoppe design herself and with a couple of assistants helped to create the corporate division that today designs all Marriott properties and keeps more than two hundred architects, engineers, artists, and designers busy every working day of the year.

It was the same with Hot Shoppe food. Experience had taught him that the food served in one shop had to cost, taste, look, and smell the same as the food served in every other shop. A shop that was inferior in any way lost customers fast. Moreover, criticism against one shop reflected, in the public's mind, against every other shop. He was discovering for his business what Frank Winfield Woolworth and J. C. Penney and Henry Ford had discovered before him, for theirs: quality control, when you mass-produce, requires standardization at the source. The more products or the more outlets, the more rigid your standardization must be.

As he had when he hired Roger Whiteford, he went to the top and hired Mrs. Ethel Savage, kitchen and menu consultant to Schrafft's of New York, in Bill's view, the best restaurant chain in the country. The construction crew built her a special test kitchen in which she strove to improve the quality and attractiveness of items already offered and to develop new ones that would add variety to the traditional Hot Shoppe menu. When a new item was offered, sales records were kept, scanned, and analyzed. Unless it was consistently popular, it was dropped. Mrs. Savage's principal task was to determine the best and most efficient way of preparing each Hot Shoppe item and then write down its recipe. These recipes were printed in little black books and distributed to every Marriott chef and manager. New recipes were added; those that failed to sell were discarded. Under no circumstances was a chef to deviate, by so much as a pinch of salt, from Mrs. Savage's original.

Bill also saw that it was necessary to insist on universal operations procedures. He wrote a small book setting forth general company policies and the way he wanted things done with regard to operations, employe and customer relations, accounting practices, and all other administrative aspects. He gave a copy to every manager and assistant manager. He held staff meetings to discuss these policies and procedures. When experience and trial-and-error proved the need for change or the formulation of new ones, this was done and incorporated into the book.

Along with all this he developed out-front changes and innovations to provide faster, more efficient and economical service, to cut costs, to make the customer happy, to get the shop talked about and written up in the papers so that when people went there they felt part of something new, bright, alive, moving with the times.

Bill had already staked out this image for the Hot Shoppes with the drive-in concept. Everybody from truck drivers to college kids, from housewives to Congressmen and diplomats saw the sense to the synthesis of automobile and restaurant—the convenience of it, the fun of it. A lot of them felt a flash of appreciation when they saw one of the clean white shops with the orange-tiled roof. It was successful. It was associated in their minds with youthful curbers, a friendly smile, good simple food, fair prices, no waiting, not only drive in, but order, eat—and drive out.

He had his electricians install intercom systems between parking stations and the kitchens, so that curbers could call in orders moments after the customers had made up their minds. By the time the curbers got back to the pick-up counters, the orders were already on the fire, or even waiting and ready for delivery. In January 1935, the time of the year when it cost the least, Bill had every store air-conditioned. That summer, sales went up and stayed up. Sometimes an idea that was good for a couple of paragraphs and perhaps a picture in the *Post* didn't work out. One manager, for example, thought of putting curbers on roller skates, so they could pick up and deliver their orders faster. "Go ahead," Bill said, "let's try it." Within a day it became evident that this practice was fraught with peril, not only for the curbers, but for windshields, plate-glass windows, frail elderly couples—anything breakable within range of flying objects. All too often a curber's skates hit a pebble or pieces of gravel, upended the curber, and sent tray, sandwiches, drinks, glasses, and cutlery soaring all over the parking lot. An all-points directive quickly put a stop to roller-skate deliveries.

More conservative, and more gratifying, was the annual citywide Waiters' Derby, run over a four-block course on Fifteenth Street below Pennsylvania Avenue, each waiter carrying a tray bearing two glasses and a two-quart pitcher full of water; and the annual citywide beauty contest to determine the prettiest waitress in the District. Hot Shoppe curbers and waitresses won first prize just about every year.

Along with all this was something else, a pervasive spirit, that pulled it all together and generated a friendly, country-western atmosphere that reflected or seemed to express Bill's smile, his firm ready handshake, his eagerness to please. Washingtonians, more than almost anybody, came from somewhere else, from farms and ranches and Main Streets all across America. They appreciated good, simple, family-style cooking, the low prices, the friendliness that made them feel easy and comfortable. These homesick country people, hungry not only for back-home barbecue but for a warm smile and a "Howdy there, neighbor," went away from the Hot Shoppes feeling good—and came back for more. It was the next best thing to a Sunday visit with the folks, and they kept the cash registers ringing.

Bill knew, and of course Allie did, too, that the Hot Shoppes were beginning to make money—not big, take-out profits, because they had more than three hundred employes now, but they could breathe a little more easily, and could think about buying from the Smoots the lovely house in Garfield Street. And they were counting other blessings, too, these days, such as their friends, the George Bushnells and the Earl Samses.

Bill had never forgotten the vicarious, intoxicating sense of success and power he'd felt riding down Fifth Avenue alone in the back seat of the Bushnells' limousine, the day Mr. Bushnell told his chauffeur to show him the sights of Manhattan when he visited New York during his mission. Yes, Mr. Bushnell had taken a liking to Bill. Maybe it was because he was such a country boy. Or because he was doing the work of the Lord up there in Vermont and Connecticut. Or a little of both.

Anyway, in the late 1920s George Bushnell had built a home near Wolfeboro, New Hampshire, on the eastern shore of Lake Winnepesaukee. The Bushnells were great friends of the Earl Samses (he was president and for 35 years chairman of the board of the J. C. Penney Company), and the Samses too had a summer home at Lake Winnepesaukee, next door to the Bushnells. As a matter of fact, they also had winter homes in Miami, almost next door to each other.

Bill had kept in touch with the Bushnells, and they appreciated it because they had no children. He admired and looked up to successful men. He wanted to associate with them, be identified with them. Not only that, he really *liked* them. So with Paul to look after the business, he didn't hesitate a minute when the Bushnells invited him and Allie down to Miami to spend a few weeks in January with them.

Bill thrived on Miami high life, more than Allie did. With the Samses' daughter Gladys and her husband,

Dean Porter, they would go to the Surf Club for dinner and dancing, then to some of the nightclubs. During the day Bill might play golf with Sams at the Indian Creek Club in Bal Harbor. Once the Bushnells chartered a seaplane and they and the Marriotts and the Porters all flew to Havana.

Bill didn't really envy George Bushnell or Earl Sams or the wonderful world they lived in. Some day, he knew, he would have his share of it, if he just lived right and worked hard and used a little common sense.

Bill and Allie enjoyed their introduction to New Hampshire and Lake Winnepesaukee and the summer homes of Tuftonboro Neck. The Samses and the Bushnells had big, comfortable, airy homes there with green lawns sloping to the lake's edge. The Marriotts had never seen anything like Winnepesaukee and the little wooded islands with the towering white pines, and there was even a golf course. They fell in love with it from the moment they saw it, and the Bushnells and the Samses were wonderful friends who treated them as members of their own families.

Another thing Bill would never forget was sitting in a big rocking chair on the Samses' front porch when the *Mount Washington,* the sightseeing steamer, went slowly by, inshore rail lined with tourists, and he could hear the guide's voice floating across the water, "And right over there, folks, is Lake Winnepesaukee's Gold Coast, summer home of the rich, where the head of the J. C. Penney Company lives. There, you can see his big white house, through the trees. . . ." And there he was, the kid from Utah who had herded sheep in the West and had sold woolen underwear in the logging camps, there he was on the Gold Coast, taking it easy, on Earl Sams' front porch.

Come to think of it, Earl and Lula Sams were just about the best friends he and Allie ever had. He'd learned a lot from Mr. Sams. He was kind of surprised in a way—

and in a way he wasn't—to hear that a lot of his own ideas about the Hot Shoppes were just like Mr. Penney's. It was Mr. Penney's policy, for instance, never to open a new store until they had a good location and until they had developed a manager they could trust, one who had started at the bottom. Good managers were just as important as good locations. Mr. Penney was a religious man, and he surrounded himself only with "good, clean-cut, decent Americans." And just as Mr. Penney did, Bill staked his whole future on the value of hard work and good employes. Mr. Penney believed that hard work was what made America great. "This is what he used to say," Sams told Bill. " 'When the mind is educated and the hand left ignorant, the person is but half-trained.'

"Of course," Sams would continue, "that isn't the only thing. The Penney stores are also dedicated to service—to the good, old Golden Rule. We sell people what they need, and we keep our prices down. We have good, clean-cut people in positions of responsibility. And we work hard—and long. Mr. Penney says, 'Nobody ever got rich working a forty-hour week.' And he's right. Mark my words, Bill, he's right."

Bill listened with appreciation—and satisfaction. It was just what he kept telling his own people: "Work hard, keep the stores clean, sell top-quality products at a low price, make people happy—that's what we're trying to do in the Hot Shoppes. If we do that, we'll succeed." That's what they were all working for. To succeed.

Chapter Fourteen

It was time to move with the expansion program. The lessons had been learned. Procedures had been developed and tested. A broad work force in all categories had been trained and indoctrinated. Hot Shoppes were a well-used, well-liked, and accepted part of the day-to-day life of Washington, and Bill was emerging as an up-and-coming young member of the business community. As for conditions in general, the economy apparently had turned the corner. Cities and suburbs were growing. There were more cars on the roads, and more roads than ever before.

Not only all these things, but Bill and Allie were buying the big house in Garfield Street without too much strain. Woody was about to come back from his mission, Russell had started on his, and Bill Jr. was almost old enough for school. The moment, Bill felt, had come. And Allie agreed.

With appropriate and now traditional fanfare—the big ads in the *Post* and the *Star*, the colored balloons, the bunting, the free root beer tickets—they opened Hot Shoppe Number Seven, in Bladensburg Road, in August 1936. In terms of existing Washington stores, it was Number Six; Number Two, in Ninth Street, had been sold in 1930, and the stores in Baltimore and Philadelphia, for bookkeeping purposes, were on a number system of their own. The Bladensburg Road Hot Shoppe marked a big move by the Marriotts: it was the first store they'd opened since 1931 and was the first of twelve that they'd open in the next five years.

But even as they went into business in the eastern part of the city, on U.S. 1 to and from Baltimore and points north, they started building Shoppe Number Eight across the Potomac, hard by the Virginia end of the Fourteenth Street bridge, on the road to and from Richmond and points south. It opened in August 1937, a year almost to the day from the opening of the shop on Bladensburg Road. Its orange-colored roof and tower, its sign of "The Running Boy" showing a uniformed curber bearing a tray in full stride—both familiar Hot Shoppe trademarks—were visible for miles around, and Bill drew on his experience with the yearbook at Weber College to write the ad copy himself: "A modern marvel in restaurant construction, perfection and completeness climaxes ten years of Hot Shoppe service in Washington! . . . All electric, air-conditioned, within five minutes of downtown Washington—the newest, smartest, finest, most modern, best of its type ever built in this country!"

Some of the trade thought Bill had made a big mistake, his first, in Number Eight. No question, it *was* the shiniest, brightest, most air-conditioned, electrified and so on of all the Hot Shoppes, including Number Five, on Connecticut Avenue. But—the location?

Bill had bought the land, about ten acres of it, from the R.F.&P. (the Richmond, Fredericksburg and Potomac railroad). The way the restaurant property was laid out, between its parking lot and four sets of R.F.&P. tracks was a teeming Waldorf of hobo jungles filled with rod-riders lolling around between freights to the Sunny South.

On the other side, between the restaurant and the Potomac, was a public beach for family outings, picnics, and swimming in the river. A couple of miles south on U.S. 1, which ran past the restaurant, sprawled a Hell's Half-Acre of roadhouses, gin mills, beer cellars, and dine-and-dance parlors. And across the street, to the west, were the runways of Hoover Airport. A heavily traveled road ran through the airport. Gates were lowered at the borders of the airfield to stop the traffic every time a passenger plane took off or came in for a landing, just as at a railroad crossing.

It was all very daring and adventurous, and caught the fancy of young people, who loved an excuse to drive out of town, even if it were only to the other end of the Fourteenth Street bridge. The clippings that Allie cut from the Washington papers began to accumulate. She would cut out every item that mentioned "Marriott" or "Hot Shoppes," and drop them in a cardboard dress box. When she had collected a dozen or so, she would mount them in large twelve-by-eighteen-inch scrapbooks. (Allie still does this—collects them all year long, takes them with her to New Hampshire in June, and mounts them in big scrapbooks on rainy summer mornings, when there isn't anything else to do.)

Louise Rowlett, the Salt Lake *Tribune* feature writer, did a story on Bill in a series on "Prominent Utahns in Washington." "J. Willard Marriott," read the headline, "Has Made Fortune with Chain of 'Hot Shoppes' in Capital and Other Cities."

The story told how Bill, Allie, and Bill Jr. were living in Senator Smoot's mansion in Garfield Street, how all eight Hot Shoppes were "veritable palaces," and how they were enthusiastically patronized by "the socially elite of Washington and stylish Chevy Chase residents." The Connecticut Avenue shop was particularly popular. "Every legation party, every political reception, seems to wind up at this spot."

Miss Rowlett did not mention Bill's illness, and pictured him on top of the Washington world. There was the story of his boyhood in Marriott, of how he trudged to grade school in the winter and herded sheep in the mountains above Ogden in the summer; how he worked his way through Weber College and the University of Utah selling woolen underwear in the logging camps of the Northwest, and the sad-funny saga of his honeymoon trip to Washington with Allie in the old Model T, and, of course, how it all began with the little nine-stool root beer stand in Fourteenth Street. But today, Miss Rowlett concluded, it was all different. Bill Marriott had arrived. "The rickety car has long since been replaced by an expensive model. He now winters in Miami and summers in Maine."

Gil Miner, columnist for the Madison, Maine, *Bulletin,* understandably was more relaxed, less self-conscious, and far folksier. His Congressman took him sightseeing one hot night in June, and they wound up at the Connecticut Avenue Shoppe for a bite to eat and a root beer. Gil never saw anything like it.

"Sunday night was so warm in Washington that a plunge into Lake Wesserunsett would have been as welcome as a free pass from St. Peter," he wrote in his column. "Congressman Smith, with whom we were visiting, decided that we should drive about for a bit and cool off. After wheeling around some of the principal sports of this marvelous city, it was thought that all could do nicely with something cold to drink. The Congressman said, 'Gil, we'll stop at a place where one does not get out of his car, and can order a hot dog or a steak and have it served right on a tray in the car.'

"This interested me and in due time we arrived at the 'Hot Shoppe' on Connecticut Avenue. Believe me, it was 'Hot!' Parking spaces for over 1,000 cars, hundreds of young men bustling about taking orders and delivering them, dressed in snappy brown uniforms with their captains in outfits so white they'd make an admiral blush! In the center of this business, the main dining room, was the mammoth kitchen.

"After we had tried the hot dogs and root beer, everybody thought we should have a repeat. Instead of signalling with the car lights as a sign suggested we do, I got out and walked up to a door and went in. I found myself in the middle of the greatest madhouse I've ever seen! I was in the *kitchen!* After almost being bowled over a dozen times by bustling attendants, a young man came over and asked, 'Can I help you?' I explained what I wanted and he said to wait a second and scurried away. One of the help said, 'You must have a drag in this league, the Big Boss is coming to wait on you personally.' Soon the 'Big Boss' returned. 'I'm Bill Marriott,' he said.

"I thanked him for his courtesy and said, 'You should take a couple of weeks off and come up to Maine and relax.' (Just doing a little State promoting.)

"He replied, 'I do—I spend a month every summer at Moosehead Lake. Do you ever go there?'

"This was the first time I had ever been able to talk things over with a living Horatio Alger. He was pleased to meet Congressman Smith, who was equally pleased to know that they had both hired the same guide (Ed King). Mr. Marriott is going to tarry awhile with the Congressman this summer and has promised to visit 'us' in Madison. Small world, what?"

This kind of publicity was gratifying after the hard struggle for recognition and standing; but Bill found he wasn't too happy with headlines saying, "Has Made Fortune," and being described as "a living Horatio Alger." "Everybody'll think I've arrived," he said, "and I don't want anybody to think that. Our company still has a long way to go."

He kept moving. A month after Number Eight opened at the other end of the bridge, Bill set out to justify a slogan he wanted very much to identify with the Hot Shoppes: "Food for the Whole Family." He liked this statement. It meant food for every member of every family, large or small, rich or poor. Moreover, it looked to the future: by building up a loyal clientele among the youngsters, you were developing customers who would stay with you for life.

All Hot Shoppes had always served little three-ounce

glasses of root beer to children at no charge, and now, for the first time, he tried a special children's meal at Number Eight. The menu itself was small, with large type and a drawing in color of the Three Bears on the cover. It offered soup, meat, mashed potatoes, stewed fruit, and milk or root beer, price 35 cents. It was an instant success. A month later, all Hot Shoppes were serving children's meals and prominently displaying the slogan, "Food for the Whole Family."

While he was broadening the customer base to support expansion, he saw that there was yet another aspect to the operations, even more important, that had to be strengthened as much as possibble. This was employe relations.

It was a decade of tensions and turbulence for the national labor movement, marked by such developments as the National Industrial Recovery Act, guaranteeing workers' rights to organize without interference and to bargain collectively; the great automobile and textile industry strikes, the Wagner-Connery Act, and the formation of the militant Congress of Industrial Organizations (C.I.O.) under the leadership of John L. Lewis.

Bill and Allie didn't need the A.F.L. or the C.I.O. to persuade them to be good to their employes; it had been their way from the beginning, and in those years, Bill formulated the policies and the philosophy that he was still talking about, thirty-five years later, when the company opened the Los Angeles Marriott.

They were all a big family, and all in business together. If everybody worked hard, led a good life, and stayed loyal to the company, they would be rewarded materially with "good measure, pressed down, and shaken together, and running over." No question but what it was a challenge. The average margin of profit in restaurants was running about three percent. Many were operating in the red. At the same time, food costs were going up, and so were wages. The thing was, you couldn't pass these increases along to the customer in higher prices, or you'd probably lose him. Bill's answer to this was great efficiency and more cost-cutting in the operation itself, and more production from everybody concerned—from him, from Allie, from Paul, from the store managers, from the whole roster of help that the company, incredibly, was now supporting: chefs, curb supervisors, waitresses, curbers, bus boys, carpenters, electricians, plumbers, designers, maintenance men, mechanics, secretaries.

On off hours, Bill and Allie would drop into a store and sit down in the back with the manager or the assistant manager and a couple of waitresses or curbers, and have an orange juice or something to eat. They'd talk shop. Bill and Allie would ask about the good things that had happened, and the bad. They went out of their way to let the employes know that they were appreciated, as people, as human beings whose connection with the company didn't end when they hung up their uniforms and went home at the close of a day's work.

Employes were trained in company programs and policies, were encouraged to work for promotion, and knew by example that Bill would always promote from within rather than seek outside, and when a curber was promoted to supervisor, or a supervisor to an assistant mangership, Bill wrote him a personal letter of appreciation and congratulations. When an employe's relative died, he wrote a personal letter of condolence. When the Connecticut Avenue curber who won the Washington city public links golf championship couldn't afford the trip to New York to play in the regional championship, Bill paid his way. When the black chef in the Philadelphia store needed $200 for an eye operation, Bill paid it. Bill and Allie instituted the custom of giving every employe a Christmas present of a day's pay for every year of service. When an employe completed five years of service, he or she received a gift from the company—a radio, a refrigerator, an electric stove, the longer the service, the bigger the gift.

It was still 1937, the year they opened Number Eight at the Virginia end of the Fourteenth Street bridge, and Number Nine at Wisconsin and Western avenues, a key four-way intersection on the line between the District and Chevy Chase, Maryland. It was also Bill's first year as a director of the Washington Restaurant Association, and the year that gross revenues looked as though they'd reach the $3-million mark, and the year that, what with keeping every shop open 24 hours a day, Bill and Allie found that they were responsible for the happiness, welfare, and livelihood of 2,000 employes and their families. To bring them closer together, they started a company bowling league and instituted an annual company outing and started a monthly house organ, named *Hot Sauce* (now more elegantly called the *Marriott Crest*).

Woody arrived back from his mission, tall, lean, debonair, and intent on marrying Judith Cannon, the girl he'd left behind on the University of Utah campus a little more than two years before. He impressed Bill by extracting from his wallet a folded scrap of yellow paper and handing it across the breakfast table his first morning back. It was a check for $300 Bill had sent his brother for travel expenses on the continent.

"Just didn't want to spend your money," Woody said.

He'd been able to save a little from Bill's monthly mission check; he'd hitchhiked around Europe; he'd saved by staying with Mormon families instead of in hotels. Bill thanked Woody and tore up the check. It was the kind of thing he would never forget.

Bill asked Woody what his plans were. Well, Woody said, he was thinking of going into law. But first of all he was thinking of Judith.

He hurried on to Salt Lake. He and Judith were married that July, in 1937, a month after her graduation from the university. Russell was still in England, with a year to go before his mission was over.

Bill was thinking so long and hard about expansion these days that for a while he paid little attention to the little development out at Number Eight between Hoover Airport and the river swimming hole.

Quite a few Washingtonians had taken to driving across the Fourteenth Street bridge to the Hot Shoppe at the other end and eating in their cars at the drive-in lot, then continuing on across the road to the airport to watch the big planes take off and land.

Some of the airlines, United, for one, had for several years been serving makeshift picnic lunches on transcontinental flights—creamed chicken out of thermos jugs, most likely, and buttered rolls and coffee—and both Boeing and Douglas were beginning to design efficient, compact galleys for the 247's and the big, new, tri-ruddered DC-4's. But for passengers on shorter trips, most in-flight meals were even more primitive, and certainly other than appetizing to passengers whose first move after fastening their safety belts was to see where their air-sick bags were located.

One day a member of an Eastern Air Transport flight crew entered the Hot Shoppe and asked for a quart of coffee to go. "Driving to New York?" the waitress asked. "No," replied the young man in uniform, "flying to Atlanta. We'll drink this on the way." It made a good six-line filler for *Hot Sauce*.

The next thing anyone could remember was that the passengers boarding planes at Hoover began buying sandwiches, milk shakes, coffee, fruit, and sometimes candy bars to take with them and eat during their flights. They carried their snacks and cartons of drinks in their pockets, in paper bags, in their hands, sometimes in their briefcases and suitcases.

Over an orange juice in a back booth one morning, the manager described this new business to Bill. Bill held up his juice glass to the waitress for a refill. "Well," he said thoughtfully, "how about that? Coming in here and buying things to eat on the plane."

"Every day," said the manager, "we get a few more of them."

They talked about this and that. When they were finished, Bill took a quick run through the kitchen, the walk-in box, the pantries, the basement. There was, he noted, a small storeroom down there, nothing in it but some empty cartons. "Get rid of those cartons," he said.

Back upstairs at the door, he shook hands with the manager. "I like the way you're running this place. Keep it up."

"I sure will, Mr. Marriott."

Halfway out the door, Bill turned, "Call me Bill from now on." He winked at the pretty cashier. "Keep those root beer mugs cold," he said. The next day, he called on the people at Eastern Air Transport.

The first meals Hot Shoppe Number Eight delivered to Eastern at Hoover Airport—first ever delivered planeside in Washington—were simple box lunches: a ham, cheese, or chicken sandwich, a small carton of cole slaw or salad, a frosted cupcake, an apple. Hot coffee and cold milk were delivered in thermos jugs, for serving in flight by the airlines' "sky girls." Deliveries were made in a company panel truck, painted orange with "Hot Shoppes" lettered on each side.

As the months went by, the service spread to American flights. Bill put a woman luncheon chef on fulltime, working in the cleaned-out and refitted basement storage room. He asked Paul to research airline feeding practices and problems. A year after that morning in the back booth, Hot Shoppe Number Eight was servicing all 22 daily flights in and out of Hoover, delivering planeside full meals, fully tested out by Mrs. Savage. The meals were individually packed, one to a passenger, in specially designed cardboard trays, with paper cups and plates, wooden forks and spoons. One full-time employe was no longer enough; the job now required six.

"It looks like it's here to stay," Bill said to his brother Paul. "Take it over and see what you can do with it."

J. Willard Marriott at Fairfield Farm.

Alice (Allie) Marriott, 1968.

J. Willard Marriott under the Tower of Jewels at the 1915 San Francisco World's Fair.

J. Willard Marriott and sisters Helen (left) and Doris.

The family of Hyrum Willard Marriott. Front row, left to right: Paul, Hyrum Willard, Woodrow, Ellen Morris Marriott, Russell, Kay. Back row: Eva, Helen, Doris, J. Willard.

Ellen Morris Marriott, mother of J. Willard Marriott.

Hyrum Willard Marriott, father of J. Willard Marriott.

Senator and Mrs. Reed Smoot on the way to a White House dinner, 1931. Mrs. Smoot is the mother of Alice Marriott.

Eastern States missionary conference, 1920. J. Willard Marriott is in the back row, second from right.

J. Willard and Alice Sheets Marriott, in front of Westchester Apartments shortly after their marriage.

J. Willard, Bill Jr., and Richard Marriott, fall 1965.

The J. Willard Marriott family. Front row, left to right, Stephen, Donna (wife of Bill Jr.), David, Sandy, Karen, Nancy (wife of Dick), Mary Alice, Julie Ann. Back row, left to right, Bill Jr., Debbie, John, Alice Sheets Marriott, J. Willard Marriott, Dick.

Nauvoo Restoration committee in front of the Carthage Jail, Carthage, Illinois. Left to right, J. Willard Marriott, Hugh B. Brown, and Henry D. Moyle, officials of Mormon church.

Bill Jr., Earl Sams, and J. Willard Marriott with a catch of mackerel and red snapper, Florida, 1940.

The original Hot Shoppe, 1927.

Connecticut Avenue Hot Shoppe, 1930, with "curbers," a new feature.
J. Willard Marriott stands in front of the Georgia Avenue Hot Shoppe, the first drive-in restaurant, in 1929.

J. Willard and Allie Marriott looking over plans for first hotel, 1955.

The Upshur Street office, 1942. Back row, left to right: J. Ridge Hikes, Lionel Thatcher, Russell Marriott, a secretary, Harold A. Candland, Edward J. Smith, a secretary, Ben E. Lewis. Front row, left to right: Paul M. Marriott, John S. Daniels, J. Willard Marriott, Milton A. Barlow, Woodrow D. Marriott.

The Marriotts with President Richard M. Nixon, in the White House Cabinet Room, October 1971.

Mr. and Mrs. J. Willard Marriott on inauguration day, 1969.

Billy Graham, J. Willard Marriott, and Bill Monroe on the Today Show, July 4, 1970, Honor America Day.

J. Willard Marriott with Bob Hope and Carl Albert, Speaker of the House of Representatives, on Honor America Day, 1970.

At Honor America Day program, John and Stephen Marriott, grandsons of J. Willard Marriott, meet Mrs. Gerald Ford.

At the Tabernacle Choir concert at the Kennedy Center, 1974. Left to right, Mr. and Mrs. J. Willard Marriott, President and Mrs. Gerald Ford, Mrs. Spencer W. Kimball, President Spencer W. Kimball, Mrs. Glenn Nielson, Glenn Nielson.

J. Willard Marriott receives wild mustang sculpture from Helen Boehm and Leonard Marks on Honor America Day.

J. Willard Marriott and Roy Rogers at the Camelback Inn, 1968.

GREAT AMERICA.
Is dedicated with pride to
Mr. & Mrs. J. Willard Marriott
who began as so many have begun
with only each other.

Together, they dreamed, and
because this is America where
dreams can come true—theirs
became the worldwide
Marriott Corporation
through their persistence, labor,
courage and faith.

As you go through this park may you
enjoy many fun-filled hours—and in leaving,
take with you a lasting sense of the
true greatness of America.

At opening of Santa Clara Great America park, Bill Jr. presents a plaque to Allie and Bill Marriott.

The New Orleans Marriott.

Chapter Fifteen

No matter how tough the tree is, Bill thought, a wind can come blowing out of nowhere and bend it, or even send it crashing to earth. In all his life he had never seen anyone die, and so it was quite a thing, he thought, to be sitting there in a hospital room, watching it happen to his father.

It was a morning in June and he was 38 and his father was 75. His father's body bulked large beneath the bed sheet, large as it had loomed and moved across the beet fields and beside the muskrat streams of Bill's boyhood.

Will had come on the train from Ogden in early spring, in time to see the last of the cherry blossoms, and they had had some good times in the big Garfield Street house, and on picnics with Paul; Woody and his wife, Judith; Kay and her husband, Ferd Kaufholz; Eva and her husband, Harold Candland; Russell, just back from his mission; and young Billy, and the baby, Dickie, whom Allie had borne that January in Columbia General Hospital.

The day before, the sun had blazed down from a milky sky, and the air was thick and heavy and saturated with moisture. King George VI and Queen Elizabeth came to Washington to spend the day with the Roosevelts, and Bill, Allie, and the two boys had driven downtown to watch the King and Queen's motorcade move slowly along Pennsylvania Avenue to the White House.

Downtown Washington in the smothering heat had not appealed to Will nor to Woody. Instead, they got in Woody's Buick convertible and drove out to Virginia to a farm where Woody boarded some horses, and went horseback riding. They arrived back at Garfield Street at about four in the afternoon, hours after the others had returned from downtown. As he got out of the car, Will somehow slipped or lost his balance. He pitched sideways and fell heavily against the open car door. He recovered his balance and held his side with his hand. Woody came around and picked up his father's Stetson from the driveway. "You all right, Dad?" "Oh boy," Will said. "That was a hard knock."

Still holding his side, he went up the front steps and through the living room to the screened-in sun porch, where the rest of the family were. "I hit myself on the car door getting out of Woody's car," he said. "It hurts."

He went upstairs, pulled down the shades, undressed, and lay down in the dim bedroom. In a little while he called down to Bill. Bill brought him some water. He was shocked and frightened at the sight of his father. Except for a gall bladder operation, his father had never been sick a day in his life. Now he lay on the bed doubled up in pain. His breathing was fast and shallow. "This is getting worse, Bill. It's real bad."

Bill called a doctor. The doctor was in the bedroom for almost half an hour. He came out thoughtful—and non-committal. He couldn't find anything wrong. But the pains in Will's side or his abdomen got sharper. The doctor gave Will some morphine, and he slept fitfully through the burning night.

The next morning Bill had an ambulance come and take his father to George Washington Hospital. Doctors now felt a lump or mass under the diaphragm, and thought it might be a cancer. But that afternoon, while they were waiting for test results, Will slipped into a coma. Now, even if they knew what was wrong, surgery was out of the question.

Bill never knew exactly when his father died. All he knew was that the family had been gathered there for an hour, maybe two, or even longer. His own eyes had been closed, and he had been thinking back, remembering his father the way he'd been long ago, remembering the struggle they'd had, and the good times they'd all had together. Words of hope and strength came to him, and he held them in his mind and heart, and kept them there as living prayers for his dying father, who would never know how much he loved him, because he himself had not known, until now.

"The Lord is my shepherd, I shall not want . . ." Through the words, it was the presence of the Lord he sought to call into the room. Then, slowly, he was aware of Allie's hand, firm on his, and he was aware that there was no more breathing, and he knew then that his father had died, there in the white-walled room, shades drawn against the June sun and heat, with the low murmur of traffic sounds outside mingling with the sound of someone crying. Even though the words of faith and hope said he should rejoice and be glad, he felt like crying too, and knew that sometime, he would.

Billy had a fever the next day, and Dickie was too little for such a long trip, so it was decided that Allie would stay in Washington with the children while Bill and his brothers and sisters took Will back home on the train to Ogden. The autopsy showed that there was nothing anyone could have done to save him. The great artery from the heart, the aorta, had ruptured. The mass the doctor had felt was a mass of blood.

The funeral was held Friday afternoon at the Ogden Twelfth Ward, there in the valley where Will had lived all his life. It was a bright, warm, late spring day, a light breeze from the west blowing, white clouds massed high over the Wasatch Mountains. Inside the church, the platform was banked with flowers, many of them, ordered by telegraph, from family friends in Washington. Then Will was buried in the Ogden City Cemetery, on a low rise that looked out over the valley toward the Great Salt Lake.

Bill didn't want to leave Allie alone with the two boys any longer than necessary. He caught an afternoon plane to Washington the next day, leaving the rest of the family there in Ogden, in the pink house on Jackson Avenue that he had bought for his parents.

Suddenly exhausted, he fell asleep almost immediately. The stewardess awakened him for dinner. After she had taken away the tray, Bill tipped his seat back and looked out the window. Night comes quickly when you're flying east, and so does the dawn. He lay back, looking out into the darkness, and thought about his father.

It had been a wonderful funeral. As he thought it all over, and the life they'd all had together, Bill recognized his father's weaknesses, his easy, amiable leaning toward sociability. And why not? He loved life and people, and he lived and worked all his life on the American frontier with sheep and cattle men whose only recreation was a big time in town. Of course he wasn't perfect—who was?—but he was, in many ways, a great man, religious, good to his family, always helping the poor and the sick.

He had a big heart. He was a happy man, always smiling, and he made people feel good. The biggest fault his mother ever found in his father was that she could work and work until her legs and back and whole body ached to put aside a few dollars for her children's clothes, say, only to discover that Will had loaned their last dollar of grocery money to a hard-up friend. But in spite of all this, he'd managed to provide for them well, better than most of the neighbors there in the valley.

Bill saw, for the first time, how much he owed to his father, what a quiet source of strength and security to them all he had been. Like many farmers who never recovered from the slump after the First World War, he had very little in worldly goods—almost nothing, in fact, to show for a long life of toil and struggle; nevertheless, Bill had known that in his father he always had someone to fall back on, someone he could depend on to do all he could to help, and to do so optimistically and with good will.

Now, perhaps for the first time since Sunday and those hours in the hospital room, Bill fully realized that his father had passed irrevocably beyond the veil. But he felt neither lonely nor abandoned. On the contrary, he knew that his father was happy, wherever he was, and knew that in a strange, loving way he could not explain, they were closer together than ever.

Will didn't leave Bill any money, or any land or anything else that wasn't heavily mortgaged, but he did leave Bill four sisters and three brothers, and to Bill they were pearls of great price indeed, particularly the brothers. He was sure lucky, he told himself, to have them in the business with him. He knew that while he schemed and dreamed of expansion, he could trust them with more and more of the day-to-day management, the constant attention to detail that would wear Bill out if he had to do it all himself.

Paul kept the in-flight catering business going and growing. Woody, likable, hard-working, interested in people, gravitated toward personnel, public relations— and golf. Bill's handicap at Burning Tree hovered around 19 or 20; Woody's was four or five. "You can tell who does all the work around this office," growled Bill. But, no doubt about it, Woody had a way with curbers and store managers, with lawyers, reporters, and Congressmen. He was an asset, all right. And in October 1939, Russell married his university sweetheart, the attractive Phyllis Brown of Ogden, at the Salt Lake Temple. Bill and Allie went to the wedding. "Don't stay away too long on your honeymoon," Bill said. "There's work to do in Washington." Ten days later, Russell went to work at the Upshur Street commissary.

Bill plunged into expansion, hiring a top architect to improve the design and brighten the appearance of the new shops. The first two were built in 1939, one in the Friendship district, the other in Silver Spring. In April 1940 he opened a second shop in Philadelphia, this one downtown, on Market Street. Between then and January 1941, five more opened, one on Rhode Island Avenue, in the District, the other four in neighboring suburbs: Rosslyn and Alexandria in Virginia, Hyattsville and Bethesda in Maryland. This brought Marriott's total to 18 Hot Shoppes, 14 in the city of Washington and suburbs, two in Philadelphia, and two in Baltimore.

As Bill's policies prospered, he let them harden. He and Allie had determined from the beginning that he did not want to run a restaurant; he was in the restaurant *business*. He learned early that he needed not just two or three restaurants, but many. This would give him a pool of labor to depend upon, to defend the business against the turn-overs, defections, failures, drop-outs that inevitably found their way on to—and off of—the payroll. This would also broaden the base of Marriott operations, so that one or two or even more unsuccessful locations would not prove catastrophic to the whole; he could simply close them down and do better someplace else. Moreover, the bigger the operation, the larger the purchasing orders in beef and milk, eggs and vegetables, and so on; and the bigger the orders, the lower the prices— savings that could be passed along to Hot Shoppe customers and their families. Most important, he'd be developing and training broad top management personnel, so that he'd no longer have to depend solely on two or three key executives to help him run the company.

So Bill was, actually, in the chain store business, in principle, the same as the great J. C. Penney. In these years, Bill was not so much living a life as he was carving out a success—forging to the top through the sure-fire formula of clean living, hard work, staying out of debt, and total confidence in the dividends, both spiritual and material, of the Golden Rule. There were no conflicts, no dallyings or diversions. You did whatever you had to do to accomplish your objective. You made whatever sacrifice was called for. You might make it gladly, or ruefully, but you made it. Bill knew by heart Mr. Penney's message to the young men and women of America: Down with soft living that will weaken your spiritual and physical muscles. Seek out the struggle that will toughen you up. Negativeness is a sin; so is self-indulgence. Bad times, such as depression or a state of war, should be challenging tests. "In such times those who are too soft, who lack the courage and stamina to strive, slacken effort. Real men tighten their belts, throw full weight into the harness of their daily activities, and pull with all their might and main. Let us choose for ourselves the hard right."

All his prosperous, expanding business and more, Bill was creating and building—had created and built—out of nothing. When most of his generation were starting out on their careers, he was far back, out of sight in the Wasatch nowhere, herding sheep, breaking his back in the sugar beet fields. Long after all these days, I once said to Bill, "You know, we've talked a great deal about your successes. How about your failures?"

Bill looked at me, puzzled, brow furrowed, as if he hadn't understood. " 'Failures'?" he repeated. "The only failures I had were temporary. When one part of the business had a bad year or two, the other parts did well, and sales and profits usually evened out. That's the way it was."

Ever since Bill and Allie had been visiting the Earl

Samses in Florida and at Lake Winnepesaukee, Earl had told Bill over and over that if he ever wanted capital, he could have a million dollars, or whatever he needed, deposited in his name in the bank of his choice the very next day. Bill naturally was awed, flattered, and intrigued. "Think of how we could branch out, all over the country!" he'd say to Allie. But always, common sense and conservatism won out. He hated the thought of going into debt. It was a weakness. It had blighted his father's life and his mother's. It would not blight his or his family's. The company paid cash on the barrel head for whatever it bought, and so did he.

But in the summer of 1940, with just about all the company's operating capital tied up in the expansion program and with the need for a new commissary pressing on his mind, Bill began to listen to what Earl was saying. The weather was beautiful that year—hot, dry days with no wind to stir up the lake; long, cool, pine-scented nights—and they would sit on the porch after dinner in their rockers and look out over the hydrangeas to the dark mirror of the lake and the peaceful mountains beyond.

"Sitting here like this," Earl said one evening, "it's hard to believe. But I think we're going to be drawn into this thing in Europe. England and Germany are bombing each other to pieces. They used to laugh at Hitler and call him a clown in a soldier suit, but Bill, I tell you—the man's a maniac."

They could hear laughter from somewhere across the still water, the trilling of crickets from the high grass behind the house.

"What do you think of Willkie?" Bill asked.

Earl rocked in silence for a few moments. "Bill, I think he's a good man. Long on ideals, short on experience, but the best man we Republicans have got. But with the European situation like it is, I don't see how we can swing the country away from Roosevelt, in spite of the third-term issue. And Roosevelt looks as though he's hell-bent on taking us to war."

Bill hadn't had much time for politics. In fact, the whole Roosevelt problem troubled him, and had for years. By nature, philosophy, and conviction, Bill was a Republican; yet his church told him it was his duty and moral obligation to support the country's leaders, no matter what.

"You'd better expand while you can, Bill," Earl said. "If we go to war, there'll be all kinds of restrictions."

"We've been doing a lot of expanding," Bill said.

"Sure you don't need some capital?"

Once more, Bill told Earl how he felt about borrowing money, most of all from a friend. "If my company has to borrow—and I hope it never does—we won't go to a friend or a bank. We'll go to an insurance company."

Earl smiled to himself. He admired this young fellow, had all the faith in the world in him, but he was stubborn as a Rocky Mountain mule.

"Bill, borrowing money, to invest in your own, growing, legitimate business, isn't necessarily a sin. It's not going to put you into partnership with Satan. You're going to increase your profits fast, this year or next. You're going to pay it back, with interest. Everybody's going to be happy. And the business is going to be that far ahead."

Supposing the country did go to war? Bill thought. And supposing they did clamp down on materials? There the company would be, commissary and offices all over the place, for years, maybe.

They sat for a moment, taking a last look across the lake. The crickets sang. The water softly lapped the sand of Earl's artificial beach. The girls had gone upstairs to bed an hour ago.

"Tell you what," Earl said. "If you don't want to borrow a million, let me buy a million dollars' worth of stock." He got up and walked toward the door, then turned to give Bill an affectionate pat on the shoulder. "Sleep on it, young man," he said.

What Earl said about war and President Roosevelt, plus the expansion program's critical need for a central commissary, persuaded Bill to accept, somewhat uneasily, Earl's offer. He and Allie and his brothers owned most of the stock in the company, and what they didn't own, employes did. Now he had to set aside something else that went against the grain: raising operating capital by turning stock over to someone outside the family, so to speak. Some people would regard it as an act of confidence and courage. Bill never saw it that way. To him, it was gambling.

In any event, a million was too much. Instead, if Earl were agreeable, he'd take half a million; the balance he would get from an insurance company and his own bank account. In return, he'd sign over to Earl the equivalent in Hot Shoppes' preferred stock, plus, as a kind of bonus, one share of common stock for every ten of preferred. By Labor Day, construction crews were excavating the new commissary's foundation at 1234 Upshur Street, N.W.

A simple, functional three-story building (to which could be added a fourth story, when needed), it brought together under one roof all the company's administrative, personnel, and accounting offices; Mrs. Savage's testing kitchens, and the company bakery, ice cream plant, butcher shop, and storage lockers. It also provided ample, centralized space for the processing and portioning of raw foods and the production of such standard items as soups, gravies, and cole slaw, which could be prepared in bulk at the commissary and distributed to individual shops as needed.

It cost more than half a million—some $100,000 more—and it was a good thing they built it when they did; President Roosevelt's reelection and the draft and the worsening situation in Europe left no doubt in anyone's mind about that. And with that problem out of the way and his increasing duties as an officer of both the District and national restaurant associations, Bill found that he was traveling and making more speeches than ever at the Rotary and Kiwanis Club luncheons and similar functions. Always one for self-improvement, he signed up for a ten-lesson course in Dale Carnegie's famous school for winning friends and influencing people. It was months before he had time for the lessons. When he finally finished the course, he hired Carnegie's Washington representative, Pat Patterson, to give it to selected employes in each Hot Shoppe, and, in the end, always the missionary, he also converted Patterson to Mormonism. But he still couldn't feel right about that preferred stock, even though it was held by a close friend like Earl. He drove himself harder than ever, so he could buy it back.

February 9, 1941, was a Sunday, a day when the headlines of the Washington papers told of the shattering raid by the British Mediterranean fleet on the port of Genoa. It was also the day when the phone rang at 4500 Garfield Street, and Allie answered it; it was her brother, Walter, calling from St. Petersburg, Florida, to say that their stepfather, Senator Smoot, had died suddenly that afternoon. The Senator and Mrs. Smoot had been visiting Walter, then chief surgeon at the Bay Pines Veterans' Hospital in St. Petersburg. He had died, Walter said, of what they thought was heart or kidney failure, or a combination of both. Walter said they were putting the body on the train for Salt Lake City. Funeral services would take place that Friday.

So once more, for the second time in little more than eighteen months, Bill went back to a funeral in the valley. This time Allie went with him. The Senator, of course, even before his death, was a legend in Salt Lake City, and thousands crowded into the great Tabernacle for the services. A gray and wintry sky lay across the valley as the funeral cortege made its way slowly south through American Fork and Pleasant Grove to the cemetery in Provo. There they buried the Senator beside his father and mother. The Oquirrhs, or "Shining Mountains" of the Paiutes, rose far across Utah Lake to the west, with towering Mount Timpanogos lost in the mist to the east.

Chapter Sixteen

Bill never believed that President Roosevelt actually wanted the United States to go to war, the way Earl and a lot of others seemed to, but for all that, what Earl said on the porch that summer evening at the lake came true, and it was a good thing that he'd listened to Earl and accepted his offer and built the commissary when he did, because four months after it opened the country was at war.

Like every other restaurant after Pearl Harbor, the Hot Shoppes headed into food rationing, help shortages as employes joined the armed forces, and a falling-off in sales because of gas rationing and diminished car use. Meat rationing inspired Mrs. Savage to devise substitutes: soufflés, vegetable platters, main-course salads. Sugar was doled out sparingly; for a while no butter was served at all. As boy curbers left for the Army or Navy, Woody took to hiring girl curbers and once even imported them by the busload from the mountain hamlets of the Carolinas. Finally, to discourage consumption of gasoline, curb service was abandoned for the duration.

Paul joined the Navy and was commissioned a lieutenant commander and assigned to the Pensacola Naval Air Station, where he had charge of the officers' club, the country club, and all the dining rooms, meals, and services. Russell also joined the Navy and was assigned to food services at the big naval base at Norfolk.

Back in Washington, with expansion plans on the shelf until war's end, Bill and Woody launched into the undramatic but essential activities of business on the home front: the daily struggle for the food, gasoline, and supplies necessary to keep the Hot Shoppes open, the air raid drills, the organization and running of a Hot Shoppes civil defense corps, development of a master plan for the mass feeding of refugees in case of wartime catastrophe.

But Bill could never let up, never rest with the status quo. He had the big, new, modern commissary. In spite of men who'd left for the service, he still had a cadre of Hot Shoppe-skilled, Marriott-trained management personnel. Where was the need that, if linked with these Marriott resources and set to rolling, would solve a problem, make life better for everyone concerned? For months he and Woody spent much of their spare time asking questions, talking to people in government agencies, war plants, defense departments. In the summer of '42, Bill and Allie bought the Gold Coast summer house and five lakeshore acres between Earl's place and that of the George Bushnells. (Bill wanted it not only for his own family, but for the use of other company executives and their children, when the Marriotts weren't there.) And this problem that was on Bill's mind was what he and Earl talked most about when they were together that summer on the porch in the evenings. He went back to Washington with the answer: mass feeding. In the defense plants and huge government complexes in and around Washington, whole families were working by the thousands. They didn't have time for lunch boxes; yet they had to eat on the job. Bill's solution: the company or the agency would provide the physical facilities; Marriott would provide the central organization, the management, and the food, and receive a fee for doing so. It was that simple.

The first customer was the Engineering and Research Corporation (ERCO) of Riverdale, Maryland. Before Pearl Harbor, ERCO manufactured civilian aircraft and aluminum-extrusion machines. Now it employed 3,000 in the production of radar components, rocket-launchers and B-29 ball turrets. Marriott took over the feeding of all three shifts from rolling lunch wagons that went from section to section within the plant with sandwiches, pastries, hot coffee, milk, and other luncheon snacks. With this project in full swing, Bill contracted to operate the huge Naval Communications Annex cafeteria, feeding thousands of government employes daily. A month after Marriott took this one on, he branched out into apartment-house catering by opening a cafeteria in the high-rent McLean Gardens complex, on Wisconsin Avenue.

As the needs arose for inner development to manage, oversee, and direct the growth on the outside, Bill set up new divisions: an industrial group for mass feeding that, when the war was over, extended Marriott catering services to the thousands employed at the Ford plant in Norfolk, the General Motors assembly plant in Georgia, and others; an architectural and design division that today is one of the most advanced and efficient in the world; a real estate division headed up by Bill's brother-in-law, Harold Candland, to scout new postwar locations and to be responsible for all real-estate negotiations and contracts.

In spite of wartime belt-tightening, Bill refused to compromise on quality. Bill Woods, the Marriott buyer, for instance, drove to the Farmers' Market every night at 10 o'clock when corn was in season and bought fresh corn, trucked in from the Virginia farms, for $1.50 a bag. He'd load it into Hot Shoppe trucks for delivery to the Upshur Street commissary, where it would be stored overnight in the cold storage meat lockers. Next day, it would go out to all the shops, still farm-fresh and sweet.

"How come we're paying $1.50 a bag for corn?" Bill asked Woods one day. "One of our competitors tells me he gets it for $1 a bag, a third less than we do."

Woods explained. The competitor paid $1 a bag because he bought in the afternoon the day after delivery, when the farmers dropped their prices to get rid of corn that had been sitting in the sun all day at the market. By this time, Woods said, most of the sugar in the corn had turned to starch.

It wasn't up to Hot Shoppe standards. "Keep paying $1.50," Bill said.

The end of the war, when it finally arrived, brought no let-up. On the contrary, Bill and his brothers were busier than ever. Returning servicemen and servicewomen needed their old jobs back, or new ones. Pent-up desire— now released—for new cars, dishwashing machines, electric stoves, television sets, and other consumer goods, combined with the cash to pay for them, set the country off on an exciting and unexpected splurge of postwar prosperity. And with the lifting of food and gasoline rationing, just about the whole nation poured out onto the streets and highways to relax, travel, and, of course, eat out.

Marriott, Stouffer, Howard Johnson, and other chain service companies unwrapped long-shelved expansion plans. Marriott got away to a fast start in January 1946 by taking over another government cafeteria—this one for the Reconstruction Finance Corporation—and by buying an existing restaurant for the first time in company history. Located in Brookmanor, Arlington County, Virginia, it was remodeled and opened for business the following April. This same year, Paul's In-Flite division reached north to the busy Newark Airport to supply all meals for all United, American, National, Northwest, Northeast, and Pacific Coast Airlines, and then west to Chicago's Midway Airport, where it served all planes of these airlines and others as well.

But this was merely the beginning. The following year, 1947, saw the start of an ambitious ten-year expansion program that would increase Marriott units from 22 in five states and the District of Columbia to more than 80, added at the rate of about six a year, in 12 states ranging from New York south to Florida, and west and southwest to Utah and Texas.

Meanwhile, in the kind of euphoric lull between the end of the war and the beginning of this new, more highly pitched phase of the company's development, Bill and Allie took a vacation trip to Mexico. From a distance, Bill hoped to get some kind of perspective on the life he was leading. The more of himself he put into the business and into the affairs of the District and national restaurant associations and the church's growing Washington Stake, the less there was for Allie, Billy, and Dickie, and for 4500 Garfield Street, and for the life that in his heart he longed for, which would have something to do with mountains and horses and big skies, hunting and fishing, ranching and sheep-camp breakfasts. He even found himself considering some kind of retirement arrangement, his brothers running the business and the Hot Shoppes moving along in orderly fashion on the formula he had established and the momentum he had generated.

But Allie, he knew, needed the trip too. With him so head-over-heels in work, and her raising the boys almost single-handedly, and her own exacting schedule of Red Cross and other home-front duties to attend to, the war years had been an exhausting, difficult, and often lonely period for her. To add to these burdens, her brother, Walter, had died of a heart attack in the fall of 1943, three months after moving to Washington from St. Petersburg.

Later in January 1946 Allie, Bill, Billy, and an old friend, Tom Ferguson of the Washington office of the F.B.I., flew to Brownsville, Texas, first stop on their journey to Mexico and Guatemala. Dickie, too young and too little to take south of the Rio Grande, was left behind in Washington.

The Book of Mormon tells how America was discovered in 600 B.C. by a small colony of Israelites who sailed east across the Pacific, from Arabia to the Pacific coast of Central or South America in a ship made, like Noah's ark, under direct instructions from God. This colony flourished and prospered over the next ten centuries. Its descendants multiplied into the tribes and nations of pre-Columbian Indians. Their sacred writings paralleled Old Testament history and belief and confidently predicted the coming of a Beloved Son, or Messiah.

At the time of the crucifixion of Jesus Christ in Palestine, dire signs and portents alarmed these nations. The Mormon prophet Nephi wrote of "a great and terrible tempest" and "exceeding sharp lightnings." Total darkness fell across the land and remained for three days.

Then, as a teeming multitude assembled in a temple, the people heard a voice from on high: "Behold my Beloved Son, in whom I am well pleased. . . . Hear ye him." The awestruck multitude, gazing upward, "saw a Man descending out of heaven." He stretched forth his hand and said, "Behold, I am Jesus Christ . . . the light and life of the world."

According to the Book of Mormon, Jesus stayed in that land for a number of days, healing the sick, restoring sight to the blind, counseling tribal leaders. After ordaining twelve apostles to carry on His work, He said, "And now I go unto the Father." Then, as the multitude stood there, a "cloud overshadowed" them and while they were "overshadowed," Jesus "departed from them, and ascended into heaven."

In the early years of the colony it had split into two camps, the followers of Nephi, called Nephites, and a band of dissenters led by Laman, called Lamanites. The natural rivalry between them was lulled by the coming of Christ, and peace reigned for nearly 200 years. Then fighting broke out again, with the Nephites as the followers of Christ and the Lamanites as shiftless, quarrelsome anti-Christs. These hostilities were climaxed about 400 A.D. by a savage conflict. Meanwhile, the heroic Nephite prophet-historian Mormon had gathered together all the sacred writings of the people and had abridged them into a single volume which he set down, in hieroglyphics, on thin gold plates. He was killed in a final battle that annihilated his people except for one survivor, his son Moroni. Moroni escaped into the wilderness with the gold plates; then, as directed by the Lord, he buried them in the Hill Cumorah, where, through divine guidance, Joseph Smith unearthed them some 1400 years later.

Bill and Allie looked forward keenly to seeing with their own eyes the areas where Mormons believe these ancient civilizations lived. Tom Ferguson would be a great help; he had made a study of the Central American origins of Mormonism.

Typically, Bill planned their itinerary to cover as many Mayan and Aztec ruins and as much of Mexico and Guatemala as they could by plane and rented car. Arrivals, length-of-stays, side trips, and departures were laid out with railroad-timetable precision. Bill told the Samses when he saw them in Florida on the way home that he and Allie had sure seen a lot of territory. But whether it was the rest and relaxation they both needed was another matter.

According to February entries in Bill's diary, they left Brownsville, Texas, on the first and flew to Mexico City. Entries for the next four days mention jai alai in Mexico City, Sunday services at the local Mormon branch, luncheon on a boat at Xochomilco, bull fights—and Mexican food that made him ill for a day.

On the fifth and sixth they drove to Cholula. "The huge pyramid here is of layers built by different generations. It has produced artifacts indicating links to Egypt and the Holy Land." From Cholula they proceeded to Pueblo, then to Chapultapec Palace, and an overnight flight to Guatemala.

Bill found Guatemala beautiful and abounding in Book of Mormon atmosphere. "City sets on top of mountains, like a diamond in a setting. Mountains are rugged. This is the land of Nephi."

In the museum in Guatemala City the travelers were thrilled by the ancient history exhibits. "Saw figurines of people at time of Christ found near Guatemala," Bill wrote. At Chichen Itza they visited ancient temples, pyramids, and ruins, took hundreds of pictures to show back home, and slept in thatched huts under mosquito nets.

At the end of a whirlwind two weeks, they split up, Tom flying on to Mexico City, the Marriotts flying to Miami via Havana.

They spent the next week at the Hotel El Morocco, playing golf with the Samses at Indian Creek, dining at the Surf Club. On the 23rd they put Billy on the plane for Washington. Never comfortable with easy living, always chafing, Bill on the 24th got in a car with Allie and drove around Miami looking for locations for Hot Shoppes. He called on Eastern Airlines people and talked to them about the in-flight services at Miami Airport.

By the 26th, a little more than three weeks after they had left home, Bill had had enough. They headed north in their gray Cadillac (a driver had brought it down from home). Bill's diary summed up the journey home: "Had a very nice trip. Very enjoyable to be alone with Allie. We had some good talks about business. Decided not to retire, but let somebody else do things and not work so hard. Good to see Dickie and be home—the best place on earth."

The next morning, Ed Brossard phoned and asked Bill to lunch. Ed, a large man with the dignified bearing of a British diplomat, was at this time president of the Washington Stake of the Mormon Church, comprising ten wards, or parishes, from Baltimore in the north to Richmond and Fredericksburg, Virginia, in the south.

Bill left the luncheon table stunned. Brossard wanted

him to accept a high church office, either as bishop of the Chevy Chase Ward or as second councilor of the Washington Stake, a post currently held by Bill's friend Ernest L. Wilkinson, the Washington lawyer and later president of Brigham Young University.

That night he talked it over with Allie and prayed for guidance. In the middle of the night, he reached a decision. He'd take the stake job. He'd just have to find the time somehow, but he couldn't say no to the opportunity to help the Church.

Two days later, the post was formally offered to Bill by Dr. John A.Widtsoe, former president of the University of Utah and an apostle of the Church. At the same time, Wilkinson was named first councilor.

To follow through on what he and Allie had decided on the drive north, Bill made Paul executive vice-president of the company, and although he couldn't find the time just then for a relaxing game of golf, he did manage to spend a Saturday morning with Billy target-shooting with pistols. Two days after that, he flew to Chicago for the annual meeting of the National Restaurant Association (N.R.A.). The nominating committee asked him for a firm commitment: would he serve as national president for a two-year term beginning in 1948, two years hence?

Wary of taking on too much, mindful of the need to conserve and protect himself, Bill said he couldn't promise; for the time being, why didn't they just put him down for the second vice-presidency? Later on, if pressures slackened off, he'd reconsider. With this off his conscience, he went to Marshall Field's and bought some presents for the boys. Next morning, after breakfast in his room, he took the 10 A.M. United flight for Washington. "Good trip," says his diary. "Very tired. Good to see boys and our home. We are indeed blessed to have so much. Brought Billy pistol and Dickie some books. Dinner at

Rosslyn Hot Shoppe. Bed at 9:30." He wasn't able to go shooting with Billy again for a long time, but he arranged to have him start riding lessons at a stable in Rock Creek Park.

It occurred to Bill that there was an untapped and excellent market for Hot Shoppes in retail sales—food to take home. After an encouraging survey in the Washington area, Paul, in March 1947, supervised the opening of the company's first retail outlet, the Pantry House, in the Rosslyn restaurant. It sold Hot Shoppe ice cream, cakes, pies, pastries, and other baked items, all made at the Upshur Street commissary in line with standard Hot Shoppe recipes. The store was an overnight success. A year later Pantry Houses were doing a line-up business in six other Hot Shoppes in the suburban perimeter of Washington.

This, of course, plus getting set for Bill's long-range expansion program which would carry the company into and through the 1950s, called for drastic expansion of the Upshur Street commissary. Only five years old, hailed as good for twenty when it opened just before the war, it was already too small. But the remodelers could hardly keep up with the growth. Before they'd finished a new annex to house Personnel, the annex wasn't big enough to hold it. Paul found offices for Personnel downtown and in the annex installed the finance department and the company print shop. This had started out as Allie's hand-cranked mimeograph machine and now comprised editorial offices and several presses turning out chits, accounting forms, letterheads, menus, brochures, place mats, and other items by the tens of thousands. In the commissary itself, refrigeration capacity was tripled, huge, cave-like ovens replaced the five-year-old ones, and the butcher shops were enlarged and rebuilt.

Bill was proud of the new commissary, and happy

with the way the country was moving into the post-war era under Harry Truman, no Republican, to be sure, but a man Bill had to admire for his small-town, heartland virtues: simplicity, honesty, self-acceptance, and his indomitable, scrappy, game-cock spirit. The demands of a war-drained world combined with war-developed technology to push the nation's production to more than 200 percent of what it had been at its former peak of prosperity in 1929. The city of Washington itself was spilling and sprawling across the farmlands of nearby Virginia and Maryland. Armies of laborers turned country roads into highspeed highways. The airport had long since outgrown Hoover Field, had given way to the fortress-like Pentagon Building, and had moved south to its present site on the Potomac, hard by the Alexandria line. The Whitehurst Freeway had been completed. A new South Capitol Street bridge provided still another link between the District and the new suburban developments across the river. The government itself had launched a $435-million office-and-agency-building program, and the presence of more than 80 embassies and legations confirmed Washington's postwar status as a world capital of the stature of London, Paris, and Moscow.

What with Bill's increased church duties and N.R.A. responsibilities, the timing was not yet right for the big thrust of Marriott expansion. But he kept building and strengthening the internal organization, establishing, for instance, a rotating 18-member Junior Board of Executives "to spread," as his memo put it, "the responsibility and experience of operating our increasingly large business among our young men of executive ability." He saw that the company acquired new locations. He and Paul added Pan-American flights out of Miami to the growing in-flight service, and took over, as well, operation of Pan-American's employe cafeteria, executive dining room, and snack bar at the Miami Airport. While all this was going on, the Hot Shoppes opened their first hotel cafeteria at Washington's Meridian Hill Hotel, and their first public cafeteria anywhere, at Connecticut Avenue and H Street, N.W.

Well, so much for his and Allie's resolve that he'd take things easier.

Inevitably, in April 1948 at the annual meeting in Cleveland, Bill was elected president of the National Restaurant Association, and that December, at the stake conference at the Mormon chapel at Sixteenth Street and Columbia Road, N.W., he became president of the Washington Stake. Three of the Church's General Authorities came out from Salt Lake City to make the change: J. Reuben Clark, Jr., of the First Presidency, and apostles Mark E. Petersen and Matthew Cowley.

There had never been any question in Bill's mind about taking the stake presidency assignment, but it put more pressure on him than ever. It meant that every Sunday he would have to visit one or two wards in the stake, speak at each one, and visit with the bishop and his councilors. Every Monday night he'd have to conduct a high council meeting, frequently until midnight or later. In addition to overseeing the affairs of the stake Relief Society, Primary Association, Sunday School, ward teaching programs, and so on, he himself took on the complicated task of working for changes in Defense Department regulations, so that lay Mormon chaplains would be allowed to serve with the armed forces in peacetime as well as in time of war. It would take him 25 years to accomplish this.

Bill, for all his life, had lived by the Mormon Word of Wisdom. This famous revelation, given through Joseph Smith at Kirtland, Ohio, in 1833, said it was the will of God that members of the Church abstain from "wine or strong drink," as well as from tobacco and hot drinks, which has been interpreted by Church leaders as meaning coffee and tea. They are to eat wholesome foods, particularly fruits, vegetables, and grains. In return, the Lord promised the Saints health "and marrow to their bones."

Nevertheless, Bill was having stomach pains all the time. He knew he was not physically abusing his body, nor was there anything essentially wrong with it. It was just that his and Allie's euphoric resolve to "let somebody else do things and not work so hard" seemed naive—and impossible. And the pressures were piling up. His Washington doctor said he needed a specialist and sent him to an expensive diagnostic clinic in Philadelphia. Three days of tests revealed that he was indeed ill: nervous exhaustion, diverticulitis (inflammation of the intestines), and a stomach ulcer.

Rest and delegation of responsibility were now enforced. He went on a hunting and pack trip out of Vernal, Utah, with his old friend Hugh Colton. Hugh remembers it to this day. After the first few days back in the mountains, Bill seemed edgy. The plodding pace of the pack mules irritated him. He couldn't wait to break camp in the morning, always impatient to push on.

One day while Bill was making a movie of the pack-horse guides and Hugh, his fractious horse turned quickly and Bill felt his ribs crack. For the next ten days, riding horses by day and sleeping in a sleeping bag at night, he suffered almost unbearable pain. Finally they went 35 miles to the nearest town where Bill got a car, and he returned to Salt Lake City. An X-ray revealed two broken ribs.

Then Bill seemed to reach a plateau. In May 1948, a month after his election to the presidency of the N.R.A., the Salt Lake *Tribune* carried a feature story by its Washington writer, Lydia Clawson Hoopes. "Success Story," read its headline. "J. Willard Marriott, Native Utahn, Builds Food Concern Employing 2300 Persons."

It was not the first article about Bill in the Salt Lake papers; but it was the first that treated him as a mature, successful businessman of the East, rather than merely a bright young fellow from Ogden who parlayed a root beer stand into a profitable string of restaurants. His picture told the difference. The blue eyes of the expensive portrait photograph were now not quite so boyish, so expectant, so open and candid; they were, rather, the eyes of a big-time executive, evaluating, appraising. His light, reddish blond hair was beginning to recede.

The text retold the by-now familiar story: how Bill herded sheep and cattle and rode the range and packed a six-shooter at 14; how he sold woolen goods in the lumber camps; his marriage to Allie, the trip east in the Model T, the A&W root beer stand, how the Hot Shoppes began, how Allie helped with the chili and the tamales and carried the day's receipts home to their apartment in a paper bag.

Today, Mrs. Hoopes went on triumphantly, the Hot Shoppes represented one of the great success stories of the times. The business that started out as a nine-stool root beer stand now grossed millions a year and criss-crossed the country.

Each year, Marriott bought 10,000 head of cattle, carloads of veal, lamb and pork, two million eggs, 85,000 pounds of butter, fresh fruit and vegetables by the truckload. All this to serve "Food for the Whole Family"—20 million meals a year, two million hamburgers, three million barbecue sandwiches, 40,000 Danish pastries, and heaven only knows how many glasses of A&W root beer.

On the personal side, Mrs. Hoopes described Bill as "quick-spoken and alert, with a ready grin—the hardest working man among the firm's 2300 employes." Hard work, in fact, was the key to his success. He always said, "No one can get very far in this life on a forty-hour week."

But this coverage was only the beginning. *Look,* the picture weekly, discovered Bill, and in one issue chose him as one of three noteworthy Americans presented in its standing feature, "*Look* Applauds—." He was in fast company: Dr. Robert L. Johnson, chairman of the Citizens' Committee for the Hoover Report, and Florence E. Allen, justice of the U.S. Circuit Court of Appeals in Cincinnati, highest-ranking woman judge in the United States. There were portrait photographs and short captions explaining the selections. "From operating root beer stands," Bill's read, "he's risen in 20 years to the top of the restaurant business. He's president of the Hot Shoppes, with restaurants in the Northeast, South and Middle West. Last year, he served as president of the National Restaurant Association."

But J. C. Penney himself couldn't have asked for higher testament to success than the one accorded Bill in June 1950, three months before his 50th birthday—a full-length article and four pictures in the *Saturday Evening Post.* A bright, professional piece titled "Good Mormons Don't Go Broke," it spread from coast to coast the story of Bill's boyhood on the range, his struggle for an education; Bill and his family, his church, his passion for cleanliness and hard work.

The fifteen Washington Hot Shoppes, the author reported, "have become an institution in the nation's capital, like sight-seeing buses, the cherry blossoms and the pigeons on Pennsylvania Avenue." Each one might be described as "an island of mechanized madness in a sea of automobiles." In addition to these, far-flung Marriott operations now included five other outside-Washington Hot Shoppes, an airport restaurant, half a dozen in-flight commissaries, eight carry-out stores, and twelve apartment and industrial cafeterias in scattered cities—a total of 47 installations employing 4,000, ranking twelfth among national restaurant chains in dollar volume of sales, and feeding 17 million Americans a year, ranging from tired housewives to J. Edgar Hoover and Eleanor Roosevelt, from dating teen-agers to screen star Madeleine Carroll and restaurant critic Duncan Hines.

It was like climbing up to the Big Basin country, up behind the Wasatch rim. He couldn't really go much higher. About all he could do now was to spread out.

Chapter Seventeen

It was ironic that in these days when he should have been feeling so good, Bill felt so bad. Everywhere he went—at the office, in the Hot Shoppe parking lots, in the commissary, at church meetings—friends and customers and everyone who recognized his picture in the *Saturday Evening Post,* whether they had met him or not, wanted to shake his hand, tell him they'd read the wonderful story, and joke that he must be a good Mormon, since it was obvious that he wasn't going broke, what with the Hot Shoppes doing something like a $12 million business last year.

But he had to force himself to smile and joke back. The truth was, he was so tired. It seemed to take all the reserves he had to open a new shop in Harford Road, Baltimore, early that July, and to keep up with plans to build employe cafeterias at the National Airport and at the Studebaker plant in Chicago later on in the year.

"What's wrong with me, Allie?" he would ask as he fell into bed exhausted night after night.

The answer was always the same. "Bill, you're working too hard. You're trying to do too much."

"I know, that's what the doctors tell me. Maybe they're right." Then, already half-gone, "Allie, could we get away for awhile—go out to Utah—go riding—see the mountains—?"

Before Allie could answer, he'd sink into sleep like a man falling into the sea. Next morning he'd feel better. "I'll slow down," he'd say. "I'll give Woody, Paul, and Russell more work to do."

They might really have gone to Utah to give Bill a rest and the breath of mountain air he longed for if it hadn't been for what happened to Earl Sams. Earl was playing golf at Wykagyl and had a stroke on the course. He was taken to the New Rochelle Hospital, where he died the next day. Lula Sams had had a stroke some years before, and she was still an invalid.

The funeral took place Tuesday, July 25, in New Rochelle, and Bill and Allie went up to New York on the train that morning and on out to New Rochelle, and stayed for the burial in Beechwood Cemetery. Earl, 66, distinguished-looking, white-haired, with the bearing of a Supreme Court Justice, hadn't been sick a day in his life that Bill could remember.

It had been raining that morning in Washington when they left. But the skies cleared as they traveled north, and a bright, late-afternoon summer sun shone on the small group of relatives and friends who gathered in the cemetery. By the time the graveside service was over, Bill felt so tired it was an effort to walk to his limousine.

They caught the late, extra-fare Congressional Limited back home, and Bill sank into his parlor car chair. What with all his traveling to Chicago and around the country on N.R.A. affairs he'd developed the facility of napping, sitting up in plane and train seats, almost at will, just by leaning back and closing his eyes and picturing himself as riding on horseback up a gently sloping canyon trail.

They were flashing past Princeton before he awoke. Allie, from the chair across the aisle, handed him a New York paper. Bill glanced through the pages. North Korean troops that had invaded South Korea four weeks ago were pushing south toward the American supply port of Pusan and engaging American and United Nations troops in a fierce battle along the Taejon-Yongdong highway. General Dean was reported missing in action, and President Truman had asked Congress for $10 billion to increase the size of the armed forces and to buy vast quantities of tanks, aircraft, ships, guns and munitions, and he wanted a $5 billion increase in corporate and individual income taxes to help pay the bill. The Broadway theater ads seemed reassuring: Shirley Booth and Wallace Ford in *Come Back, Little Sheba,* Mary Martin and Ray Middleton in *South Pacific,* Ray Bolger (one of Bill's favorites) in *Where's Charley?*

Another time, they might have stayed in New York for dinner and a show and spent the night; now, though, he was glad to be going home.

Going back in his mind beyond the sad, unhappy things that had happened and were happening, putting them aside until he got home anyway, he wished he had felt better and could have enjoyed some of the good things of the past month or two: seeing Paul's little girl, Rebecca, for the first time, and seeing his sister Kay's two cute kids, Kay Ellen and Carolyn, and Billy's graduation from St. Alban's, the National Cathedral School for Boys, where all his classmates—naturally—called him "Hotshoppe" and where he earned the best grades you'd ever want a son to get; and being with Dickie, who was at St. Alban's too, and earning a name for himself on the tennis courts. And there was the nice story in the Washington papers about Allie's collection of Dresden china and Meissenware that she'd started back in 1940 with eight pieces, which were all she could afford, from Buchorn's gift store in Salt Lake City. Now she had more than a hundred pieces, including a set of Dresden plates designed especially for Marie Antoinette. Each plate bore the monogram "MA" fashioned in tiny pink roses. "Allie," he'd exclaimed, "of course you have to have them! Those are your initials, spelled backwards!"

Even the biggest event of all Bill had had to drag himself through, and he'd been Washington chairman, too—the unveiling of the statue of Brigham Young in the Capital rotunda on the first of June, which would have

215

been Brigham's 149th birthday. Mark Evans, the famous Washington radio commentator, had helped Bill a lot. He was an Ogden boy, a Mormon, and had been, like Bill and Ernie Wilkinson, president of the Weber student body. Mark knew everybody, and, to Bill's relief, had taken over most of the arrangements work. What a wonderful day! Mabel Young Sanborn, almost 90, the Prophet's only living daughter, had been there, and George Albert Smith, president of the Church, and Governor Lee of Utah, and Vice President Barkley himself had made a speech—there beside the 10-foot marble statue carved by Mahonri Young, the Prophet's grandson, and before a throng of distinguished guests, amid clusters of sego lilies, Indian paint brush, sage, and rabbit brush that he'd had flown from Utah to add a touch of Utah to the occasion.

Bill looked out the window at the vague blur of the Pennsylvania landscape reeling past and out of sight. The long train sped south, toward Baltimore.

The skin of his face had turned strangely sallow. The doctors entered his room at Doctors' Hospital with sheaves of test reports and said that he was suffering from a disease that, in him, at least, had evaded detection until then, possibly because so little was known about it. It was a liver ailment called hepatitis, which had afflicted American soldiers based in Italy during World War II. How long had he had it? A year, maybe, possibly longer. Perhaps he'd contracted it in Mexico. In any event, there was severe damage to the liver. As for treatment, it was still experimental: intravenous glucose, penicillin, total inactivity, and rest—in bed, in the hospital.

They wanted him to stay eight weeks; he stayed six, and left the hospital still weak, grateful to Paul, Woody, and Russell for carrying on with the Baltimore opening and the expansion planning. He was also filled with a pervading homesickness for mountain and sky, river and forest, sun and rain and country stars; if he were going to survive, they were, he felt, his only chance.

They had to have a place outside Washington, he told Allie, close, but at the same time deep in Virginia—deep enough to ride a horse in, to hear the morning stillness in. They spent long summer and fall afternoons on the back roads west of Washington, in the smoke-blue Blue Ridge mountains, in Rappahannock and Culpepper and Madison counties, looking at land and farms for sale.

But, his own needs aside, it was easy to rationalize a ranch in Virginia. If the cold war turned hot, it would be a place for the family and even Marriott employes to head for in case of atomic attack. Secondly, if they had a ranch they could raise their own cattle and sheep to provide beef and lamb for the restaurants and cafeterias. Only a few months back, a Midwest stockyards strike had cut their wholesalers off for weeks. It taught them a lesson: they needed an auxiliary meat supply. Finally, Bill and Allie wanted a country place so that management personnel could take their wives and families out of the city on Sundays or weekends and have picnics or cookouts and get together around a campfire and sing, Western style.

One perfect October afternoon, the Shenandoahs dreaming in the autumn haze across the valley, over toward Front Royal in Fauquier County, they found what they'd been looking for. They were led to it by a real estate agent who said they ought to take a look at Fairfield Farm, the old Marshall place, with the Rappahannock headwaters, only 20 feet wide even in the spring flooding season, running through it. Kind of neglected, he said, ever since the Baroness with her two boys had left it and gone back to Europe a couple of years ago. But it had nigh on to 3,000 acres of the best grazing land in Virginia, and an old manor house built in 1814 by James Marshall, brother of John, the great Chief Justice. And the price, he reckoned, would be right.

In Bill's words:

"It *looked* like a ranch, it looked like the West, at the foothills of the Blue Ridge mountains about four and a half miles east of the Skyline Drive, east of the Shenandoah range. Beautiful, beautiful country, great grazing country for cattle, sheep and horses. It was owned by Baroness Jeanne von Reininghaus Lambert. Her husband was an Austrian Rothschild and they owned a big share of the Bank of Belgium. They had two boys, and since the boys were part Jewish they were afraid that the Nazis would take them away if Germany invaded Belgium. So she brought them to America and bought this property as a refuge. We heard that it was for the King of Belgium, too, if he needed it.

"It had this beautiful old Manor House with brick walls eighteen inches thick and rooms 25 feet square with ceilings 16 feet high, but it had fallen into disrepair, and when the Baroness started to recondition it, she couldn't get the materials because of the war. A quarter of a mile away was a little log cabin where James Marshall's slaves had lived, and she had this rebuilt. She added an upstairs bedroom and a downstairs bedroom and two bathrooms on one end and a kitchen on the other end, and rebuilt the cabin itself into a nice living room with a fireplace. This is where she lived until about 1948, when she went back to Belgium with her sons.

"She never did do anything with the Manor House. When we first saw it, one of the main rooms was full of oats and barley just piled on the floor, and the house was in terrible disarray. After we bought the property we put it back in shape and restored it. Now it's sound and beautiful again, the way it was when Marshall built it.

"A little later we added two other pieces of property (through one of them flowed Fiery Run) so that now it has about 4500 acres of land all in one piece, and we call it Fairfield Farm and Fiery Run Ranch.

"For several years we raised cattle for our commissary. Not only beef cattle, but lambs. But our business got so big that we could supply only a small portion of our needs, and it became cheaper for us to buy all our beef from the beef company in Iowa City.

"We had a big sheep barn at the farm with a loft in it. In the spring, we would put bales of hay all around the loft and lay down a red carpet on the ramp built for the entrance and have some great parties for all our management people. We always had a square dance caller and music for the parties, and I think the best times we ever had down there were during those years, in the early part of the time when we owned the place.

"Finally the barn became too small. So then, on about five acres of ground in back of the Manor House, we built a big pavilion with a large fireplace, and, at the other end, a kitchen. The pavilion was fitted with glass doors along two sides; we could slide these back and open up the whole building. It had a lot of grass area where people could play volleyball and baseball. We would have ponies for the kids to ride on, and we set up a place for horseshoe-pitching, so that when we invited the men we invited their whole families with them.

"For years now we've had several parties there during the spring and summer. Attendance is six, seven hundred, sometimes a thousand people at one time. And they all have a great time. It's one of the things we do for our company from a morale point of view. Sometimes our grandchildren bring their friends from school and use it for a dance or a hamburger cookout.

"Also, we named a lot of our products we manufacture in our commissary 'Fairfield Farms' products, after the place. And we developed a good breed of quarter horses for driving the cattle and pleasure riding. We have a lot of trails over the ranch, beautiful trails for riding. We have some jeeps there also.

"Did it cure the hepatitis? Well, I came out of it alive, which for a while I never thought I would, and eventually my liver became completely healed and I had my health back again. Riding a horse out there in those mountains and getting out in the open had a great deal to do with my recovery. It took some time, too, since all through the years I've been so busy I've never been able to stay down there more than one or two days at a time. Usually one night and a day, unfortunately."

Even before he was out of the hospital, the new shop on Park Road had opened, and then, that December, the Hangar Cafeteria at National Airport. The next year, 1951, the company opened five more stores, including one in Salt Lake City where both Bill Jr. and Dick would start learning the business from curb service up, while students at the University of Utah. At the same time work was proceeding on two new shops in Maryland and on a cafeteria for the Rand McNally building in Chicago.

It was in October 1952, in Detroit, while campaigning for the Presidency against Adlai Stevenson, that General Eisenhower promised to end the "police action" in Korea, now beginning its 32nd month. "That job," he said, "requires a personal trip to Korea. I shall make that trip . . . I shall go to Korea."

Eleven days later, the Presidency was his. By a popular vote plurality of more than six million, sweeping 39 states and 442 electoral votes out of a possible 531, the nation went Republican for the first time in 20 years. And on November 29, Eisenhower went to Korea.

Before he left, Eisenhower had thrilled Mormons everywhere by naming Ezra Taft Benson his Secretary of Agriculture. Idaho-born, a year older than Bill, Benson was one of the Church's Twelve Apostles.

On the January afternoon that Eisenhower was inaugurated, moments before Chief Justice Fred M.

Vinson administered the oath of office, the sun broke through the clouds of what had been a bleak and chilly day and shone warmly on the throng gathered in front of the Capitol. When the ceremony was over, the new President turned to the thousands jamming the Capitol plaza to hear his inaugural address. Tension gone, he flung up his arms in an exuberant V-for-Victory salute. The thousands cheered, and were his.

There were two inaugural balls that evening, one in Georgetown University's McDonough Gymnasium, the other in the National Guard Armory. The Marriotts attended the latter. But before the ball, they gave a small dinner party for 36 at the Columbia Country Club. Bill and Allie were proud of their guest list, and well they might have been; Secretary of Agriculture and Mrs. Benson, whom they'd known for years; Secretary of the Treasury Ivy Baker Priest and her husband; the David O. McKays (he was president of the Mormon Church), the Brossards, the Stewarts, and even Mother Alice Smoot. The women wore mink jackets and "Mamie" bangs, the men, including Bill, wore white tie and tails, white scarves with their tailored Chesterfields, and silk top hats. Every picture taken of them that evening might have been captioned "On Top of the World."

It all made Bill feel that the time was right for a fundamental change, one of the very few that have occurred in his life, or in the life of the Marriott Corporation. The time was right to let the business take off and grow with the economy, grow with the country, branch out, find its way logically into new extensions, like water flowing over the ground. The hitch was, it would take a lot of money. New money. He and Allie and Roger Whiteford and his brothers had been talking about it for months, ever since the previous summer, in fact, when the Republicans nominated Ike for President.

Years ago, he'd come across something Emerson had written that expressed how he felt about borrowing and how to build a business. He'd copied it down and had given it to his secretary to file. "The true way now of beginning is to play the hero in commerce, as it has been done in war, in church, in schools, in state,—not begin with a borrowed capital, but [he] must raise an estate from the seed, must begin with his hands, and earn one cent; then two; then a dollar; then stock a basket; then a barrow; then a booth; then a shop; and then a warehouse; and not on this balloon of credit make his first structure. Franklin, William Hutton, and many New England merchant princes are men of this merit."

That's how he and Allie had done it. They'd raised an estate from the seed, had begun with their hands, with root beer and mugs that cracked in cold water and sticky nickels in the cash register, and the fifty-cent ledger with the ruled lines. For 25 years they'd shunned credit like the spotted fever. But meanwhile, the little nine-stool root beer stand had grown to 45 eating establishments in nine states and the District of Columbia, 13 Pantry Houses, an in-flight meal service for a dozen airlines, various Federal agency and industrial cafeterias extending from Miami and Atlanta to Norfolk and Chicago. They employed more than 3,000 and provided them with up-to-date group insurance, princely incentive premiums, and generous other fringe benefits. They served how many millions of customers a year—twenty? thirty?—and the last time anyone counted, the company in 12 months dished out 400 tons of hamburger, 4.5 million rolls, 55 tons of bacon, 75,000 beef carcasses, seven million eggs, 250 tons of seafood, mountains of potatoes, vegetables, fruits and sugar. In 1952, the company's gross income had reached an all-time high of $19,737,935.86, nearly triple what it had been only seven years before, at the end of World War II.

Meanwhile, both he personally and the business of

222

which he was the driving force had reached a critical decision point: either play it conservatively, hold to the present line or, at the most, inch ahead from savings; or generate expansion capital, probably by going public, keep on growing, take the risk with eyes open, stake the future on the driving faith he had in himself.

He could not have told even Allie when he made up his mind that he was going to take the company ahead. But he knew he was on solid footing. He had a good Harvard man for financial vice-president, Milton Barlow, with whom he discussed his plans. Marriott had behind it 25 years of growth, a wide reputation for good food and fair prices. Marriott had always made a profit, had always paid its bills on time, had never overextended itself or backed unorthodox ventures. The company had gone far indeed on its earnings and insurance company loans; but for the magnitude of expansion he had in mind he needed more equity capital, much more. And the best place to get it, it seemed to him, was the stock market. Other Washington firms had gone public and had prospered: Julius Garfinkel, the Goldenberg Company, the Hecht Company, Woodward and Lothrop. In addition to the corporate advantage, it would have a personal one as well: it would allow him and Allie to withdraw some of their own capital from the company and diversify their investments.

The month after President Eisenhower's inauguration, through the Washington brokerage firm of Johnston, Lemon & Co., Hot Shoppes, Inc., offered for public sale 229,880 shares of common stock at $10.25 a share, and 18,000 shares to its employes at $7.54 a share. This represented about one-third of the company's 704,800 shares. The remaining and controlling two-thirds stayed with the family: Bill and Allie, Paul, Russell and Woody, with Roger Whiteford as trustee for Bill Jr. and Dickie. Johnston & Lemon had never seen anything like it. In two hours of trading, every share was gone.

Chapter Eighteen

The company came out of it, Bill always said, like a bronco busting out of a rodeo chute. Within five years, its 45 locations increased to 88, its 3,000 employes doubled to 6,000, its operating revenue rose from $21 million a year to $38 million. Sales increased at the rate of 20-25 percent a year, and profits climbed at an even higher rate—34 percent, for example, for the company's fiscal year ending July 28, 1957, when they toppled $1 million for the first time: $1,138,348 for fiscal year 1956-57, as compared to $847,987 for fiscal year 1955-56.

In order to give the new stockholders representation outside the Marriott corporate family, Bill drastically changed the make-up of the board of directors. Though they retained their company title, salary, and responsibilities, he dropped from the board four vice-presidents: Paul, John S. Daniels, Sid Wilcox, the company executive in Philadelphia, and Milton A. Barlow, who also served as secretary-treasurer. He himself stayed on as president of the company and chairman of the board. Allie and Roger Whiteford stayed on. And he added two "outsiders," James M. Johnston, senior partner of Johnston, Lemon & Co., and Eric Johnston, president of the Motion Picture Association of America. Bill had great respect for Eric Johnston. Johnston could sit down with the script of a 30-minute speech, study it for an hour, and then that evening get up at the banquet table and deliver it verbatim. "You've got to have brains to do that," Bill said.

To Bill's relief, the company remained a Marriott family operation, even though it had, so to speak, opened its doors to the public: the new board endorsed his and his management team's programs with only perfunctory comment. The new stockholders, holding stock that climbed past $15 a share, then edged up over $20 and on toward $30, sat through annual meetings with an air of happy complacency, laughed appreciatively at his jokes, and applauded warmly when the meeting was over.

The company soon opened a number of standard Hot Shoppes in the District and its environs and thrust out strongly in industrial and institutional feeding: at Eastman Kodak and Kelly Springfield plants in Georgia and Maryland, at Philip Morris in Richmond, the Du Pont nylon plant in Waynesboro, Virginia, the L.B. Smith plant in Miami, Children's Hospital and American University in Washington. They also took on government installation and agency feeding, such as the Rossford Ordnance Depot in Toledo, Robins Air Force Base, near Macon, Georgia, the International Monetary Fund staff and offices in Washington. They drove an opening wedge into the growing fast-foods business with their first "Mighty Mo" curb-service unit in Queen's Chapel Road, named for a new double-decker hamburger that, in turn, had been named in honor of the famous battleship, *U.S.S. Missouri,* by the winner of a company contest. In-flight service expanded with the addition of Braniff Airlines and an even brighter feather in Paul's cap, the commission for blue-ribbon service to Air France flights from Chicago to Paris. Catering the flights from the other end: Maxim's of Paris.

In addition to this kind of expansion, Marriott went gunning for Howard Johnson territory and came up with contracts for nine Hot Shoppes on the New York-Albany stretch of New York's new million-dollar-a-mile Thruway from Manhattan to Buffalo, and for three more on Florida's new Sunshine Parkway. It had distressed Bill for years that company divisions and departments had outgrown the Upshur Street buildings and had spread all over town, executive offices and commissary in one location, Finance and the Print Shop in another, Architecture, Procurement, Personnel, and Employment in still others. To solve this problem, the company bought ten acres on River Road, just across the District line in suburban Kenwood, and proceeded to build a new home office. The spacious new headquarters, themselves soon rendered inadequate by company growth, were opened in May 1955, the same month that, in a foreshadowing of things to come, Allie was named assistant treasurer of the District of Columbia League of Republican Women. Proudly Bill took possession of his handsome office: custom-made teakwood desk and buffet; polished Texas longhorns over the fireplace with the brand Interior Decorating had designed for him, the running "JM" hand-tooled on the leather that bound their butts together; wormy chestnut paneling; hand-woven raw silk curtains. On the wall went the latest but not the last of his many awards, *American Restaurant* magazine's "Hall of Fame" plaque, the "Oscar" of the trade. Two years later, the 30th anniversary year of the founding of the company, he could add another, the Award of Achievement Scroll of Washington's Advertising Club. In his acceptance speech at a Presidential Arms luncheon, Bill gave his three basic rules for successful advertising: (1) reach the greatest number of people at the least possible cost; (2) reach the greatest number of people *continually*; (3) make a distinct and lasting impression on them *continually*. For every 24 hours a visitor is in Washington, Bill said, he is exposed at least once and possibly as many as 15 times to Hot Shoppe advertising. This was one good reason for the Hot Shoppes' growth.

Sometimes, particularly after the fanfare about the Twin Bridges Motor Hotel, the media—tastefully or not—accorded Marriott a kind of it's-all-in-the-family acceptance that money couldn't buy. A Washington *Star* joke, for example, told of the little boy who went to Sunday School in Chevy Chase. Proud of his cards illustrating scenes from the New Testament, he showed them off to his friend. His mother in the next room heard him say, "This shows Jesus in the manger . . . This is Jesus at school . . . This is Jesus in the temple . . ." Long pause as he studied a picture of The Last Supper. Then, triumphantly, "And *this* is Jesus at the Hot Shoppe!"

The Twin Bridges project, advertised with Barnum and Bailey fervor, was to both company and community the most exciting development of all in this phase of the Marriott expansion program for the significant reason that it was the company's first venture into hotels. Its beginnings went back to 1950, when Bill bought the eight acres of land in Virginia from the Richmond, Fredericksburg and Potomac railroad for $60,000 an acre, intending to build a new office and commissary building there.

Originally part of the estate of George Washington Parke Custis, Martha Washington's grandson and adopted son of the General, the property adjoined the strategic one-acre piece on which Hot Shoppe Number Eight was located, the one at the end of the Fourteenth Street bridge where they'd started the airline box-lunch service for planes flying in and out of Hoover Airport. The airport had been moved down the river and had been replaced by the bleak battlements of the Pentagon, but every motorist coming from or driving to the south still had to pass the property, and the number of cars going by was increasing at the rate of thousands a month.

The Korean armistice was signed in July 1953, and the nation seemed again in a buying, optimistic, let's-get-out-and-see-the-country mood. Congress was talking about a $40 billion coast-to-coast system of federal highways (authorized in 1956), airline people accurately predicted that passenger jets would soon be flying in and out of National, and right there within a six-iron shot of Number Eight's parking lot, Federal Bureau of Public Roads engineers were making surveys for a futuristic maze of cloverleaf approaches to the Virginia end of the Potomac bridges.

It began to be obvious to Bill and the other directors that here, where everything was happening, was a dramatic location for a motor hotel. In April 1955, the month they moved into the River Road headquarters, Bill called a press conference to announce that Marriott intended to build on its Virginia property a 370-room hostelry that would represent "the logical extension of Hot Shoppes' traditional concern for the American family on wheels." Quite splendid by the standards of the day, it would cost $7 million, be the largest motor hotel in the world, and offer a host of customer-oriented amenities: air-conditioning, soundproofing, drive-in registration arcades, a glass-walled Hot Shoppe overlooking the swimming pool, a rooftop observation deck from which to view the Washington skyline across the river, 21-inch TV sets in every room, king-size double beds, wall-to-wall carpeting, baby-sitters on call, and so on.

To a fair-sized element in Washington, for varying reasons—political, competitive, environmental—all this came as a shock and an outrage. How come such a thing as a Hot Shoppe was ever permitted there in the first place? demanded the Sunday *Star*. There it was, next to the north and south lanes of two of the nation's busiest highways, U.S. 1 and Shirley Highway, in what was probably the prize restaurant location in the United States. A few hundred yards from the restaurant, linked by connectors to these arteries, ran three other heavily traveled roads, Routes 50, 29, and 211 (since relocated), to vast regions of Virginia countryside across the Potomac. Not only this, but crossing the property to the north was the George Washington Memorial Parkway to National

Airport, Alexandria, Mt. Vernon, and points beyond. And, to cap it all, even if you *flew* into Washington and sat on the right side of the plane, you couldn't miss Hot Shoppe Number Eight, just below the right wing as you coasted down the final leg of National's most frequently used landing pattern. It was to the south of the restaurant and all the connectors, about half a mile away, between them and the East Coast tracks, that Marriott proposed to build its motor hotel.

There had been quite a flurry over the Hot Shoppe acre back in 1949, when the District Highway Department and the Federal Bureau of Public Roads wanted it for the approaches to the new Fourteenth Street bridge. Sorry, Bill said, but the Hot Shoppe had been there since 1937, and when the Highway Department, anticipating the approaches, started buying up all the surrounding land, its then chief, Captain H.C. Whitehurst, had promised him that whatever happened the Hot Shoppe could stay there. Of course, Captain Whitehurst, unfortunately, was now dead, but no matter: that's what he said. District officials countered with a demand for an option to buy the land within ten years. Bill said that if they'd give him a long-term lease on it for the Hot Shoppe they could have it—for $1 million. The officials said this was too much for them to spend on an acre of land in Virginia, and gave up. "We ought to have known better," one of them growled. "Every time we want to improve a strategic spot in the District, we find a Hot Shoppe sitting right in the middle of it."

The spirit of resignation on the part of the opposition, plus substantial community backing in favor of the project, cleared away the obstacles, and the 11-building complex began to rise there on the right bank of the Potomac, a ten-minute drive across the bridge from the Lincoln Memorial, the Washington Monument, and the White House. The opening ceremony took place on a bright but chilly morning in January, a few days before President Eisenhower's second inaugural. Outside, the building had been completed on time, but inside, it was a nip-and-tuck finish. The Marriotts themselves, in fact, had been up until after midnight hanging guest room pictures. Allie wore a beige tailored suit and held a sheaf of long-stemmed roses. Bill wore a dark suit and tie, white shirt, white carnation pinned to his left lapel. At their side were their good friends Secretary of Agriculture and Mrs. Ezra Taft Benson and Senator Arthur Watkins of Utah. Together the Marriotts grasped the shears and symbolically cut the broad ribbon that stretched across the front entrance. Flashbulbs flickered, a band played, people cheered. For better or for worse—Bill was confident it was for the better—Marriott was in the hotel business.

Filling a need and filling it with service and accommodations of quality, Twin Bridges was immediately a success. It still is.

In Washington there are no dividing lines between private lives and public lives, and if you're in business in the District it's even more complicated. You have a dozen balls to keep in the air instead of three or four. The more involved you are, the more involved you tend to get.

In April, three months after President Eisenhower's inaugural, for example, Allie was supervising arrangements for a National Symphony fashion luncheon. Then both Marriotts attended the Morris Cafritz's elite "at home" Easter party at their mansion in Foxhall Road, just around the corner from 4500 Garfield Street. After that it was opening night at the opera, and after that, out to Warrenton for the Virginia Gold Cup race over the timber course of William E. Schlusemeier's Broadview Farm. A few months in Washington to direct the public stock offering, and it was time for a Palm Springs vacation with George and Lenore Romney. In the fall, they crossed the Atlantic for a quick tour of the Continent. Back in Washington, they began to see a lot of the Bensons and their family. It was through the Bensons that they met the Eisenhowers.

In fact, one bright December Tuesday, in bitter, 15-degree weather, President Eisenhower, Secretary Benson, and a motorcade of 32 overcoated and mufflered Secret Servicemen drove out to Fairfield Farm. There in the Manor House the President changed into long woolen underwear, khaki trousers, heavy shirt and sweater, scarf and windbreaker. He put on his brown snap-brim fedora and went down to the cottage to see Bill, in bed with the flu. "How're you feeling, Bill?" the President asked. "Well I sure feel bad, Mr. President," Bill said. "I turned a hundred pheasant loose on the farm for us to hunt when you and the Secretary get back from Front Royal, but my doctor here tells me I can't get out of bed at all this afternoon if I want to have dinner with you this evening. So I guess I have to stay here." (His doctor had come from Washington with him.) The President's smile was a blend of sympathy, concern, and encouragement. "That's some hat you've got there, Mr. President," Bill said. "Out here on the ranch, you ought to have a real cowboy hat—"

The President and Secretary Benson motored the 12 miles to the government research station at Front Royal to inspect its black Angus, Herefords, and shorthorns. As they drove back to the Manor House, the early December dusk closed in fast. It was too cold and too late, they decided, to hunt pheasants. They went upstairs to change. Log fires snapped in the Manor House fireplaces. The lights on the big Christmas tree cast a warm glow over the candlelit living room. Homey kitchen noises came from somewhere in the back as the help prepared dinner. In the high-ceilinged dining room the long table was set and waiting. The clans gathered: Mamie Eisenhower and her mother, Mrs. John Doud; her sister and her sister's husband, Colonel and Mrs. Gordon Moore; Mrs. Benson, the four Benson girls, Barbara, Beverly, Bonnie, and Beth, and the two Benson boys, Reed and Mark, and Mark's wife; Allie, of course, and Mrs. Smoot, visiting for the holidays; Bill Jr. and Dick. Bill, temperature down, feeling stronger, came up from the cottage. After dinner, around the living room fire, everyone was charmed and moved by the Bensons' "family home evening" program, typical in spirit of those conducted in most Mormon homes every Monday night. The program closed with a hymn and a prayer. In separate limousines, the Eisenhowers, the Bensons, and the Secret Servicemen drove back to Washington.

A few days after Christmas, Bill bought a Borsolino western hat at Saltz's in Washington, enclosed his card, and sent it to the White House. He received a note on White House stationery: "Dear Mr. Marriott: When I returned to my office Monday morning, I found the hat you so kindly sent me. I am truly grateful to you for remembering our conversation and making certain that I would be properly outfitted Western-style. With warm regards, Sincerely, [signed] Dwight D. Eisenhower."

Bill Jr. was by now in the Mediterranean as supply officer on the carrier *U.S.S. Randolph,* and when she put into Cannes for ten days Bill and Allie flew to the Riviera to brighten up his shore leave. But they were back in time for the opening of the new River Road headquarters, and before they knew it they were in Salt Lake City for Bill Jr.'s marriage to Donna Garff in the Mormon temple.

Even with all the excitement, turmoil, and exhaustion of opening their first hotel, Bill and Allie found time and energy to work for the President's second inaugural, in 1957, Bill as vice-chairman of the Festival Committee,

Allie as hostess and floor committeeman for the ball itself. Then that spring, at the request of the State Department, they spent three weeks in Russia as members of an exchange group of American hotel and food industry experts, studying Soviet methods of mass food production, inspecting farms and factories, visiting universities, sampling Russian food in hotels, factories, restaurants, and cafeterias.

So, with strange irony, the going got tougher, requiring a different order of strength and nerve. Before the company went public, Bill had been personally liable for just about everything; if the company collapsed, Marriott collapsed. Now, however, he and Allie were financially safe. No matter what happened to the expansion program, they and the boys would be comfortable for the rest of their lives. As far as the company was concerned, Bill was in a sense set free—free to push ahead faster with expansion, free to take risks that he never would have taken before. But also, for the first time, free to pack it all in and spend the rest of his life on the farm, at the lake, in the Grand Tetons hunting and fishing with his Utah friends. Every waking moment of his life and even in his dreams the West, the outdoors, the outdoor life called to him; sometimes he could shut it out and sometimes he couldn't. Now at last, if he wished, he was free to go. And yet—

The year 1958, an eventful one in the Marriott family, started for Bill with a bracing ride on Golden Guber, his young palomino stallion, down to the barns and then across the farm's rolling, winter-bound hills. The farm was lovely in the clear, frosty New Year's morning. As always he left it with a pang—"A beautiful place. Hard to leave," he wrote in his diary—and drove with Allie back to Washington, and then to the home of Bill Jr. and Donna for New Year's dinner and a visit with Debbie, their new little granddaughter. Bill's diary entry for the long and contented day concluded with the old resolution, familiar but bright and beckoning as ever, "Hope to make 1958 more sensible and take care of my health and do more good. The Lord has blessed us abundantly. We are grateful."

Bill showed slides of the Russian trip a lot that month, to members of the National Geographic Society, for example, and officers of the Quartermaster Corps, and he was invited to join the board of the Chesapeake and Potomac Telephone Company. "It's a real honor and a compliment," he said to Allie and, of course, he accepted. He flew to Chicago on business and back, worked all the next day at the office, then went home and worked that night in his study until 12:30. He had a doctor's appointment the next morning and was in the doctor's office at 8:30. The doctor took a lot of blood for a liver test.

That was the 29th. On February 3 he had an executive meeting scheduled, plus an afternoon flight to New York and tickets to *Romanoff and Juliet* that night (they'd be taking off from Idlewild for Puerto Rico the following day), and his stomach seemed to be aching all the time, so on the first of the month he saw the doctor again. The liver test reports were back and showed that it was 15 percent deficient. "You ought to get some rest," the doctor said. "Take it easy in Puerto Rico. Play some golf."

The day they left New York was pretty much spent traveling—checking out, cabbing to Idlewild, in the air to San Juan, checking into their ninth-floor room with a balcony at the Caribe Hilton, and then dinner, as planned, with a hotel architect and his wife from New York. Afterward, Bill lay in bed with his mind going a mile a minute. "There's a big opportunity here," he told Allie. "Leo told me about the tourist boom in Puerto Rico. We have to think about taking over a hotel here. We might even build one."

They spent the next three days riding around in a rented, chauffeur-driven sedan, inspecting possible hotel sites and looking over some of the newer hotels that had been built to capitalize on the tourist boom. On the fourth day they looked at more property, then packed and took the plane to St. Thomas, where they checked in at the Virgin Isles Hotel. Bill Jr. and Donna flew down from Washington the next day. They were getting ready, Bill Jr. said, to break ground for the new motor hotel, the one in Rosslyn at the Virginia end of the Francis Scott Key Bridge, just a mile or two away from Twin Bridges. That was fine, Bill said, but there were still a lot of problems to solve. They all looked forward to a wonderful winter vacation together in the sun.

They went swimming and lay on the beautiful white and deserted beach, listening to the wind rustling in the palm trees: they looked at fish in a glass-bottomed boat and cruised over to St. John, fishing off the stern as they sailed. Then on the fourth day after Bill Jr. and Donna arrived the whole nice time blew up. Something awakened Bill at 4 that morning. He couldn't get back to sleep. He worried about what was going on back at River Road and all the various problems that only he could handle and the decisions that he needed to be there to make. He couldn't stand wasting any more time doing nothing in this idle, indolent place, spending all this money. The more he fumed about it, the worse it seemed. At 8:30 he woke up Allie, and Bill Jr. and Donna in the adjoining room, and told them to pack and get ready to leave. They could catch the 1 o'clock plane back to San Juan and get a connecting flight from there to Miami, and be in Miami—and, thank God, back in America—that night.

Allie and Donna managed to get in some shopping and at 12:30 sharp they were at the airport to board the flight to San Juan. The plane was late. Bill was furious because no one had told them. The hot Caribbean sun beat down on the terminal. One hour passed, then another. It was 4 before they lifted off. When they arrived in San Juan, they learned there would be a two-hour wait until the next plane to Miami. They cabbed out to the Caribe Hilton. Bill phoned Leo to come over. While Allie and the kids had dinner, Leo took Bill to look at the new Hotel San Juan and some property that would make a fine location.

It was a long, tiresome, three-hour flight to Miami and almost midnight when they arrived. The temperature was in the high 40s. An icy wind tore at their light tropical clothes as the porter and the cab driver struggled with their luggage. Only Bill was cheerful as the cab pulled away from the terminal. He looked out at the familiar street signs and billboards, the twinkling lights of Miami. "Sure is great to be back in the good old U.S.A.," he said.

They stayed in Miami two weeks. On the fourth day, Bill had stomach trouble and spent the day in bed. Then he developed a chest cold that traveled to his head. Allie, too, came down with a head cold and a sore throat. Nevertheless, Bill was constantly on the phone to Washington. The hotel architect flew down for conferences about the Rosslyn project. At Bill's insistence, Roger Whiteford came down as well. He drove around with Bill Jr. to look at hotels and sites in the Miami area, rushed together a bid for the hotel to be built at the Miami Airport (it was too high), looked at possible sites in Fort Lauderdale, tried a round of golf or two, riding in carts, but it was too windy and he felt too bad all the time to enjoy it. On the night before they left he wrote in his diary that both he and Allie were "sick and tired of this place. Prices awful. Room $40 a day, meals $5-$10 each. Tipping every time you move."

The next day, he had a meeting with the president of National Airlines and came away with a contract to provide in-flight feeding for all National flights out of Miami. "To hotel, packed, and on 3:45 P.M. National to Wash.," his diary entry reads. "Sure glad to be on our way home. Arriving 7:30. Home Sweet Home . . . Home Sweet Heaven."

But after a euphoric few days, filled with pleasure at being back at the office, March was no better. As early as the third, he wrote in his diary, "All tired out and sick. Discouraged. Worried about business. Can't get feeling well. Stomach very bad."

Then he spent a couple of days at Fairfield Farm. He rode the trails on horseback, drove the forest roads in his jeep, did some sheepherding, breathed the Blue Ridge air and smelled its promise of spring, ate dinners that Allie cooked, slept more soundly, returned to work feeling better.

He took a trip to Philadelphia to look at the City Line site the company was about to take over for the third motor hotel, the first outside the District area, and to inspect the Philadelphia shops. Sid Wilcox drove him to New York the next day and from there they drove north to the New York Thruway to Albany, stopping off at every Thruway Hot Shoppe. It was a discouraging trip. Somehow, somewhere, they had to find better managers.

Because a snowstorm closed down the Albany airport, he had a harrowing drive back down the Thruway to Newark, where he caught a flight for Washington. It was 10:30 the following night before he finally caught up on all his paperwork and correspondence. At last he climbed the stairway to the second-floor den and took his little diary out of the desk drawer. "Am tired of all this pressure," he wrote. "Wish I were a Mormon missionary or a rancher. Bed at 11."

One thing that kept Bill going that spring was the letter he'd received from Congressman Henry Aldous Dixon of Ogden, a former president of Weber College, inviting him to deliver the college's commencement address at the end of May in the Ogden Tabernacle. "The homefolks would appreciate it no end," the Congressman wrote.

Bill accepted, naturally. He mapped out his next ten weeks. On March 20 he, Allie, and Bill Jr. would fly to Dallas to look at possible motor hotel locations on Stemmons Expressway and to check the Braniff in-flight commissary at the Dallas airport. Bill Jr. would stay there to work out the location deal, and Bill and Allie would fly over to Camelback for a few days, going on to Salt Lake City April 7. Bill would leave Allie there for a visit with her mother and with Dick, now a sophomore at the University of Utah, and would fly back to Washington via Chicago. Toward the end of April he'd fly to New Orleans and Atlanta to check out possible motor hotel sites to consider after they got Philadelphia and Dallas started. Then they'd have a beautiful May in Washington and on the farm, and along about the 28th—commencement was on the 31st—they'd fly back out to Utah.

When Allie returned to Washington she brought her mother with her for a spring visit. And—brightest day of the spring!—Bill received word from Ernest Wilkinson, president of Brigham Young University, saying that while he was out there to deliver the Weber College address, he might find time to drop down to Provo. They had something there they wanted very much to give him: an honorary degree, Doctor of Laws.

But Bill was feeling poorly, and now he was worried about whether he'd be physically able to give the commencement address and receive the degree. He wasn't sleeping well, and the cough still hung on. Finally he had his doctor make reservations and appointments for him at the Mayo Clinic in Rochester, Minnesota. He wanted all the tests and all the check-ups and the best medical advice money could buy. Reservations at Mayo were also made for Allie. She had come down with shingles, a painful skin and nervous disorder. The doctor echoed Bill's question: "What caused it? My guess is—worry over you."

Mayo doctors gave Bill a thorough check-up. A week after his arrival, the doctors told Bill that his cold and cough were cured. There remained two things wrong: his liver was still deficient and he had a "nervous stomach." Their recommendation: get lots of rest; take life easier. Yes, Bill agreed, overwork, too fast a pace, got him into trouble every time. But he'd learned his lesson. From now on, it was going to be different. As for Allie, injections and hospital rest and regimen had done her a world of good. The shingles were clearing up. She felt fine.

Back in their rooms at the Kahler Hotel, the world seemed bright again. Bill felt very fit indeed. His doctors had told him what to do and this time, for once, he was going to take their advice. Allie's distressing illness was over. Better yet, her worries about him were, too. As they did their last-minute packing, he glanced at his watch. He picked up the phone and called a bellman. "Step on it," he said. If they got their bags downstairs in time and checked out without any delays, they could just catch the six o'clock flight to Chicago. He could be back at his desk bright and early in the morning. But they'd have to hurry.

The Weber commencement program was on a Sunday evening, windless and very warm. Even before the opening selection by the choir, many of the 327 members of the graduating class and the more than a thousand family members, friends, and guests in the audience were fanning themselves with their programs. On the speakers' platform with Bill were William P. Miller, president of the college, and, to Bill's pride and pleasure, his old friend and former president, Aaron Tracy, now in his seventies.

Bill had worked hard on his speech. Allie thought it was too long and he himself suspected that it was; but it represented his best, the words of wisdom he really wanted to pass along to these fine young people. He called it "Building for Strength."

Reading off a script typed in big type, he told of his years at Weber and how much he owed to Aaron Tracy. He told of selling woolen underwear in the northwestern logging camps. He spoke at length about the trip to Russia, and the Russians, and what a threat their growing might was to the free world. "We must build for strength or our doom is certain, and our unhappiness sure," he warned. To succeed, he said, young people today should find work they like to do and are interested in; they should learn how to get along with people; they should try to develop and use common sense; they should develop their imagination; they should be willing to make changes, to keep abreast of changing conditions. Finally, he said, more important than all these are three other qualities: unselfishness in service to others, good personal habits, and a strong faith in God. "These things make for character in a man," he declared.

Then he concluded with an inspiring quotation from Dr. Ray Lyman Wilbur of Stanford University. "Happiness is a true goal of man, but it comes through striving, not through drifting. To halt, to be satisfied, is, in part, to die. Life is an adventure and can be glorious, but not for the parasite. . . . To live—to grow—to have a family—to seek new paths—and to help the less fortunate—are the goals . . . we call life."

Everyone in the tabernacle stood up when he was through, many of the older ones with lumps in their throats, eyes misting, remembering the days when they and Bill and his brothers and sisters had all been kids together, fishing, going barefoot, milking cows, cutting beets, playing ball, going to school, laughing, fighting, being scared, being proud, yearning, loving, living, growing up . . . They clapped for a long time, until President Miller finally had to step to the podium, hold up his hand for silence, and announce that it was time to get on with the awarding of the diplomas.

A few days later, Bill and Allie, the Stewarts, and the Coltons drove from Salt Lake City down to Provo and the broad walks and lawns of the Brigham Young University campus. They had an early dinner together, talking about old times and their early days together in Washington. And now their old Washington friend Ernie Wilkinson was president of BYU, and their old Washington friend Ben Lewis was provost.

Though it had been an early spring in the valley, traces of snow still lingered high on the slopes of Timpanogos, looming northeast of the campus. Bill noticed them as they all walked together to the George Albert Smith Fieldhouse, where the commencement exercises were to take place. Allie kissed him; the others shook his hand.

Then there he was, on the platform in his black, velvet-faced silk gown, tasseled mortarboard sparely on his head, with the half-dozen others to be honored, and the more than a thousand young men and women of BYU's graduating class, ranged in long deep rows on both sides of the podium, the filled auditorium silent, waiting for Ben to open his presentation:

"President Wilkinson—an Old Testament prophet once wrote '. . . Your old men shall dream dreams, your young men shall see visions.' It is my privilege today to present a person who, as a young man, saw a vision and whose vision has materialized into one of the great businesses of our time. I speak of John Willard Marriott. . . ."

Eloquently, Lewis told of Bill's childhood in the dusty valley eighty-five miles north, of Bill's college and university days, his marriage to Allie, his success in Washington, his service to the Church.

"John Willard Marriott," he concluded, "stands as a giant among men, one who loves the Lord and his fellowmen with all his heart. For the outstanding accomplishments of his life and for what he represents, Mr. President, I commend him to you as worthy to receive this university's most distinguished award of Doctor of Laws, *honoris causa.*"

A wave of applause swept through the auditorium. Then smiling, Bill rose and crossed the platform toward Ernest Wilkinson and the waiting scroll.

Chapter Nineteen

In November 1958, the board of directors of the Marriott Corporation elected Bill Jr., 26, executive vice-president in charge of its newest and boldest venture, the multi-million-dollar motor hotel program; and if Bill, the father, even for a fugitive moment sensed—as most leaders sooner or later must—even the dimmest intimations of his own mortality, his own ultimate dispensability, no one, not even Allie, knew it.

From his earliest boyhood they had been very proud of Bill Jr. At St. Alban's, some of his friends would remember him as a serious, hard-working student who got good grades, who was mostly all work and very little play, who didn't care much or perhaps wasn't big enough for football but who put together a fair-to-middling game of tennis. He liked machinery, its concentrated energy and power, and terrified Bill and Allie with the way he tore up the course in the summer speedboat races at Lake Winnepesaukee. In his last years at St. Alban's he drove a fire-engine red Ford convertible that, when he reached the University of Utah campus, turned into a flame-red Jaguar Mark IV. He struck his friends as very competitive, some would say compulsively so. Like most competitors, what mattered most to him was winning. What he hated most was losing—even, they said, at Ping Pong.

In the 1950s, as now, western campuses had their share of young men and women who, like Bill Jr., came from backgrounds of new wealth, security, and status, whose families had struck it rich in wartime or postwar oil, ranching, mining, real estate, shipping, defense industries. Some of them drove Mark IV's too, and thought nothing, say, of flying their dates from Salt Lake to

Phoenix for a Mexican dinner, spending as much for plane fares in one evening as poorer classmates spent for everything in a whole month. The different breed—serious, nondrinking, aware of their responsibilities, eyes and mind on the future—was in the minority, and of this minority Bill Jr. was one. He dressed unpretentiously, dated Donna Garff of Chi Omega, Mormon daughter of a professor of speech, studied hard, achieved monotonously high grades, walked off with the business school's and Navy R.O.T.C.'s top honors. In addition to all this, he made an off-campus career of learning the family business at the Hot Shoppe that the company had opened in Salt Lake City in 1951.

Every morning at four he converged on the restaurant with the breakfast chef. During his last two years at the university he worked his way from station to station, from the hot dogs, ham and eggs, and hamburgers of the grill to the chocolate malteds and strawberry sodas of the fountain, and in the back from deep-fat fryer to salad block. Then graduation, and duty aboard the *Randolph* with its crew of some 2,000, where he was in charge of ship's stores and mess operations. When Bill and Allie visited him on the *Randolph* at Cannes, they could hardly believe that Bill Jr., who still seemed only a boy to them, was dealing with sharp French salesmen, driving bargains for everything from sides of beef to cashmere sweaters. After he and Donna were married, he joined the company in Washington and for six months worked in restaurant operations, then transferred to advertising and public relations for another three months. When that was over he was assigned to the Twin Bridges project. He was in charge of pulling it all together in the last hectic months of construction and operation. Then, finally, he programmed the triumphal opening itself.

The night of the stockholders' meeting when Bill Jr. was made vice-president in charge of hotels, Bill and Allie had gone with Mark and Lola Evans to the Shoreham for dinner and to hear Nelson Eddy. It was a celebration and they had something to celebrate: not only Billy's vice-presidency, but the fact that they'd been able to report to the stockholders the best year in Marriott history—sales of $40,783,549, up 18 percent from the previous year's sales of $36 million, and almost double the sales of $21 million plus of five years before.

The Marriott Corporation, tightly wound, single-minded, was pushing ahead hell-bent for more units, a broader base, higher earnings. It opened a new Char-Broiler at Bailey's Cross Roads, across the line in Virginia; scouted locations for new Mighty Mo's; and opened its first luxury restaurant, the Sirloin and Saddle, at the Twin Bridges motor hotel, ushering in a whole new division and a whole new level of success—and problems. All the endless flights, conferences, and negotiations, the thrust and parry, clash, conflict and compromise over money, site, insurance, equipment, furnishings, publicity, construction, and a thousand other things finally did, after all, come to an end of sorts and Bill Jr.'s hotel division broke ground for the 500-room Dallas Marriott on Stemmons Expressway, and for the $10-million Philadelphia Marriott and its exotic Kona Kae Polynesian restaurant a block off the heavily traveled Schuylkill Expressway. In-flight expanded its already sizeable facilities at New York's Idlewild Airport to handle Eastern Airlines' expanded schedule of daily flights, 104 in all, made possible by its new, three-story terminal.

Meanwhile Dick Marriott, now 19 and a cum laude graduate of St. Alban's, took a leave of absence from studies at the University of Utah to fly to Australia for his two-year Mormon missionary service; and Bill Jr. and Donna had their first boy, Stephen, in April 1959. Two months later Stephen's big sister Debbie, dressed in a white organdy frock with a pink satin sash, and helped by her grandfather and Dina Merrill, the actress, cut the symbolic yellow ribbon that stretched across the front entrance of the new hotel on the rise above the Virginia end of Washington's Francis Scott Key Bridge. Holding the big shears in both hands, she closed them on the ribbon with a big snip. The ribbon parted. Eight hundred spectators cheered. Flash bulbs flickered. "I did it," Debbie said. Marriott's second motor hotel, the Key Bridge, was officially open for business.

Bill was pleased and happy about it, of course. He was finding from the Twin Bridges experience and all the planning for this motor hotel and the ones in Dallas and Philadelphia that he liked the hotel business. You served people so much more basically. You took them in and provided them with food, shelter, safety, and rest.

Two days after the opening Bill and Allie left with the Evanses for Toronto to visit the Nelson Davises (he was a wealthy Toronto banker) on their 90-acre estate and play a few rounds of golf. But Bill wasn't feeling well, and he stayed in bed with a fever and sore throat. A few weeks later he was at the doctor's office again for still another check-up, and X rays showed a spot on his left lung almost the size of a 50-cent piece. A malignancy? Dr. Geier couldn't say. He advised another trip to the Mayo Clinic.

Neither Bill nor Allie said very much on the plane to Rochester. Bill dozed, or pretended to doze. Allie read, or pretended to read. What was there to say, until they knew? The operation, performed in Methodist Hospital, took two hours.

"Do you smoke?" the doctor had asked Bill in the pre-operation interview. No, he didn't. "Then I doubt if it's cancer," the doctor said. And it wasn't. The "spot" was actually a cluster of pods formed by tiny fungus-like spores inhaled into the lungs, very probably during one of Bill's trips to the Southwest. In the normal course of development, the pods burst, scatter their seeds throughout the lung, and cause the disease known in the Southwest as valley fever, or San Joaquin Valley fever, a severe flu-like illness.

It was three weeks before they let Bill go home, and when he recovered it turned into a pretty good autumn after all. The farm was especially beautiful that September and October, and President Eisenhower had promised him last December that he would come out hunting this year. It had been at a White House musicale after the President's dinner for a number of ambassadors and their wives. After everyone had gone through the line, the President made his way across the reception room to Bill and Allie and chatted with them for ten minutes or so. He told Bill he had bought some Hot Shoppe stock at 15 for his grandchildren, and wished he could have bought more. They laughed about how cold it had been when he visited the farm with Secretary Benson. Bill asked him how many quail covies he had at Gettysburg and the President said only three, but he'd made one discovery at Gettysburg: the number-one quail feed was Scotch broom. Bill invited him out to Fairfield next year. The President flashed his wide, warm grin. "You bet—I'd be delighted." Then he and Mamie said good night and left the reception, and all the society page reporters crowded around Bill and Allie wanting to know what the President had said. "Just personal things," they laughed.

The date for the President's trip to Fairfield was set for November 16. The farm never looked lovelier. The Manor House was spruced up and waiting. All the barns were freshly painted. On a trip to New York with Bill Jr., Bill had gone to Abercrombie and Fitch's and bought for the President a 20-gauge mahogany-stocked Browning shotgun.

But on Thursday the 10th the President came down with a heavy chest cold and went south to Augusta,

Georgia. He got word to Bill that he was sorry, but he just couldn't make it this time. He made up for it, however. He left on December 3 on his bold and celebrated 22,000-mile swing around three continents—Africa, Asia, and Europe—and 11 nations, returning on December 22, in time to light the Christmas tree on the south lawn of the White House. The next morning Tom Stephens, the President's appointment secretary, called Bill. "Can you make it to the White House tomorrow morning at 10? The President would like to see you."

Bill arrived promptly at 10 with boxes of Christmas candy for the Eisenhowers and their family, White House aides, and others, and with the President's shotgun. Rising from his desk in the Oval Office, the President looked cheerful and fit. Bill, who had expected to present the gun, wish the President a merry Christmas, and leave, was there for 45 minutes. They spent 15 minutes assembling the gun, the President insisting on doing it several times without Bill's help. "He was like a little boy with a new toy," Bill said. Facing the big French doors, he whipped it to his shoulder, followed an imaginary pheasant on the rise over the terrace, and snapped the triggers on the empty chambers. "It's light and it's a beauty," he said. "I'll take it to Augusta with me and have the caddy strap it to my golf bag. We're always flushing out quail down there."

Early in his Army career, when stationed in San Antonio, he and Mamie learned to love Mexican food, so in the early 1930s, when they were transferred to Washington, they went to the Connecticut Avenue Hot Shoppe at least once a week for chili and hot tamales.

"Could Mamie and I get some sent into the White House, so we could have a real oldtime Mexican dinner?" he asked.

"Anytime you want, Mr. President. Just say the word."

The President was serious, and so was Bill, but the order never came. The President only had one more year in the White House. It was an election year and probably, like Bill, he never really had the time for the things he wanted to do.

This was the New Year's resolution that Bill entered in his diary for January 1, 1960: "Make today as perfect as I can and tomorrow will take care of itself and yesterday will be another memorable event." If he stopped to look back, which he almost never did, he could survey quite a substantial collection of yesterdays to remember.

The company of which he was co-founder and president and had started with a nine-stool root beer stand and cash reserve of $200 now encompassed 83 units in ten states and the District of Columbia. The company now grossed almost $55 million a year and employed 7,000, upon whom depended perhaps another 20,000. His own personal net worth topped, conservatively, $10 million and his annual salary amounted to $115,000, highest paid to any executive in the District of Columbia, including the President of the United States. He owned a large, comfortable summer place in New Hampshire, a well-stocked, 4500-acre ranch in Virginia, a stately home in Washington, six or eight riding horses, and five or six automobiles. Allie, a talented hostess who was just beginning to win prominence in the Republican party, remained devoted, loyal, all he ever needed and wanted in a wife. His sons too were all he could desire.

Yet, for all this, Bill bore down harder than ever. His heavy work schedule deprived him of time he thought he should be devoting to reading history, current events, and, most of all, the Bible. His solution: don't cut back on work, read faster. He hired Evelyn Wood, the speed-reading expert, to come to Garfield Street at 8 o'clock several mornings a week to teach him how to read a thousand words a minute. In 1959, he'd been "released" as president of the Washington Stake; instead of spending more time at Burning Tree or the farm he took on Sunday School and Aaronic priesthood classes at the Mormon Church. No matter how he felt, he was there at 9 o'clock every Sunday morning.

Moreover, he was now on four boards in addition to serving as chairman of his own: Riggs National Bank, Chesapeake and Potomac Telephone Company, Acacia Mutual Life Insurance Company, and George Romney's American Motors. This took constant study of reports, surveys, analyses, projections, and other material necessary to a responsible directorship, as well as attendance at lengthy, sometimes argumentative, often boring monthly meetings, which always seemed to coincide with some unpredictable crisis in his own affairs.

Allie also was busier than ever. In March 1959 she was named a member of the Republican State Committee for the District of Columbia. In recent years, sons grown, husband almost totally absorbed in business and church, she had turned to civic affairs and politics. While she devoted more time than ever to Marriott Hotel and restaurant interiors, she was an active member of the Rheumatism Foundation of Metropolitan Washington and of the Women's Committee of the National Symphony. Along with Mrs. E. Ross Adair, wife of the Congressman from Indiana, she founded "Welcome to Washington," a hospitality program for embassy wives and other women from foreign countries living in Washington. And she was a vice-president and assistant treasurer of the District League of Republican Women.

In October of that year, after only seven months of the State Committee, Allie's name was entered as a dark-horse candidate for an interim position on the Republican National Committee. To just about everyone's surprise, including her own, she was elected.

In office until the unexpired term she was filling ran out the following May, she buckled down to an ever more arduous schedule of Republican meetings, climaxed by the tumultuous convention in Washington in April for GOP National Committeemen and women from all over the country. On May 3, in the District Republican primaries, she was elected to her own four-year term as GOP National Committeewoman, without opposition.

Neither Allie nor Bill hastened back to Washington after the Republican convention in Chicago in late July had nominated the Richard Nixon-Henry Cabot Lodge ticket. Instead they flew to Utah, Allie to visit her mother, Bill to visit his mother and to ride into the Wasatch Mountains with Ken Garff, Hugh Colton, and Roland Parry for trout and sage hens. After that, almost as if avoiding Washington and the formative days of the November campaign, they spent several weeks in New Hampshire.

On election day they watched the returns on television with the Shipleys, the Evanses, and Bill Jr. and Donna. After dinner Allie left for Republican headquarters in the Sheraton Park, to welcome the Eisenhowers. When it looked as though John F. Kennedy would win, she came home, and the gathering broke up.

Marriott stock had split two-for-one that year. The company had declared a 100 percent stock dividend and had opened 12 new establishments, bringing the unit total to 86 and making it the third largest restaurant chain in America. Annual sales had crested at nearly $55 million, another all-time record.

Yet night after night Bill was unable to sleep. Reaching the top was only half the battle—the easier half. After that came a totally new kind of warfare, the fight to stay there, to outsmart, outwit, and outsell the competition. To do this, the company had to grow. Yet every expansion move opened up another competitive struggle, like opening up another front in warfare. Your flanks grew more exposed, more vulnerable. Your army of employes grew bigger, more mechanized, more impersonal. And the values he'd always believed in and lived by—were they valid in the confusing, turbulent world of the 1960s? Certainly they were to him, if anything, more valid than ever, gyroscopes in the storm. But people on every side, youth in particular, seemed to be questioning them.

The August before the election it suddenly struck him that in spite of all the good financial news, not only did he not have it made, he had a lot of problems—new problems that sometimes seemed to be carrying him right to the brink of the falls. The way he saw it, the company was plunging into debt like a ne'er-do-well crap shooter, and it was Bill Jr.'s hotel division that was responsible. They'd borrowed $2.7 million the previous year for the Philadelphia project, and now he and Milt Barlow, the company's executive vice-president, were saying they needed to borrow another $12 million within 24 months to complete the Dallas hotel and proceed with others they were planning for Boston and Atlanta.

He had never foreseen top management personnel problems, yet they certainly existed. The company now was so big he couldn't possibly run it himself, the way he wanted to. "Make today as perfect as I can and tomorrow will take care of itself and yesterday will be another memorable event," he'd written in his diary as a goal to strive for. Was his drive for perfection a weakness, a subtle form of sin? He would never see it that way. Never quite to suceed in perfection was only to be human, a little lower than the angels, but to *strive* for it was the Christian imperative; the sinning lay in the falling-short. And this was happening too often, in too many places.

There was a period when these problems depressed his usually buoyant and optimistic nature and made him short-tempered, hard to get along with, super-critical. He told Paul that he was too careless and inefficient to make a good executive. He lashed out at Woody for failing to tighten up the operation of the Hot Shoppes division. He knew that Milt Barlow ached to succeed him as president; Milt was certainly an asset to the company, but Bill's deepest feeling about him was that he lacked the warmth and empathy that an inspiring leader must have. The successful leader must be a people's man, not just a financier. But who else was there to take over? Bill Jr., the only real leader in sight, was still too inexperienced, too unseasoned.

Right after the inauguration Bill and Allie left on a trip around the world via New Zealand, where they would pick up Dick on his release from missionary service, Southeast Asia, Hong Kong, Japan, Greece, Italy, France, and England. Mark Evans drove them across the snow-covered countryside to Friendship Airport and their plane for Salt Lake City. That night they dined at Hotel Utah with Allie's mother, the Coltons, and Donna's parents, Royal and Maxine Garff. The next day they visited their mothers.

Bill would often remember trying to learn to ride a surfboard at Waikiki, how humid it was in Hawaii, how thin Dick looked when he met their plane at Auckland, how hard it was to find lamb stew in New Zealand where they had all those sheep, the lights on the hills of Hong Kong, the Emperor's Palace in Tokyo, the Taj Mahal, the Parthenon, and, of course, the thrilling changing of the guard at Buckingham Palace.

But in all their travels he never saw anything to match the loveliness of the spring at the farm that April, when they got back: the greenness of the meadow grass along Apache Ridge, the breathtaking glory of the dogwoods, the cornflower blue of the sky that arched above Big Horn. Being back there again filled him with a peace he never knew anywhere else except maybe in the high country of his childhood. Travel was a wonderful thing. But no matter how many oceans he crossed, his home and heart were here, on the familiar trails, under his native sky.

Wednesday, July 12, was to be the opening of the Marriott Motor Hotel in Philadelphia, at City Line and Monument Road, hard by the Schuylkill Expressway and Fairmont Park—300 rooms, the Kona Kai, a Polynesian specialty restaurant, a Sirloin and Saddle, an Olympic-sized swimming pool, parking for 500 cars. Allie and Bill drove up from Washington Tuesday morning to help Bill Jr. with preparations for the grand opening ceremonies. They found the hotel "beautiful," as Bill put it, "but a real mess." Painters, electricians, carpet-layers, and half a dozen other work crews were racing frantically through last-minute installations. Trucks pulled up with deadline deliveries of entire inventories of glassware and crockery, kitchen utensils and curtains, bed linens and floral arrangements.

One room, at least, the Sirloin and Saddle restaurant, was finished. A little before noon they sat down and ordered lunch. Moments later Allie was called to the telephone. It was long distance: Max Dean, manager of the Hotel Utah. The maid had found Mother Smoot lying across the bed in her suite, dead of an apparent heart attack. It had been sudden and swift; there were no signs of struggle or suffering.

When she returned to the table, Allie was quiet, in control, not yet ready for the grief, the heartbreaking ordeal of acceptance that would come before the day was over. She had talked with her mother only the night before, and she had seemed very happy. She looked forward eagerly to leaving at the end of the week for Washington to spend the summer with Bill and Allie and her great-grandchildren.

"It was a blessing that she never got old," Bill said. "She was still young and beautiful. She was a queen in every respect."

Bill put in a telephone call to Salt Lake City, to Royal Garff, Donna's father, and then to their old friend, Harold B. Lee of the Council of the Twelve Apostles, and asked them to help make funeral arrangements. He and Allie and Dick would get an early flight out of Philadelphia the next morning. Bill Jr. would stay to see the opening through; there was no one to take his place.

The big home at 4500 Garfield Street was filled with a thousand things that recalled Mother Smoot to Allie and Bill, things she had given to them when she and Senator Smoot moved away from the house and back to Salt Lake City. Not only these material things, but ever so much more poignant, the lingering echo of her voice, her remembered laughter, the warmth, the love with which she invested every room.

Little by little Bill and Allie were comforted, as we all are in our own ways, by the words of a hymn, the sound of the sea, a glimpse of stars, the clasp of a hand, a baby's smile, a look of love—and finally their faces and lives turned forward again with the spirit and mood of that Christmas season, the jingle-bells excitement and eagerness of their grandchildren, the casual references of Dick, home for the holidays, to a girl in his junior class at the University of Utah. Perhaps they'd met her? Nancy Peery? A blonde, cute, real pretty, in fact, and sang in the university choir? Did they know her folks, the Taylor Peerys, of Palo Alto? Did they ever notice how many college kids were getting married these days, while they were still in college?

Mrs. Peery announced the engagement in January at

a luncheon in the Hotel Utah Sky Room, and they were married two months later in the Salt Lake Temple. Bill and Allie had flown up from Camelback a few days before and had taken everyone out to Millcreek Canyon for a wedding breakfast at Log Haven restaurant. After the wedding the families all flew to San Francisco for the wedding reception and dance at the Menlo Club, near Palo Alto. Then, amid showers of rice and a clattering of tin cans strung out from their rear bumper, the newlyweds wheeled down the drive, Camelback-bound on their honeymoon. They would be back on the campus at Salt Lake City in time for the opening of spring term. (The next summer Dick and Nancy would both graduate from the U., Dick receiving honors in business, and Nancy receiving a bachelor of science degree in elementary education. With the permission of President A. Ray Olpin, Bill, who offered the invocation at the commencement, would be allowed to hand them their certificates.)

In the months that followed, Bill was busier than at any period he could remember. It was an eventful year, 1962 was, blasting off to a thrilling start when Colonel John H. Glenn Jr. completed three orbits of the earth in spacecraft *Friendship 7* that February (Glenn's wife and children watched his televised Bahama splashdown in a second-floor suite at the Key Bridge Marriott, still known as the "Glenn Suite"). Two activities, next to family and church, would pretty much dominate Bill's life, and one of them would be a developing interest in politics. Allie's participation—in 1963 she would be named treasurer of the Republican national convention—would involve him, vicariously, on the fringes of national party affairs; but it was his belief in his old and good friend George Romney that got him to caring more about elections than he ever thought he could.

Twice in his lifetime Bill would be close to an

American and a Mormon in the running for the Presidency of the United States, and both times it would be George. As president of American Motors, George had gained national press notices by preaching the gospel of his economy compact car, the Rambler. He took the company from the brink of bankruptcy to the point, two years later, where it couldn't turn out Ramblers fast enough to keep up with the demand.

There followed the usual journalistic accolades to success: a full-length article in *Saturday Evening Post*, a *Time* cover story, ten pages of text and pictures in *Life*. The whole country knew George as a Bible-quoting advocate of clean living who got up at five every morning, didn't drink or smoke, set an alarm wrist watch before speaking so he wouldn't talk too long, and brought to bear on every decision he made a go-for-broke belief in himself. "You've got to have confidence, and enough of it," he always said, "to bet every last dollar on yourself."

Two weeks before Glenn's historic space flight, George came under Republican party pressure in Michigan to run for governor the next November. Bill flew to Detroit for the American Motors board meeting and spent the night at the Romneys' Swiss-chalet home in Bloomfield Hills. He woke at seven the next morning to find that Walter Cronkite had already been there for an hour, interviewing George ("Slow down, George. You're walking too fast!") on his mile-and-a-half morning hike. Everyone had breakfast afterward except George, who was fasting for three days in order to reach his decision with clear mind and spirit.

The next day George made the front page of newspapers all over the country. He had reached a decision after seeking guidance "beyond that of man." He was asking for a leave of absence as president and chairman of American Motors in order to run for office. He was certain that he would win and be the next governor of Michigan.

"He's a great guy. Some day, he may be President of the United States," Bill said when he and Allie heard the news that evening. They knew he'd be needing help. They sent him $12,000 for his campaign, and that May Bill agreed to help head up fund-raising for the Romney campaign in the District of Columbia.

They all backed a winner, a Republican who, paradoxically, seldom permitted the word "Republican" to appear in his campaign literature because he believed that "issues are more important than parties and candidates. Principles are more important than men." While former Vice President Nixon, in California, was losing disastrously to the incumbent Democrat, Romney, in Michigan, was defeating the incumbent Democrat by some 70,000 votes. No other Republican had been elected governor of Michigan since 1948.

Ironically, it was this victory that for a few hours in June 1964 made Romney a front-running candidate for the Republican nomination for President, and that, at the same time, made it impossible for him to accept the position of leadership that popularity and party politics had thrust upon him.

For most of 1963, most Republicans who would ordinarily have sought the nomination were holding back; why enter an election that President Kennedy was sure to win? And George Romney had still another constraint: he had promised the people of Michigan that if elected governor, he would run for a second term in 1964.

As it did so many lives and destinies around the world, the assassination of President Kennedy rearranged within the space of a few hours the entire political scene in the United States. In due time, Republican candidates began to press forward: Senator Barry M. Goldwater of Arizona; Henry Cabot Lodge, ambassador to Vietnam; Governor Nelson Rockefeller of New York; Governor William W. Scranton of Pennsylvania. As for Romney, he swore that he wasn't a candidate. But he told a National Press Club luncheon meeting in his honor, in Washington, that if his party drafted him, he would respond "like every other concerned American." That is, he would accept.

In the spring primaries of '64 Lodge won in New Hampshire and Rockefeller won in Oregon, but Goldwater won the big one, in California, and emerged the leading contender for the nomination. With the GOP convention in San Francisco only a month off, a choice of some kind had to be made at the Governors' Conference in Cleveland the second week in June. The conference had hardly opened before Romney electrified it with an attack on Goldwater conservatism. Scranton, Rockefeller, and Governor James Rhodes of Ohio hailed Romney as the dynamic new leader who would wrest the nomination from Goldwater and lead the party to victory over Lyndon B. Johnson in November. For a hectic thirty-six hours it appeared as if he would indeed take on Goldwater. But, what about his pledge to the people of Michigan? In the end, he had to keep his promise. Leadership of the anti-conservatives fell to Governor Scranton.

At San Francisco, where Allie, as national convention treasurer (the second woman ever to hold the position), arrived with 100 pounds of checkbooks with which to pay $650,000 in convention bills, Senator Goldwater won the nomination on the first ballot.

On election day Bill and Allie flew to Detroit to be with George and Lenore. They met at the Romney-for-Governor headquarters in the Detroit Statler. As they had been two years before, early returns were discouraging. It looked as though Lyndon B. Johnson would not only carry Michigan by a wide margin, but would sweep all other Democratic candidates into office. When it was all over, Goldwater did go down to defeat in Michigan by an overwhelming 1,250,000 votes. But Romney, in the face of all the odds, won by 350,000 votes.

As they left for their hotel suite, Bill shook hands with George and said something he'd been thinking for the past three hours. "George, this makes you the Number One Republican in the country. It's up to you to take the lead and unite the party, and go on to win in '68. You can count on us to help you do it." All over the country many Americans were going to bed thinking the same thing.

Chapter Twenty

The major concern that dominated Bill's life in these years was still, of course, the company—ever challenging, always calling for more than his best, sometimes frustrating, even discouraging, often filling him with a sense of accomplishment few men would ever know.

The problem that had been wearing him down for months was still there: how to control the company's almost runaway growth and at the same time find or develop the quality management it had to have to remain uniquely Marriott. And this was related too, and was now even more pressing: Who could succeed him as president?

Mixed feelings arose. There were days when he doubted his own effectiveness and knew he ought to step aside, whether he had a successor or not. But then the next week he'd be in Philadelphia or Dallas, staying at the Marriott Motor Hotel. The landscaping and the building itself would be so beautiful, and the interiors Allie had helped to design would be so lovely, and there'd be so much cheerful bustle in the lobby and the restaurants, that he'd suddenly experience a deep rush of feeling that could only be called love for this place that his company had created and for the bright, outgoing people who worked there. This feeling, these moments, made him want to hold his job forever.

To begin to come seriously to grips with the management problem, he called Jim Durbin in Las Vegas. Years before, Jim had been assistant manager of the Hotel Utah. His personable manner, attention to detail, and enthusiasm for his work had impressed Bill. Then Jim had left the Utah to work for the Del Webb corporation in Arizona and Nevada. While managing the Pioneer Hotel in Tucson, Arizona, he'd been voted the state's outstanding young businessman of the year. Then he was transferred to Nevada. What would he think about coming to work for Marriott? Bill asked. No rush; take your time and think it over carefully. Meanwhile, he brought in for the restaurant division another bright young executive, G. Michael "Mike" Hostage, from Proctor and Gamble. He also took on Brigadier General H. H. Shaller, U.S.A., retired, as his personal assistant. The general, he thought, had definite management potential.

But he still could not bring himself to turn the presidency over to Milt Barlow. Or, for that matter, to anyone else he could think of. While he racked his brain for a solution, he commissioned a management engineering firm to examine the company's executive structure, and studied its report carefully. Early in November 1963 he reached the only possible solution: he himself would have to take control more firmly than ever. At an executive committee meeting on the sixth he announced his decision with clarity and power. "For much too long," he said, "the top management of this company has been lacking in drive and purpose. It has not been able to agree on matters vital to the interests of the company and stockholders. I've probably been remiss in standing to one side. I've been hoping that some kind of strong, unified management team would emerge from all this. But it hasn't. Consequently, as of now, I'm going to run the company the way it used to be run until we can solve our problem. I'm still president and chief executive officer. Until further notice I intend to exercise those prerogatives." Of the five members of the executive committee, three were Marriotts. This was the way it was going to be.

A month later, almost to the day, a shift occurred. Milt, convinced at last that he'd never be president, told Bill that he'd like to leave the company. He'd stay on a year, even more, until some of the management problems were settled, but then he'd like to devote more time to his own affairs. Bill, saddened but at the same time convinced it would be for the best, said he'd take it up with the board.

He could never tell when he started thinking about Bill Jr. as president. Thirty-one years old, a wonderful boy, but just a kid, really (what had *he* known at thirty-one?), long on fancy business school ideas, short on practical Hot Shoppe know-how. He couldn't see any of his brothers in the president's chair. Bill Jr. as president some day? Of course. It was inevitable. But not now. Not yet.

At its next meeting, the board of directors acceded to Milt's request. He was a capable, talented executive; he had contributed much to the company and was still valuable to its operation, but it would be unfair to let him think he had a future as president. That was Bill Jr.'s job, as soon as he was ready.

"I'll stay on until then," Milt said.

"We'd all appreciate that very much," Bill said.

Don G. Mitchell, president of General Telephone and chairman of the board of the American Management Association, an authority on corporate management procedure, was a new member of the Marriott board. To Bill's astonishment, he spoke up. "Why wait?"

"What do you mean?" Bill asked.

"Why not put him in now—and get organized?"

Three days after Christmas Bill took the first step. He wired Jim Durbin in Las Vegas and offered him $35,000 a year plus a handsome array of collateral benefits to go to work as Bill Jr.'s assistant—and probable successor—as head of the Marriott hotels division. Jim wired back the next day. He'd be there—with bells on.

Shortly after the first of the year Milt handed in his resignation as executive vice-president. In recognition of his continuing value to the corporation he was made vice-chairman of the board and a member of the executive committee until a new vice-president was named. Bill felt as though he had been released from prison. He summed it up in his journal that night, "A great relief for all."

Bill asked Bill Jr. if he thought he was ready to become executive vice-president and chief operations officer of the corporation. He was young for the job, but he had worked through just about every department there was, he'd been head of the hotels division now for five years, and he knew all about the company's financial programs and policies, its real estate and employe-relation policies. But was he ready for the responsibilities, the wear, tear, and stresses of competition? Could he take the physical punishment? Was he ready for all the sacrifices? Did he really *want* them?

Bill Jr. hardly had to answer these questions, and his father knew this as well as he did. Ever since the days when he'd opened up the Salt Lake City Hot Shoppe with the chef at four o'clock in the morning, his whole life had been preparing him to say yes to every one.

There followed a week of intensive brainstorming discussions with Booz, Hamilton management consultant people about the reorganization of the Marriott corporate structure. Bill Jr. enrolled in an American Management Association seminar for corporate presidents to be held in February in Hamilton, New York.

The board meeting at which Bill Jr. would be appointed executive vice-president of Hot Shoppes, Inc., would take place at River Road on Tuesday, January 21. The understanding was that if all went well, he would, as soon as possible, be moved up to the presidency, with Bill remaining on as chairman of the board.

Bill couldn't sleep the night before the meeting. He lay in the dark of the bedroom, thinking. Finally, he got out of bed. Without waking Allie he went downstairs to his study and turned on the tall reading lamp. The desk clock said it was a little after four. He found a pad of paper and a pen and began to write what his mind and heart had to say.

January 20, 1964

Dear Bill:

I am mighty proud of you. Years of preparation, work, and study have shown results.

A leader should have character, be an example in all things. This is his greatest influence. In this you are admirable. You have not taken advantage of your position as my son. You remain humble.

You have proved you can manage people and get them to work for you. You have made a profit—your thinker works. You are developing more patience and understanding with people, more maturity.

It is not often that a father has a son who can step into his shoes and wear them on the basis of his own accomplishments and ability. Being the operating manager of a business on which probably 30,000 people depend for a livelihood is a frightening responsibility, but I have the greatest confidence you will build a team that will insure the continued success of a business that has been born through years of toil and devotion by many wonderful people. I have written down a few guideposts—all born out of my experience and ones I wish I could have followed more closely.

Love and best wishes.
Sincerely,
(signed) Dad

Bill's "guideposts" were written on separate sheets of stationery. There were 15 of them.

1. Keep physically fit, mentally and spiritually strong.
2. Guard your habits—bad ones will destroy you.
3. Pray about every difficult problem.
4. Study and follow professional management principles.

Apply them logically and practically to your organization.

5. People are No. 1—their development, loyalty, interest, team spirit. Develop managers in every area. This is your prime responsibility.

6. Decisions: Men grow making decisions and assuming responsibility for them.
    a. Make crystal clear what decision each manager is responsible for and what decisions you reserve for yourself.
    b. Have all the facts and counsel necessary—then decide and stick to it.

7. Criticism: Don't criticize people but make a fair appraisal of their qualifications with their supervisor only (or someone assigned to do this). Remember, anything you say about someone may (and usually does) get back to them. There are few secrets.

8. See the good in people and try to develop those qualities.

9. Inefficiency: If it cannot be overcome and an employe is obviously incapable of the job, find a job he can do or terminate *now*. Don't wait.

10. Manage your time.
    a. Short conversations—to the point.
    b. Make every minute on the job count.
    c. Work fewer hours—some of us waste half our time.

11. Delegate and hold accountable for results.

12. Details:
    a. Let your staff take care of them.
    b. Save your energy for planning, thinking, working with department heads, promoting new ideas.
    c. Don't do anything someone else can do for you.

13. Ideas and competition:
    a. Ideas keep the business alive.
    b. Know what your competitors are doing and planning.

c. Encourage all management to think about better ways and give suggestions on anything that will improve business.

b. Spend time and money on research and development.

14. Don't try to do an employe's job for him—counsel and suggest.

15. Think objectively and keep a sense of humor. Make the business fun for you and others.

There was no opposition to the change at the top. Bill Jr. had been a vice-president of the company and president of the Marriott Motor Hotels division for six years. During that period division sales had increased tenfold and the division itself had grown from zero to four big motor hotels whose accommodations were bright, modern, of excellent quality, whose rates were by no means cheap, and which, regardless of season, operated at a steady eighty-to-ninety percent of capacity. Another achievement credited largely to his leadership was Marriott's successful invasion of the specialty restaurant field through the Sirloin and Saddles, the Sirloin Inns, the Fairfield Inns, the Kona Kai at the Philadelphia Marriott. With a record like this, his age, going on thirty-two, was not a liability. It was an asset.

The big company news of the summer was Hot Shoppes' annual report for the period ending July 26. Sales had reached another high that year of $84,726,000. Net income after taxes was also up to an all-time high of $3,110,000, representing growth of 68 percent in the last five years. Other figures supported Bill's concern about expansion, his fears that they might be riding a runaway horse: 17 new units opened during the year—three cafeterias, three restaurants, six turnpike and parkway establishments, and five institutional feeding outlets—making 120 units in all. And more were on the way: a 500-

room motor hotel two blocks off Atlanta's Peachtree Street, in process of construction; another big motor hotel about to go up in Saddle Brook, New Jersey, at the intersection of Interstate 80 and the Garden State Parkway; still another almost ready for the groundbreaking in Boston, and three others on the model boards, not to mention a new Hot Shoppe carry-out service that Woody's restaurant division was planning for the family trade.

To keep all this moving ahead, to stay in front of the competition, to hire, train, and indoctrinate the right kind of employes, to watchdog expenses, to plan and build for the future—all this required a diverse, motivated, and loyal cadre of corporate officers and divisional executives, 26 in all, including five Marriotts: Bill, Allie, Bill Jr., Paul, and Woody.

As the summer wore on and Bill watched his son take hold as the hard-working, precociously skillful captain of this team, he saw no reason to wait any longer. Every word he'd written in his January letter to his son was true, and always would be. It was high time that he and Allie got a new president.

The statement that he read at the annual stockholders' meeting that November at the Twin Bridges hotel was brief, to the point, and no surprise to those who'd given any thought to the executive realignment that had taken place in January:

"For nearly four decades I have headed our company's operations, and—with the help of many dedicated, talented people—I have been privileged to see the business grow from a small root beer stand to a major national chain with annual sales which are now approaching the $90 million level.

"I feel it is my responsibility to our shareholders to turn over the operating management of the company to a younger man.

"Our board of directors feels that the outstanding job done by J. Willard Marriott, Jr., both as executive vice-president of Marriott Hot Shoppes and as president of the Marriott Motor Hotel Division, has qualified him to assume the responsibilities of president of the corporation.

"However, I expect to be around for a long time as chairman of the board to assist in every way I can to be helpful to the continued growth and development of our company."

Of the company's total 7,572 stockholders, some four hundred were present—Hot Shoppe employes and housewives, car salesmen and government workers, mail carriers and bank tellers, retired accountants and school teachers, a cross-section of Anytown, U.S.A. The proxies of several thousand of the absent were on the desk of secretary and assistant vice-president Betty Cushwa. There was a move from the floor to adopt the board's recommendation. Then a seconding.

From the podium Bill looked down into the hundreds of upturned faces. Attendants stood here and there in the aisles with portable microphones for those wishing to address the meeting.

"Any discussion?" Bill asked.

The attendants scanned the audience for a lifted hand, or someone rising to his feet. No one moved.

"All in favor raise your right hands."

Every right hand in the audience went up. Some raised both hands. On the platform where the corporate officers sat, everyone stood up. Hands outstretched, Bill and Allie converged on their son—and successor.

The stockholders broke into cheers. It was all in the family. The whole thing was so unbelievable. Such a success story. So corny. So wonderful—so American. It made them feel warm all over. They felt as if they belonged to the family too.

Chapter Twenty-one

The New Year, the new life, the years now of the patriarch, began innocently and peacefully enough at the farm, a beautiful morning of icy sunshine, crackling log fire in the cottage fireplace, a stick-to-your-ribs breakfast with Mark and Lola Evans and their two young daughters, who had spent a quiet New Year's Eve there in the cottage with Bill and Allie.

TV sets on, they watched the Rose Bowl parade from Pasadena all the rest of the morning. About noon a high overcast began drifting eastward over the Shenandoah ridge, and at some time during the first quarter of the football game it began to snow, blowing in from the ridge. Bill got out the toboggan and tied it behind the jeep and pulled the Evans girls, the sound of the engine, crunch of snowtire rubber against the snow, their songs and laughter drifting through the New Year's night.

The next day the Evanses drove back home to Washington and Bill and Allie went for a long walk along the plowed roads, to the duck pond, and then back to the cattle barns, and saw that their manager had everything in good shape for the winter months ahead.

Bill was still nervous about the expansion program—Bill Jr.'s projections called for a steady 15 percent a year—and he lost sleep over the millions of dollars of borrowed money that financed the program. But it seemed to be the new wave in corporate affairs. He tried hard to hold his tongue at executive board meetings, and not to criticize. It went against the grain of principles that he'd founded the business on and governed his life by and built the family name and reputation on, but—what could he do? He had to admire these driving, compulsive young men with their computer analyses and critical paths. They did show an increasing profit every year. The company moved faster, was more efficient, more imaginative, bolder in branching out, tougher and leaner in its marketing, thought bigger, served more millions of Americans. Yet there were times when he felt as though he were standing by hypnotized or dreaming, watching it move closer to the edge of the precipice. He spent less time at the office, tried to stay out of decision-making sessions that Bill Jr. should handle, began to work on problems involving his estate, gravely and conscientiously gave Bill Jr. elder-statesman views in such matters as minimum wage, company-union relationships, corporate tax affairs, real estate transactions, profit-sharing policies, restaurant and motor hotel locations—just as gravely, just as conscientiously as his own father, forty years before, had taught him how to cut sugar beets, how to plant corn, how to mend a corral fence, how to clean a .30-30, how to comfort a lamb that had strayed from its mother.

The shape of things to come seldom announces its presence among us, but later on—much, much later—Bill and Allie, looking back, could see that it was there, latent and masked, in the events of the third week of January.

On Monday the 18th, George and Lenore Romney flew down from Michigan for President Johnson's inaugural. They were Bill and Allie's house guests, staying in the second-floor guest room. The next day they all went to the Governors' Reception at the Statler Hilton. George and Lenore were clearly the most popular couple there. President Johnson himself came by the Michigan state booth to shake their hands. "Pick up the phone, George," he drawled, "just pick up the phone. Call me at the White House—anything you want—any time."

At the National Armory inaugural ball the night of Wednesday, the 20th, the Marriotts and the Romneys shared a box. Allie naturally was prominent as a high-ranking member of the Republican National Committee, but all evening long people crowded up to shake George's hand and congratulate him on his dramatic victory in November. It was clear that most of the Republicans there that night considered him the party's white hope who would lead them to victory in 1968.

Bill was proud of his old friends. "George and Lenore sure are a great couple," he said to Allie. "Everybody loves them—no doubt about that." He couldn't help but dream a little. Four years from now—why not? George was a crowd-pleaser. He was dynamic and energetic. He got things done. He had sound, proven, successful, business-like ideas. Above all, he was a religious man. He believed in God and in the sanctity of the family and in the divine inspiration that guided the writing of the Constitution of the United States. In short, he was the leader that the whole country was crying out for. And then, four years after that, in '72, Bill could see him in a national landslide winning through to a second term.

George and Lenore, in the White House, for eight years? In America nothing was impossible. Look at how far he had come, in this very city. "You know," he said to Allie, "they might just make it."

Other pressures began to build on Bill. In February, between trips to Florida and Puerto Rico, he flew to Salt Lake City for talks with Church officials about the complicated task of securing equal recognition from the armed forces for Mormon chaplains, even though they were lay ministers, and about the Nauvoo restoration project, which, in his opinion, was getting too costly. He left for home worrying about these matters, and saddened by a visit with his mother. It was evident that she was slipping rapidly.

In early June, shortly after a trip to Europe, the

University of Utah awarded him an honorary law degree, and he gave the convocation the next day to graduates of the university's college of business.

Meanwhile, Dick had graduated from Harvard Business School and had joined the company, and would eventually captain the entire fleet of Marriott restaurants. Bill Jr. was moving the company ahead at a clip that took his breath away. The new Junior Hot Shoppe division, Marriott's entry in the highly competitive hamburger-French fries-fried chicken-and-milk-shake field, was off and running at three Washington locations; ten more were scheduled to open this year, and fifteen or twenty next year. The Saddle Brook Marriott Motor Hotel ten minutes from the New Jersey end of the George Washington Bridge opened; work had started on a Houston Marriott near the Astrodome; Mayor Richard J. Daly had broken ground for the 12-story Chicago Marriott at O'Hare Plaza just off Kennedy Expressway, and two days later the company announced plans for a Boston Marriott on the Cambridge side of the Charles River. The annual report for 1966 would show that the company for the first time had shattered the $100-million barrier and then some with sales of nearly $124 million, up 25 percent over the previous year in the largest percentage and dollar gain since it went public in 1953. In a *Washington Post* story Bill Jr. commented amusingly on the phenomenal expansion and growth of the company. "As my father is always saying, he owed $2,000 when he first came to Washington in 1927 as a young man. Now he owes $20,000,000, and that, he says, is progress." Bill always had a good sense of humor, and the rare quality, most always, of being able to enjoy a joke at his own expense. Sometimes he thought this was a pretty good crack and told it on himself with wry good nature. More often, however, he didn't think it was funny at all.

There was a high-level Republican strategy meeting at

the Statler-Hilton in June, which George attended along with Ike (down from Gettysburg), Thomas E. Dewey, Ray Bliss, chairman of the Republican National Committee, and Allie, one of the four vice-chairmen. And then, perhaps the most memorable day of the year was the August day they Gulfstreamed from National Airport to Gettysburg for Ike and Mamie's midsummer lawn party. The top Republican leaders spoke with serious concerns about the Presidential campaign three years in the future, and about how desperately the nation needed a Republican victory. It was too early to be specific about candidates, but after listening to Ike talk, and General Lucius Clay and Dick Nixon and George Romney, everyone there felt that George would be the one to head the ticket. On the way back to Washington, Bill totaled up the pledges of financial support for George's campaign that he'd received during the afternoon. Including his own, they came to more than $60,000.

Almost a year to the day from the lawn party in Gettysburg, Cliff Folger flew up from Washington to New Hampshire. He and Bill went for a walk under the lakeside pines, Bill showing Cliff the trails that he'd cut and cleaned out. They had a good dinner with Allie and sat on the porch in the cool of the evening and talked, mostly about George. Even though the convention was still two years away, and even though George was running in the fall for a third term as governor of Michigan, the pace was picking up. In March George had come down to go with Bill to the Gerald Ford reception at the Capitol Hill Club and to speak to the Young Republicans. And then in June, a week before he and Lenore came down again for the party Allie gave at Garfield Street for Ray Bliss and Senator Dirksen and other Republican VIP's, George had appeared coast-to-coast on TV, on *Face the Nation,* and had made a strong statement against President Johnson's

Vietnam policies. The following Sunday there had been the long *New York Times* story that said George not only *looked* like a Republican Presidential candidate, he was beginning to *act* like one. It said he was far out in front of others new to the national scene—Charles Percy of Illinois, for example, and Mark Hatfield of Oregon. Of course he had to watch for the conservative GOP candidates, such as Ronald Reagan or Richard Nixon, but his friends were saying that George couldn't lose.

There was an illustrated, eight-page profile of George in the September 5, 1966, issue of *U.S. News & World Report.* By a twist of fate that hindsight would render ironic, this issue carried two main cover lines. The first read, "General Greene Tells the Story of the Vietnam War—Interview with Commandant, Marine Corps." Bordering the lines was a photograph of the handsome, haunted-looking, 58-year-old General Wallace M. Greene, who said in his interview that "tremendous progress" had been made in the Vietnam war in the last seven months, "progress which to me augurs of a definite victory." Below that cover line was George's: "Romney—Republican Hopeful for '68?—Profile of a Candidate." Next to this, balancing off General Greene's picture above, was an almost straight-ahead portrait photograph of George, now 59, with graying hair and a clean-cut, open, unsophisticated, challenging face. The text ranged far and wide across George's life and career. It was scrupulously objective, saying, in effect, that here was an exciting, dynamic, successful man who was leading Richard Nixon as the Republican choice for the nomination and who might be the next President. Bill liked the quotes of his own that the authors used, describing him as "The Governor's friend and fellow Mormon—J. Willard Marriott, millionaire owner of a motel and restaurant chain." Bill was quoted as saying, "George is a very religious man, but not sanctimonious. I don't know of anyone who has more integrity, decency, and honesty than George Romney. He's a doer, a good manager, an executive. That's what we need in government."

On November 8, election day in many parts of the country, George was elected to a third term as governor of Michigan by more than 500,000 votes, and pulled a Republican U.S. Senator and five Republican Congressmen into office with him. It was the big win that the king-makers had been hoping for.

Now that Bill was nationally identified with George, his phone, both at home and at the office, rang incessantly with calls from all over the country. And the pace picked up still more speed.

At a meeting at Twin Bridges, George made it official: Len Hall, the former Republican national chairman, was to be the over-all manager of the Romney campaign. The general policy committee was to consist of Len, Cliff Folger, Max Fisher, Bill, and Robert J. "Jack" McIntosh of Port Huron, Michigan, who would be national manager of operations. The finance committee produced a list of well-to-do Republicans who quite possibly could be counted on to contribute $25,000 each toward the Romney campaign chest. The finance committee called them "Early Christians." George's skull sessions, which took place at Twin Bridges and at Garfield Street, where he and Lenore were staying, were long and tough, with heavy emphasis on foreign affairs.

The Romneys and the Marriotts flew to Puerto Rico for Thanksgiving at the Dorado Beach Hotel. George was national news now. Everywhere they went newsmen pinned him down for planeside interviews. Smiling, frosty blue eyes appraising the questioner, radiating confidence, he lashed out at President Johnson's "Great Society" program, excessive concentration of government power in Washington, excessive federal control over agriculture. He wanted to see the people back in control of the economy. He wanted to see an end to the moral decay that beset the nation. He wanted to see Americans everywhere put religion back into their lives and return to the wholesome values of family life. He felt that for the nation this was the bridge over the troubled waters and perhaps our only hope. Bill felt that way, too.

Nelson Rockefeller had just been reelected to a third term as governor of New York. He and Happy happened to fly down for Thanksgiving in Puerto Rico, too, and were also staying at Dorado Beach, in his brother Laurence's home. On Monday, November 21, the Marriotts, the Romneys, and the Rockefellers lunched together. Then George and Governor Rockefeller held a joint television news conference, with George doing most of the talking.

Both *Time* and *Newsweek* that week carried cover pictures of the front-running candidates for the Republican nomination. On both covers George's picture was at the top. The others were all ranged below: Rockefeller, Reagan, Percy, Hatfield, and Senator Edward Brooke of Massachusetts. They called this meeting between George and Rockefeller "The Dorado Summit," and did some speculating. Maybe Rocky was thinking of backing off from George. George was in trouble with Goldwater and his conservative wing, because he had refused to support Goldwater against LBJ in '64. This still powerful element in the party was said to favor none of the front five, but, instead, Richard Nixon. Moreover, George's weaknesses were beginning to show: a lot of voters were beginning to find his "holier-than-thou" image hard to take, and they couldn't tell where he really stood on Vietnam and other key foreign affairs issues.

Nevertheless, when they left San Juan the Saturday after Thanksgiving, George and Bill took with them all they could have asked for: Governor Rockefeller's promise of support in money and personnel, and delivery to Romney of New York convention delegates. George already had Michigan's delegates wrapped up. Senator Hugh Scott and Governor William Scranton had promised him Pennsylvania's. Things were looking good for Miami in '68. Late November Harris and Gallup polls had George comfortably out in front, endorsed by 54 percent of the voters as against President Johnson's 46 percent.

For a while, as Christmas approached, Bill had to bear down on business. Bill Jr.'s expansion program now involved a capital outlay over the next five years of $110 million. Where would it all end? Right now they were spending $1.5 million for the St. Louis airport site and another $1 million for the Charles River site in Boston, and on December 14, his mother's 98th birthday, a really major deal went through whereby Marriott took over the Robert C. Wian Enterprises of Los Angeles, which owned 23 Big Boy fast food restaurants in Southern California and controlled the franchise operation of more than 500 others all over the country. Included in the package was Big Boy Properties, a real estate firm owning several other restaurants. Total sales and franchise income, about $15.2 million a year. The price was slightly under $9 million, paid in Marriott Corporation stock.

Two days after Christmas Bill and Allie flew to New York for an all-day policy meeting with George. Len Hall, Cliff Folger, Max Fisher, and Jack McIntosh were there, and three others in from Detroit: Dr. Walter DeVries, George's executive assistant; Richard Van Dusen, a lawyer who had served as George's legal adviser, and William Seidman, a partner in a Detroit accounting firm. After a day-long discussion, they reached a major strategy decision to take the next step toward a formal declaration.

George talked to the Associated Press reporter from the telephone in the bedroom of the suite. Yes, he had called this meeting of his close friends and advisers to ask their help in reaching a decision about his candidacy. Well, asked the reporter, what did they decide? George replied, "It will be at least six months before I make up my mind."

Bill got on the phone as the committee spokesman. He told the reporter who was there and identified each one. He repeated what George had said, and then added: "However—and you can quote us being unanimous about this—all of us think Governor Romney will be a candidate. I personally am sure that he will run. I think he has a good chance to win the Republican nomination, and a good chance to be the next President of the United States."

The next day, there were Bill's quotes in the New York *Times,* the Washington *Post,* and just about every other newspaper in the country.

It was, Bill thought, like raising the sluice gate of a beet field irrigation ditch. By the New Year's first weekend, he was on the phone morning, noon, and night. Reporters from Washington and Detroit newspapers kept coming to the house. He had to be calm, cool, friendly, diplomatic, authoritative, walk the taut highwire of their probing questions. This was not his *metier.* The world he knew and loved best was a world of action and achievement, with no time or patience for sly verbal fencing. "I'm in for something," he wrote in his diary. "Big—too big for my time. But I must help a friend and a good and fine couple."

A few days later he and Allie attended a dinner for Washington newspaperwomen. Halfway through the meal Bill felt suddenly ill. Allie drove him home. He went to bed racked with chills and fever.

Still sick and weak, he went to the office the following morning but drove home before lunch and went to bed.

Two hours later, he felt a sharp violent pain in his back, between the shoulder blades.

"Allie!" he called.

Allie ran up the winding staircase. She stripped back the bedclothes and massaged his back where it hurt. She called their family physician. It sounded like indigestion, he said; he'd stop by on his way home from work. When he examined Bill a little after five, he said that Bill's blood pressure was high. He gave Bill an injection of Demerol. He gave Allie some nitroglycerine capsules. "If he gets chest pains during the night, give him one of these and wait five minutes. If the pain is still there, give him a second capsule and wait another five minutes. If he needs a third one, give it to him, and call the ambulance."

Bill had a bad night. At 7:30 the next morning Allie called the Bethesda-Chevy Chase rescue squad and then phoned the doctor. He said he'd meet them at Doctors' Hospital. Bill was rushed to the intensive care unit, and within the hour blood and enzyme tests had been taken. The tests left no doubt. Heart attack.

One week in intensive care, the doctor said. Private hospital room for two more weeks. Then Bill could get up and move around the house but just on one floor—not up and down stairs. Of course, any kind of stress was forbidden. No worries. No tensions. Minimum of phone calls, and absolutely none of an upsetting nature. Another attack, and—well, it just might be terminal. In fact, at his age, it probably would be.

Cold air puts a strain on people with a heart condition. As soon as Bill could travel, Allie took him to Miami and the warm sunshine. But he wasn't out of the woods yet, not by a long shot. Mild exercise was good for him, though, so they walked slowly up and down the sidewalk in front of their apartment house every morning and afternoon, and soon he was feeling stronger. They finally returned to the farm after Easter, to the smell of alfalfa and the heart-lifting loveliness of the flowering dogwood. But Bill still felt weak and was too tired even to go trail-riding in the jeep.

Time drifted slowly by, days muted by weariness and weakness and the wonder at being alive at all, like the survivor of a shipwreck rescued far out at sea. The familiar, the everyday, took on a touch of the miraculous: Stephen, Bill Jr. and Donna's little boy, standing proudly at attention before him in his new Cub Scout uniform, a baby colt born at the farm with a white star on its forehead, the reaching, touching, busy, tender little hands of Dick and Nancy's flaxen-haired, blue-eyed girls, Sandra and Julie Anne.

He had a bad time in the spring and in the early part of the summer. And the George Romney situation, of course, would *really* upset him if he let it, but his doctors and Allie and everyone close to him kept telling him that he just had to stand to one side, try to remain aloof. George was still fighting, but it was obvious that his campaign was floundering. His organization seemed riddled with dissension; moreover, it was running out of money and was even closing down its Washington office.

"Why?" Bill asked Allie. "Why do I get so involved and work so hard for my friend when I don't even have the time or strength to go to my own office? Why?" He couldn't understand it. Thank heaven, Bill Jr. was doing such a superb job with the company. At least he didn't have *that* worry on his mind. "I don't know," he'd say. "Maybe the Lord wants George to be President of the United States—and wants me to help him all I can."

Bill was getting stronger all the time, but even so, that July was a strenuous month. On the fifth and sixth they gave two receptions for the Romneys at the Anchorage, their home in New Hampshire, working for weeks ahead of time to get the place in order—windows washed, lawns mowed, flower beds cleared and weeded, new porch awnings installed, tennis court patched and conditioned, the turkeys, hams, lobsters, shrimp, cheeses, breads, and sauces prepared, all kinds of beverages arranged for, and ice and crackers and the thousand and one other things always necessary for parties. The purpose of the receptions was to launch a vital phase of George's campaign, the phase that would climax the following March with the New Hampshire Republican primary.

The first reception took place on the evening of July 5. It started to rain at about five that morning and rained heavily until early afternoon. What with TV camera crews and reporters swarming over the place wanting to interview George and Lenore, Bill and Allie, Cliff Folger and Len Hall and George's PR staff people, and with Allie and the kitchen help trying to prepare the buffet for the reception, it was nerve-wracking chaos most of the day. But it started clearing at about six. By the time all the guests had arrived, New Hampshire political, industrial and educational leaders and their wives, some two hundred fifty in all, the sun came out and Bill and Allie were able to move the party outside.

Friday, the seventh, the Marriotts gave another reception just like the previous one, except that this one was for publishers and editors of New England newspapers and their wives, and was much smaller—about a hundred guests in all. They ate and drank heartily, found George inspiring and Lenore delightful, and said they all had a wonderful time. Maybe George's campaign had been sagging during the spring months, but it looked good now. He was out in front in New Hampshire. All they had to do now was keep him there.

That summer and fall Bill counted heavily on the farm to restore him firmly again to the living. And this it did. "I'm still a country boy at heart, I guess," he told Allie. "The farm, the peace and quiet—they make me live."

And as for the business, well, it was hard to see how it could be doing any better than it was under Bill Jr.'s leadership. He still thought they were expanding too fast and borrowing too much money, but he just had to put a lid on his feelings and live with them. No more policy arguments. No more criticism, just constructive advice—when requested. Doctor's orders. Anyway, how could he complain? At the annual shareholders' meeting just before Thanksgiving, the company would again announce record earnings this year of $146 million plus, up 18 percent over last year, and another record net income of more than $6 million, also up 18 percent over the previous year. Operating units increased from 150 to 206, including 12 new Hot Shoppes Jr.'s; the 22 Big Boy restaurants in Southern California plus the 600 Big Boy franchise units; Bill's favorite hotel, the Camelback Inn, first existing hotel acquired by the company and bought for $3 million late in the summer; a new $10 million central supply and quality control facility called Fairfield Farm Kitchens; and the beginnings of Marriott's international In-Flite service with new flight kitchens in Caracas, Venezuela, St. Croix in the Virgin Islands, and San Juan, Puerto Rico.

Yet, for all the doctors' orders and the good days and the prosperity of the company and his own recovery from the attack at the back of his heart, Bill lived with the Romney campaign heavy on his mind.

The campaign, which had started out so hopefully a year ago, was now in serious trouble and foundering. As far back as the previous May, Bill had gone to Walter Reed Hospital to see President Eisenhower, still one of the Republican king-makers. Ike had aged poignantly since Bill had seen him last, but his smile was as magnetic and his mind as keen as ever. "I like George Romney," he had said. "He's a good executive. But Vietnam has hurt him."

And again, in August, just a few weeks after the receptions in New Hampshire, Bill paid another visit to Ike at Walter Reed. Ike hadn't eaten anything solid in five days and looked frail and weak. But he liked Bill's company, and liked to talk with Bill about his Gettysburg farm and his black Angus cattle and the golf at Palm Springs. Only one reference to politics. "I think," Ike said, "that the Republican candidate will be Nixon."

In one vital respect, George's critics were right: on the Vietnam question, the burning issue of the day, he was fuzzy, ambiguous. Most Americans were either hawks or doves—for the war or against it; believed in it or were outraged by it. George's position, someone said accurately, represented "a guarded endorsement of U.S. involvement." It just wasn't good enough. In early April, with 470,000 U.S. troops fighting in Vietnam and General William C. Westmoreland, the U.S. commander, asking for 210,000 more, George made a speech in Hartford, Connecticut, the first major policy speech on Southeast Asia of his undeclared candidacy for Republican nomination for President. It was intended to set the record straight on how he felt about Vietnam. First, he said, it was "unthinkable" that the U.S. withdraw from Vietnam. Our military effort must succeed. We don't want "massive escalation," however; what we do want is to provide a military shield for South Vietnam, and to continue negotiations for "peace with amnesty."

Bill, when he read about it the next day in the Washington *Post,* was distressed and unhappy. "Peace with amnesty?" What did that mean? The speech was obviously a patchwork compromise between the hawkishness of George's old-hand political advisers and the doveishness of his young Michigan speechwriters. Democrats, on the other hand, were delighted. It was just what they'd been saying all along. In fact, George Christian, President Johnson's press secretary, issued a statement saying that the Administration agreed completely with Governor

Romney. "George Romney," he said, "deserves the gratitude of the American people for maintaining our great tradition that politics stops at the water's edge." Bill got on the phone to other members of the Romney policy committee. They agreed: the speech was a disaster. George was listening to too many advisers. Or, more accurately, to the wrong ones.

But George was a fighter. He had loyal people with him and was sure, particularly after the New Hampshire receptions, that he could hammer out something positive on Vietnam and other international questions before the March primaries.

Four months later, on national television, George himself just about tore to shreds his chances for the nomination. He said that while on a tour to Southeast Asia with nine other governors in 1965, he had been "brainwashed" by American generals and diplomats into believing that the United States had to fight in Vietnam.

The way it happened was that on the last day of August, George taped a question-and-answer show with Lou Gordon, a Detroit news commentator. When he came back from Vietnam two years ago, Gordon said, George had declared it "morally right and necessary" for the U.S. to pursue the war in Vietnam. Now, however, he was talking about "peace with amnesty." The two statements didn't add up. How about that, Governor Romney?

"Well," George replied, "I just had the greatest brainwashing that anyone can get when you go over to Vietnam—not only by the generals, but also by the diplomatic corps over there, and they do a very thorough job."

Since then, he continued, he'd given further study to the Vietnam situation. "I have changed my mind, in that particularly I no longer believe that it was necessary for us to get involved in Vietnam to stop Communist domination of Southeast Asia."

The interview was telecast in Detroit on September 4.

The next day, the New York *Times* carried the story under the headline "Romney Asserts He Underwent 'Brainwashing' On Vietnam Trip." That night on the national networks, the whole country saw a thirty-second news clip of the Gordon telecast. Accurate as the statement might have been, its timing couldn't have been more unfortunate. Democratic National Chairman John M. Bailey said Governor Romney had "insulted the integrity of two dedicated and honorable men"—General Westmoreland and former Ambassador Henry Cabot Lodge, who had been responsible for the briefings. But George wasn't about to take anything back. Instead, he went even further and said the Johnson Administration itself, including Secretary of Defense Robert McNamara, had not been telling the people the truth about the war. And that's what he meant by "brainwashing"—"not the Russian-type brainwashing, but the LBJ-type—the credibility gap, snow jobs, manipulation of the news."

Reactions came thick and fast. Former Ambassador Lodge said he'd never brainwashed anybody in his life. Secretary McNamara said he doubted that George could recognize the truth when he heard or saw it. The Detroit *News,* which had always supported George as governor of Michigan, advised him to withdraw from the campaign and support Governor Rockefeller as the Republican nominee. On top of these and others, the interesting comment of the Nixon-for-President committee: Campaign chairman Henry Bellmon called a news conference at the Washington Hilton and said George Romney had shown "damaging weakness" as a candidate for the Presidency. He was obviously unable to cope with top foreign policy questions. As one political writer noted, Democrats and Nixon Republicans alike were delighted that George Romney seemed to have destroyed himself with a single phrase.

Nevertheless, standing by his guns, still convinced

that he could win and with the dogged support of Governor Rockefeller and other Republican moderates, George, at a jam-packed press conference in Detroit on November 18, formally declared himself a candidate and announced that he would enter the New Hampshire and Wisconsin primaries. He pledged the nation that when elected, he and the victorious Republican party would lead the country "back to morality and out of the Asian land war in which we've become mired."

Bill passed up a campaign committee meeting in Detroit on the first of November. He explained to Allie, "I just don't feel like going up there and getting into an argument with George's staff people there in his Detroit headquarters." He'd gone to the farm instead. Then, just before Thanksgiving, he had lunch with Len Hall in Washington. In spite of George's optimism, Len agreed that things didn't look too promising. "Vietnam," he said, "was George's Waterloo." Even so, the king-makers remained loyal and pledged $1 million in their own names to keep the drive going until the New Hampshire primary on March 12. Bill felt bad about it. He knew how much of themselves and how much faith and love of country George and Lenore were putting into the campaign, how much it was costing them in personal and physical stress, what it was doing to their lives. He still believed in George, and always would. It wasn't his fault. You just couldn't run for President of the United States, in those days anyway, with a made-in-Detroit campaign.

In the meantime, Bill had other things on his mind, particularly worries concerning Ellen, his mother. She'd be ninety-nine on December 14. He thought of her out there in the little pink stucco house in Ogden, weak and bedridden, with her sight and hearing fading. Bill had seen her twice this year, the first time in July, right after the Romney receptions. Lying against the pillows in her bedroom, white hair neatly brushed, she looked well, recognized both him and Allie, and seemed contented. But she kept asking where they lived, and was surprised when Bill told her they lived in Washington. The second time had been in the fall, when he'd gone out to Utah alone about the last phases of the chaplain negotiations and some meetings of the Nauvoo Restoration committee. At first his mother didn't recognize him, asking his sister Doris who this stranger was. But then she remembered, and cried for happiness.

It was on Monday, December 11, that things started to go wrong, when Bill called Doris to ask about Ellen. "Mother's failing," Doris said. "She's caught a bad cold. Remember the trouble she was having with her eyesight and hearing when you were here in October? Now she can hardly see or hear at all."

Bill felt exhausted all that week; he had to drive himself to keep going. Then, on the morning of the 20th, Doris called and said that the cold might be developing into pneumonia. She'd called an ambulance to take Ellen to the hospital.

Bill went to the office and tried to work. After lunch he met with Len Hall at Len's office. Len and Cliff Folger and Max Fisher and, of course, Governor Rockefeller were doing everything they could to keep George Romney's campaign alive. But he'd been to Vietnam again, and since his return it was all he could talk about. Meanwhile, Nixon was staying off stage, quietly building support, keeping George "out at the point," as he said, where George would draw the pre-primary heat and fire. Somehow, Bill and Len agreed, they *had* to move George on to less emotional, less divisive subjects.

Bill could never remember whether he was talking or Len was, but without warning a shattering pain hit him in the head and neck like a soft-nosed bullet. Gasping from the shock, he half-rose in his chair, then pitched over.

It was only after two days of oxygen, medication, electronic monitoring, intravenous feeding, and the closest kind of observation that the baffled doctors said Bill seemed out of danger, for the time being, at least, and that Allie could take him home. What had happened? They really didn't know. Whatever it was, it wasn't a heart attack. Bill and Allie were both relieved and disturbed—thankful to be spared another cardiac crisis so soon after last winter, yet, what was this new thing they had to worry about? When would it strike again?

At home, Bill seemed all right for a day or two. Then his head began to ache again, the pain knifing through his brain with every heartbeat. The day after Christmas he was back in the hospital, for three more days of intensive tests. Finally, on the 29th, the doctors reported that the results of the tests—the brain scans, the X rays, the electroencephalograms—all were negative. There was no tumor nor evidence of damage or impairment. Discoloration of the spinal fluid, however, seemed to confirm their suspicion: a burst blood vessel in the brain. Bill, they were quite sure, could recover. But he'd have to follow orders: bed rest for 30 days, complete submission to the long, slow, recuperative process, and a drastic change to a way of life free once and for all from stress and contention.

That was the day, in the hospital in Ogden, that Ellen died. Doris called Allie and finally reached her at the hospital. "She died in her sleep," Doris said. "The doctor said she just wore out." The funeral was to be Wednesday, January 3, in Ogden.

That evening the doctor told Bill. He took the news quietly. It was almost as if he'd known. Sorrow, yes, but gladness too. Dying was not the end. It was, rather, the leaving of a darkened room, a going forth into light, into a new life. He was silent for a while, lying back against his pillows, eyes closed. Then he looked at the doctor. "The funeral—when is it?"

"Wednesday."

"Is there any chance—that I—?"

The doctor shook his head. None at all. It would be a week or more before he could even leave the hospital to go home, a few miles away. "Everybody will understand that you were very ill and could not come," the doctor said. He leaned forward and placed his hand on Bill's. "And your mother, she too will understand."

As the New Year began, Bill felt a little better. Those ten days in the hospital had been a dream, a hazy montage of voices and visions, panic and pain, light and darkness, the feeling of helplessness, awareness of warmth and caring in the touch of loving hands, surrender to the something inside that trusted them with his life. Those days had changed his whole world. In his moments of strength, he talked with Allie, with the doctor, with his sons. He began the process of adjustment to new realities. Obviously, as far as George was concerned, he could do no more. Even if George should win in New Hampshire and go on, in July, to win the Republican nomination and run for the Presidency in November, even if all this happened, it was unlikely that Bill could get involved. That's how necessary rest and harmony were to his health.

He went home in an ambulance on January 6 and three days later got out of bed for the first time. On the morning of February 2 he and Allie flew to Phoenix, to the sun, the dry healing warmth, and the desert country he had been yearning for.

All the while Bill had been in the hospital and up until the last week in January, Allie had made entries in his diary, though there were some days when the pages were blank. Now Bill was back to keeping the diary, and for the day of their arrival in Arizona even his terse entry managed to convey his delight at being there, his resilient optimism, the spirit of thanksgiving that he never failed to express when he was back in the outdoors. "The inn is really beautiful," he wrote. "The nicest spot on earth . . . ideal, sunny. . . ."

It did indeed seem to be a place where life and time stood still, still as the baking desert air, still as the statuesque saguaro, still as the distant Salt River Mountains, low and mirage-like against the horizon.

Then page after page of Bill's journal went blank. Back in New Hampshire, George Romney campaigned from village to village, stood smiling and shaking hands at mill gates in the snow as workers came thronging off their shifts, made speech after speech at town meetings and on icy street corners in a stouthearted fight against Nixon. In the last days of February when the polls told him the struggle was hopeless, he withdrew his name from the primary ballot. No entry in Bill's diary told the story. Two weeks later, when Nixon won overwhelmingly in New Hampshire, the diary pages remained as empty as the desert sky.

Chapter Twenty-two

For months after their arrival home in Washington, the air of the River Road headquarters was filled with expansion news. A Roy Rogers Western Roast Beef Sandwich Shoppe, first of a new type of instantly successful Marriott restaurant venture, opened in Falls Church, Virginia. Marriott stock split two for one for the third time in less than eight years.

In August, the Marriott Corporation went on the Big Board of the New York Stock Exchange with the ticket symbol "MHS" and selling at $32\frac{3}{4}$. In October Marriott opened and expanded Camelback Inn as a luxury condominium resort. A month later the company opened its new 350-room Houston Marriott and announced at the annual stockholders' meeting plans to construct its biggest hotel yet, the 1020-room, $24-million Marriott next door to the Los Angeles International Airport.

Once in a while, when he stopped to think of how fast and how far Bill Jr. was moving with the company, it all but took Bill's breath away. On his 68th birthday, in fact, he and Bill Jr. locked horns over the company's expansion policy and program. On that very day the dynamic young president had signed the papers for the Los Angeles Marriott investment and for a $28-million, 42-story convention motel in New Orleans. At the same time, the company was enlarging six of its existing hotels, had six more under construction—and its real estate teams were out looking for still more locations!

Bill couldn't sleep that night. He knew Bill Jr. and the management staff he'd built up were bright, top-notch people. Certainly the company's steady growth of 15-20 percent every year, year in and year out, proved it. But he couldn't help it. He'd never forget how just about every big hotel in the country went bankrupt in the depression.

Maybe, he thought, it was time for him really to step aside, to get out of his son's way. He was too old to change now, too old to travel at his son's speed. Bill Jr. was a jet-propelled 707, while he was an old-time DC-3, flying too low and too slow to be of much use today.

Yet at the same time, he couldn't help remembering the time at the annual meetings, at church meetings, at awards banquets in Washington and New York, when pride in Bill's and Dick's achievements had made his heart sing. True, they didn't always agree, but when was that so strange, for fathers and sons? He knew they'd disagree again in days to come. But he knew, too, that they'd make his heart sing again.

In late October, anticipating a Nixon-Agnew victory in the November elections, Cliff Folger brought Bill a message from national Republican leaders. Because of his standing in the Washington community, his administrative experience, his generous contributions to the Romney and Nixon campaigns, and the party leadership contributed by Allie as vice-chairman of the Republican National Committee and treasurer of the national convention, they were hoping that Bill would serve as chairman of the 1969 inauguration.

Bill and Allie talked it over, lived and slept with it—and couldn't refuse. In mid-November, eight days after Nixon defeated Senator Hubert Humphrey for the Presidency, the White House announced Bill's appointment as chairman of the parade, receptions, balls, concerts, and other festivities marking the inauguration of the 37th President of the United States on Monday, January 20, 1969. Allie was appointed special assistant to Bill, a vice-chairman of the general committee, and chairman of the Distinguished Ladies reception.

Happily Bill plunged into nine weeks of whirlwind preparations that swept him and Allie far from the round of corporate affairs; assembling and directing from inauguration headquarters in the Pension Building an army of staff personnel, committee members, and volunteer workers that finally numbered more than 3500; supervising arrangements for inaugural concerts by the Mormon Tabernacle Choir and the National Symphony Orchestra; helping Mark Evans, the inaugural ball chairman, with setting up the six balls and hiring the nine name bands and 25 to 30 smaller, local groups that would provide music; holding press conferences; debating liability contracts with lawyers; dashing all over Washington to give talks, appear on television, be interviewed on radio; planning the seven-division parade that he and Allie would lead down Pennsylvania Avenue and that he swore would last no longer than two-and-a-half hours. (He kept his word—and won the appreciation of the crowds that lined the broad thoroughfare as the floats, bands, and marching units moved west toward the White House reviewing stand.)

Every day and night in the week preceding the inauguration seemed progressively swifter—through Allie's Distinguished Ladies reception on Saturday, the concerts and the governors' reception on Sunday, and then Monday, the climactic inauguration day itself: the President's prayer breakfast, the impressive swearing-in ceremony at the Capitol's east portico, the top-down convertible ride with Allie at the head of the inaugural parade, and finally with Mark and Lola Evans and the President's official party to the gay, noisy, jam-packed inaugural balls—all six of them—where an estimated 50,000 danced the whole night through.

Financially, the inauguration was the most expensive in history; its bills totaled well over $2 million as compared to the $1.6 million spent on President Johnson's inauguration. On the other hand, it cleared almost $1 million, more than an inauguration ever had. Much of this Bill and his committee were able to turn over to the District of Columbia for the improvement of schools and playgrounds and for other civic welfare projects. A portion of what was left paid for permanent night-lighting fixtures for the exterior of the White House. Once more, Bill had brought home honors, acclaim, and success.

Bill could remember when the big events in his and Allie's lives were the opening of a Hot Shoppe, the winning of a restaurant association award, Bill Jr.'s or Dick's promotion from one grade to the next in June, a good crop of corn at the farm. Now he realized that the highlights were beginning to be of quite a different order. Then it had been mostly doing, achieving. Now it was mostly giving.

No matter how little or how much he earned, he had, like most Mormons, paid tithing to his church all his life: 10 percent or more, before taxes. Over the years he'd given far more than a tenth of his waking hours and abilities in church work, and money in addition to the tithe in gifts to mission programs, the Nauvoo Restoration project, and building of chapels and general church projects.

Now in the April after the inauguration, President James Fletcher of the University of Utah announced the biggest single gift Bill had ever offered and the largest single contribution the university had ever received: $1 million in Marriott stock to complete the financing of the university's huge new $7 million library. Constructed of concrete and glass on five levels, surrounded by plazas and terraces and with a capacity of 1.5 million books, it had been opened in 1968 and was clearly one of the most distinguished and best equipped university libraries in the nation. In appreciation, President Fletcher said, it would be named "the J. Willard Marriott Library."

On Friday, the day before Utah's summer commencement, Bill inspected every floor and corner of the building with President Fletcher. The naming and the dedication ceremony took place at 5:30 o'clock Saturday afternoon, August 16, on the library's wide east plaza. It was a gathering of several hundred state, city, and university officials, faculty members, the Marriott family and friends. President Fletcher spoke, as did Gifford Price, a former student body president, and Elder Richard L. Evans of the Council of the Twelve Apostles, member of the Utah State Board of Higher Education, and known throughout the nation as the author and deliverer of "The Spoken Word" on the weekly radio concerts of the Mormon Tabernacle Choir.

"We look back," said Elder Evans, "to the making of a man: to hard work and the early responsibilities and realities of a sheep and cattle ranch; the missionary; the salesman; college student; and to the time, forty-two years ago, when, with an unreliable Model T, and a very reliable and beautiful bride, he set out for Washington. . . . It is wonderful to live in a land where a boy from nowhere, with nothing, can go anywhere. . . ."

In brief remarks, standing against the background of the campus and university buildings in the dark robes of his doctorate, Bill told what an honor it was to make a contribution to the university that he, his wife, his two sons, and their wives had attended. "It's a magnificent library. I can't imagine a better place to leave my name for my children, and for their children."

Amid a planting of young evergreen ground cover there stood a massive slab of travertine marble eleven feet long and four feet high, now covered with crimson drapery. At a word from President Fletcher, Bill Jr. and Dick lifted it back and to one side to reveal the gold-leaf inscription, "J. Willard Marriott Library."

In the waning light of the westering sun the ceremony

was over. From the north and northwest, the Wasatch ridges looked down, as they had on Brigham Young and his tattered band of pioneer saints a hundred and twenty years before. Then they looked down on a desert wasteland. Now they looked down on the broad streets of a thriving city, and on a university within the city, and on a library, a shining temple of knowledge, that bore the name of the boy from nowhere.

The spring of 1970 was a turbulent and tragic time in Washington and indeed across the nation, a time cruelly at odds with cherry blossoms and bland April air. Throughout America anti-war demonstrations erupted, often violently, with bloody confrontations between Far Right extremists and long-haired revolutionaries of the New Left. The trouble, turmoil, confusion, and potential for dark tragedy generated a countermovement that, it was hoped, would be nonpartisan—a movement to "honor America" and the principles and ideals for which it stood; a movement to recognize its shortcomings, its unfulfilled promises, but more than that, to unite in regenerated appreciation of what was gloriously right about America.

On May 26, in view of his success with the inauguration, Bill was asked to head a committee to produce a patriotic and religious program in Washington on the approaching Fourth of July. Such an event would give thousands of Americans something they sorely needed—a chance to have a picnic, get together out in the open air, hear inspiring words and music, listen to a band, see some spectacular fireworks, and in general enjoy a wonderful, oldtime Fourth of July celebration.

In Bill's life, much had already happened that year. Dick had been appointed vice-president in charge of Architecture and Construction; Allie was now in the thick of new responsibilities as chairman of the President's Advisory Committee on the Arts for the Kennedy Center; the company was negotiating for the take-over of Bill's favorite New York hotel, the Essex house on Central Park South; the 307-room Crystal City Marriott had opened across the Potomac in Virginia not far from the Twin Bridges, and so had the new Marriott hotel at Dulles International Airport. To cap all this, Dick and Nancy had had their fourth baby, their fourth girl, and they'd named her Mary Alice.

So it was almost with a feeling of relief that Bill accepted the assignment at once and turned his energy and drive to what he did best: organizing, administering, getting people to work together toward a common goal and in a common cause, in this instance all the more challenging and inspiring because the cause, he was convinced, was America—next to God, the highest cause he knew.

Within a matter of days, he'd set up headquarters at 1725 DeSales Street, N.W., had chosen Major General Charles S. O'Malley, Jr., one of his top inaugural aides, as executive director, and had put together a committee whose membership ranged from former Presidents Harry S Truman and Lyndon B. Johnson to Hobart Lewis, from Bob Hope and Billy Graham to AFL-CIO President George Meany, from the NAACP's Roy Wilkins to Coach Vince Lombardi and Golfer Billy Casper.

There followed five hectic weeks of telephoning, press conferences, radio and television interviews, sessions with hard-working members of his sub-committees about scores of details. He managed three days off, the first weekend in June, for a trip to the Weber College commencement exercises in Ogden, to receive from his old school an honorary degree as doctor of humanities.

The day itself, the Fourth, was hot and muggy. Bill and Allie had breakfast, then drove down Foxhall Road and across the Key Bridge to the Crystal City Marriott. There they met Billy Graham and went over the details of the morning's program. At 10:40 they crossed back to the District over Memorial Bridge and wound down to the Lincoln Memorial. Before the seated figure of President Lincoln was the platform for the Armed Forces color guard; below that, the speakers' platform; then the gathering crowds on the grass all the way back to the reflecting pool and down both sides of the long pool to the lawns beyond. In the distance loomed, majestically, the tall thrust of the Washington Monument.

Around the Lincoln Memorial it was a festive, patriotic, family-picnic crowd that had come, some 45,000 strong, not only from the capital itself, but by chartered plane, special trains, and caravans of flag-flying buses and cars from New York and Chicago and Atlanta, and from all the countryside in between, hot and happy thousands who had gathered together to honor America.

Simply and movingly, the program did just that, and united the crowd in what, for the times, was a unique and profoundly touching affirmation of faith in this divided land. Speaking first, Bill welcomed the people. He asked them in coming together to help "rekindle the spirit of patriotism and respect for individual liberties which have made America great." He said, "We want to demonstrate to the world that despite its imperfections, America is still the greatest country on earth . . . 'A land choice above all others.' "

There were cheers and waving of flags when Kate Smith finished singing "God Bless America," and again when Billy Graham rousingly called upon them to "Let the world know that the vast majority of us still proudly sing, 'My country 'tis of thee, sweet land of liberty.' America needs to sing again! America needs to wave the flag again—the flag that belongs to all Americans, black and white, rich and poor, liberal and conservative, Republican and Democrat. . . .

"We have stood tall in America in most areas, but on this Independence Day, I call on Americans to bend low

299

before God and to go to their knees as Washington and Lincoln called us to our knees many years ago. No nation is ever taller than when on its knees. I submit that we can best honor America by rededicating ourselves to God and the American dream. . . ."

Billy Graham's closing words rang out over the reflecting pool like a blast of trumpets: "I say to you today, 'Pursue the vision, reach toward the goal, fulfill the dream—and as you move to do it, never give in. Never give in! Never! Never! Never!' "

The 45,000 rose to their feet in a storm of applause.

Pat Boone, the television star, led the crowd in the singing of "The Star Spangled Banner"; Bishop Fulton J. Sheen delivered the benediction; then a sky-shattering barrage of aerial bombs, one for every state and territory in the Union, crashed high in the sky over the Lincoln Memorial.

That evening, the weather still hot, still muggy, a festive crowd estimated at 450,000 thronged to the grounds of the Washington Monument for a variety review of entertainment that featured Bob Hope as master of ceremonies and a supporting cast of performers that included Jack Benny (and, of course, his violin), Red Skelton, Dinah Shore, Dorothy Lamour, Glen Campbell, the New Christy Minstrels, and others. At the end, the throng rose to its feet to sing "The Battle Hymn of the Republic." The stirring anthem, full of union and strength, carried far down the Mall toward the distant dome-lit Capitol, far out across the Tidal Basin toward the Potomac. The aerial bombs burst in the night and the sky gushed with rocket-fire, and the day that honored America was over.

Moving slowly with the crowd, Bill and Allie found their way to their car and started back along the traffic-clogged drives to the Twin Bridges Hotel and the Chesapeake Room buffet supper for the entertainers and committee members. They could tell from the comments, the laughter, the looks on people's faces, that for most of them it had been a happy day. Those who had come, those who had been there, were proud to be Americans. All over the country, there were millions who felt the same way.

There weren't and never had been half-way measures, compromises, with Bill. He worked as hard as he could, and he played as hard as he worked. If he had something on his mind, he said it. If there was something that needed to be done, he ordered it done or did it himself. "Make today as perfect as I can and tomorrow will take care of itself and yesterday will be another memorable event." That's what he had written in his diary on the New Year's Day of his sixtieth year. Never quite to succeed in making it totally perfect was, of course, to be human, a little lower than the angels, but to strive to do so in the Lord's name was the essence of the Christian life. And if he stopped to look back, which in these years he almost never did, he could survey half a lifetime of yesterdays that, collectively, represented an event most would term not only memorable, but remarkable.

But he never did, and perhaps never would, learn to hold back; he never did, and perhaps never would, admit that he had limits. When he went to New Hampshire "to rest," to get away from the strain of corporate life, he worked, physically at least, harder than ever. Less than three weeks after organizing and seeing the Honor America Day celebration through to the last midnight bomb-burst, he was at the Anchorage swinging an axe, clearing out trails, cutting timber from the big lot Bill Jr. had bought for his new house. "I sweat terribly and overdo," he wrote in his diary. "But I love to work."

Suddenly Bill and Allie seemed to be traveling all the time: to new Marriott hotel openings in Kansas City, in Miami, and in New Orleans; to Jamaica and London,

Madrid and Athens, Cannes and Agadir, always checking on possible hotel sites wherever they went. And they took part in the dedication of the new Mormon visitors' center at Nauvoo, Illinois, and in the ceremonies for the gala premieres at the opening of the Kennedy Center's Eisenhower Theater and Opera House and Concert Hall.

As early as June of 1972 Bill had been asked if he would take on the chairmanship of the inauguration committee again in the event of a Republican victory in November. Bill was a loyal party man, had been from the days of President Hoover and Senator Smoot on down through the Eisenhower years and George Romney's stalwart run for the Presidential nomination.

His relationship with President Nixon was cordial but formal, without the warmth and personal bonds that had naturally developed between Bill and President Eisenhower. So when the invitation to be inaugural chairman again came through, his inclination, as he noted in his diary, was "to quit while I'm ahead." Besides, he'd promised Allie. A few days after the 1969 inauguration, he told her he'd never do *that* again. Even for the President of the United States, it was too much. Half-joking, Allie asked, "Can I have that in writing?" Bill got a sheet of paper and wrote, "To Allie: I promise I'll never run another inauguration. (signed) Bill." Allie folded the note and put it in their wall safe. It was still there.

As the election approached, however, his resolve weakened. It would by no means present the complicated problems in management that the 1969 inauguration had. The random approach that he'd confronted then had struck him as ridiculously amateurish; even before the Pension Building headquarters had been dismantled, he'd allocated $30,000 of inaugural proceeds to the Booz, Allen and Hamilton management-consultant firm in Washington to computer-design a master plan and critical path for the next inauguration down to every last detail, from official license tags to invitation lists, from swearing-in ceremony to ballroom balloons.

Approached a second time toward mid-October by a member of the Cabinet, Bill still backed off. "I'll think it over. I don't want to do it. But if the President insists—"

No one was better qualified. No one could do a better job for his community, his party, his President. This outweighed personal considerations—and, Allie reluctantly agreed, the little note in the safe. A week later Bill was inspecting his new committee headquarters in the Tempo B building—temporary military barracks, in southwest Washington, near Fort McNair. He learned that he had at his disposal 55,000 square feet of freshly painted, well-lighted floor space, a 400-car parking area, and a staff of six coordinators from the White House.

So, once again, he and Allie were plunged into the coordination and supervision of 3500 staff and volunteer workers, and into the production of a $4 million spectacular that would draw people to Washington by the tens of thousands and involve a dozen major events of national interest and import: a Vice President's reception, a two-and-a-half hour "Salute to the States," an American Heritage Festival, three inaugural concerts at Kennedy Center, the swearing-in for the second term of the 37th President of the United States and his Vice President, a one-hour, 143-unit parade down Pennsylvania Avenue, six black-tie inaugural balls, and a White House prayer breakfast—not to mention all kinds of dramatic security measures (such as the President's bullet-proof reviewing stand) to guard against mob or terrorist violence, if it should occur.

For all the intelligent and willing help they had, Bill and Allie found themselves in an exhausting repeat performance of 1969; a day-and-night round of phone calls and committee meetings, press conferences, luncheons, radio and television appearances, arguments over concert orchestras, ball invitations, and free ticket lists, hammering out bartenders' contracts, liability insurance policies, souvenir book and program texts. "As an honorary chairman, Mrs. Marriott, what are you doing for the inauguration?" a Washington reporter asked Allie. "My job," Allie replied firmly, "is to keep the chairman on his feet."

Never stinting himself, never holding back, Bill kept up the destructive pace. It was not only the inauguration. On Friday, December 15, for instance, he was awake at 4:30 A.M. He read in bed, worked out on his Exercycle, and was dressed and downstairs for breakfast at 7:15 with Don G. Mitchell, vice-chairman of the Marriott board. At 8 he and Mitchell were at 5161 River Road for a meeting of Marriott's executive committee, to discuss and vote on spending $250 million on the corporation's newest venture, three "Great America" theme parks, two of them to open in the Bicentennial year of 1976. The committee voted millions more for new hotels and the enlargement of existing ones. After the meeting, Bill went to NBC's Washington studios for the taping of an inaugural program to be broadcast the following Sunday. He went home, had lunch, took a nap, and woke to find that he couldn't speak above a whisper. He worked in his library at home all afternoon, doctored his throat, regained the semblance of a voice, changed into black tie, and took Allie to the Kennedy Center for a dinner honoring Secretary of Transportation John Volpe.

Finally Bill's resistance gave out and he went to bed with a devastating case of flu the day before Christmas; he stayed home, most of the time in bed, right on through the beginning of the New Year. Returning to work long before Allie or anyone else thought he should, he resumed inaugural affairs full-time on January 10. From then on he stayed with them to the end—through the last long days of preparation, through the state receptions and the state concerts, through what the papers called "the massive crush" of the inaugural balls, through the final reception at the White House for the still victory-flushed members of the Republican National Committee.

When it was all over and they'd had a few days of rest, Bill and Allie were glad and proud that they'd played a dominant role in another Presidential inauguration; but at the same time, it would be good to get away from Washington and out to Utah.

On a Friday a month after the Marriott Library dedication at the University of Utah, Bill had stopped off in Salt Lake City on his way home from the coast and had talked with his old friend Ben Lewis, Brigham Young University's executive vice-president. They'd driven down the valley to Provo, a growing mining and farming community of 53,000 forty miles south of Salt Lake City, and strolled the broad walks of the mountain-sheltered BYU campus. Like many American universities, BYU had grown steadily since World War II; its student body now totaled more than 25,000, most of whom were Mormons.

To Bill, always repelled by hippyism, by the "New Left," the "New Morality," and other manifestations of the prevailing American youth culture of the 1960s, the BYU students bustling brightly to and from their classes were an inspiring sight. In accordance with the university's dress code, the men were short-haired, clean-shaven; the girls wore dresses, sweaters and skirts, or *modest* (as the code stressed) pant suits. "Look at these fine young people!" Bill exclaimed. "None of them walking on the grass, all of them on the sidewalks, where they should be, and not a beard or a long-hair in sight. They're a credit to America."

"Yes," Ben agreed, "we're mighty proud of our student body, Bill."

"So am I," Bill said. That afternoon, before he left to

catch his plane to Washington, he pledged more than $1 million toward the big new $8-million student activities center that the university was planning to build along the northern border of the campus.

It turned into quite a structure—a massive, rectangular building with rounded corners, exterior of concrete and buff-colored brick, flat roof, seating capacity of 23,000 (more than that of New York's Madison Square Garden), bigger in area inside than two football fields side by side, the largest on-campus arena in the United States. From the beginning it was called the Marriott Activities Center, a fitting name, said the university steering committee, "not only because he gave a large gift to help make it a reality, but also because—like the life of Mr. Marriott—this building is destined for doing: for serving, for believing, for achieving."

The formal dedication service took place at the center on a late Sunday afternoon, before a filled auditorium. In contrast to the noisy exuberance of the previous night's basketball crowd, a religious mood pervaded the arena as Harold B. Lee, president and world spiritual leader of the Mormon Church, opened the program. There was music by the BYU Philharmonic Orchestra and the university's combined choruses. The university's welcome was extended by BYU's president, Dallin H. Oaks. Marion G. Romney, second counselor to the church's First Presidency, offered the dedicatory prayer. Then Ben Lewis introduced Bill.

"Bill Marriott," he said, "demonstrates that a man can be a religious leader as well as a giant in business. He has attained a reputation as a man of wealth, but he accepts the premise that the earth is the Lord's, and that he is the steward of the things in it for the benefit of mankind."

Bill's response was short and moving. At 73, he stood before the audience of young men and women as one of them, but one of them who had made his mark in the world beyond the mountains and now had come back home to share with them his wealth and the wisdom of his years:

"This is one of my greatest days—to be with the leaders of the Church and the students of BYU. I realize that my contribution to this university is a small one. But I consider the investment I made here to be the best investment I will ever make. . . . You students are building a good Mormon image here. Remember that change is good, if that change lifts us up. Discipline yourselves. Discipline is the greatest thing in the world. Where there is no discipline, there is no character. And without character, there is no progress."

To close the program, the orchestra played and the combined choruses sang three verses of the triumphant Mormon hymn, "The Spirit of God Like a Fire Is Burning." On the fourth and final verse, President Lee and President Oaks, Elder Romney and Ben Lewis, Bill and Allie, and all the 23,000 people there joined in and filled the great hall with hosannas.

The weeks and months that followed passed swiftly, came and went like the day after tomorrow—weeks and months of springtime in Arizona, of the tragic summer of the Watergate hearings and the Watergate trial, of the happier New Hampshire summer and hiking with his grandchildren, tennis with Nancy and Dick, golf at Bald Peak with Bill Jr. and Mark Evans, boat rides on the lake at dusk in the *Dolphin*. Before he and Allie realized it, the many-memoried summer was gone. It was a bright and breezy September, and they were in Los Angeles for the opening of their biggest hotel yet, the Los Angeles Marriott. The smiling, sombreroed *mariachis* played "Guadalajuara!" in the lobby, and the famous guests were beginning to arrive for the opening festivities. In one of the conference rooms, much smaller than the one the employes had gathered in the previous afternoon to listen to the Chairman, Bill, Bill Jr., and Jim Durbin, president of Marriott Hotels, sat at a table on a low dais, facing twenty-five or thirty reporters in a press conference. I had arrived the day before and sat toward the back of the room, taking notes like the others. "What, Mr. Marriott," a reporter from one of the Los Angeles papers asked, "has given you the most satisfaction in life?"

Bill thought for a moment, framing his reply. "Well, I've had many satisfactions in life, and hope to have many more," he began, "but I think that, up until now, anyway, it has been turning over to my two sons the results of all the good things that have happened to their mother and me, since we started out in life together forty-six years ago, and started out in business in Washington . . . to render a good service to people . . . for a good purpose."

And he began recalling for the reporters how it all began—the honeymoon trip in the old Motel T, the little root beer stand on Fourteenth Street, how it opened the day Lindbergh flew the Atlantic, and all the trouble they had with the root beer mugs cracking so loudly you could hear them across the street—memories of two American lives, of two who had pioneered as bravely as their westward-trekking grandparents and whose toil and faith, like theirs, had brought forth substance from the American dream, had helped keep the dream alive, so that it might be dreamed again.

Chapter Twenty-three

On a chilly, windy April afternoon, Bill and Allie, Bill Jr. and Dick and their families, and Marriott corporate executives officially opened the first of three Marriott Great America theme parks at Santa Clara, 40 miles down the Peninsula from San Francisco (the second would open at Gurnee, north of Chicago, in May).

Only a few knew the crises that Bill and Allie had weathered in the last seven months. During these months he had suffered four heart attacks and had been in intensive care units in four hospitals. These crises had buffeted and exhausted them; and to their friends they were a brave and inspiring sight as they sat on the speakers' platform, hats and overcoats on, smiling and chatting with Santa Clara city officials. Bill and Allie were there from Arizona because it was an eventful day in company history, because after all these years they still got a thrill out of openings, and because—well, they wouldn't have missed it for the world.

The scene was one of movement, bustle, excitement, anticipation. Bright pavilion banners snapped in the west wind. A military band played jauntily beside the platform. Before the platform stretched a reflecting pool several hundred feet long, lined by the olive trees, walks, benches, and lamp posts of Carousel Plaza, already filling with thousands of the festive opening-day throng. At the pool's far end rose the majestic, white and gilt, double-decked carousel named Columbia, world's largest, with its more than a hundred carved and painted lions, tigers, cats, ostriches, camels, pigs, and horses to ride, and a sky-piercing spire 10 stories high. On all sides of the pool and carousel extended the park's 200 acres—its shops and boutiques, its theaters and restaurants, its heritage-evoking replicas of early and country America, its aerial trams, flume boats, Ferris wheel, plunging roller coasters, and some thirty other thrill rides, all free for the single price of admission.

When Bill was introduced, his voice came over the loud speakers as firm and strong as ever.

"Your great thrill is going to be the rides. My great thrill is to see this wonderful park finished. One of the strongest needs in America today is a place—lots of places—that will bring the families of our country together, where they can laugh and play together, where the rides and the entertainment are good, and the food is good, and they don't cost a week's pay.

"That's what we're trying to bring you with this park and the others like it that we're going to open. We hope it gives you many fun-filled hours, and a deeper appreciation of the heritage that has made this the greatest country on earth. Have a good time, and come back soon."

The symbolic moment of the opening arrived: the starting of Columbia. Bill and Allie stepped to the left of the podium, to a tall, ratcheted lever resembling the grip on a San Francisco cable car and wired to activate the merry-go-round's controls. Allie grasped the lever with her right hand, Bill with his left. Leaning on it together, they pushed it slowly forward. In the distance, the lights of the carousel came up slowly. Its calliope and drums, cymbals and bells began to play. Bill and Allie stood back and clapped and the throng around the reflecting pool waved and cheered as the two levels of the great carousel began to turn.

If it hadn't been 1976, that might have been enough. But since it was, there was another occasion that nothing, not even doctor's orders, could keep Bill away from: the celebration of America's 200th birthday. Two days after the Santa Clara opening, he returned to Camelback and his semiweekly check-up and treadmill exercises at the Arizona Heart Institute in Phoenix. He still carried nitroglycerin pills and always traveled with oxygen handy. On May 10, he was back in his office on River Road, taking control of arrangements for the Honor America program at Kennedy Center on the night of July 3, when President Ford would signal the opening of the two-day national Bicentennial holiday.

It was the seventh year of Bill's chairmanship of the American Historical and Cultural Society, which had sponsored and produced the Honor America Days, and of all its programs, the historic occasion made this the most significant. Twenty-two hundred friends and guests of the society crowded into the Concert Hall for a soaring tribute to America by stage and television personalities and for the singing of stirring hymns and anthems by the Mormon Tabernacle Choir—coordinated to almost the last detail by Bill personally in weeks of committee conferences and production sessions. Comedian Bob Hope and the Rev. Billy Graham were there to speak, as they had been at the first, unforgettable Honor America day program at the Lincoln Memorial in 1970.

Bill's message was characteristically brief and to the point, nine short paragraphs.

"Our purpose—our only purpose—in organizing 'Honor America Day,' " he said, "has been to rekindle the spirit of patriotism and respect for individual liberties, which have made America great. We want to demonstrate to the world that, despite its imperfections, America is still the greatest country on earth—'A land choice above all others.' "

In sounding the keynote of the Bicentennial celebration, President Ford stressed not the excitement of the present, but the promise of the future: "Here we are on the eve of our 200th, the greatest Fourth of July any of us will ever live to see. . . . Let's look to the third century as the century in which freedom finds fulfillment in even greater creativity and individuality."

President and Mrs. Ford and Bill and Allie, in accordance with stage directions, were seated on the stage for the first portion of the program. When the President finished speaking, they left the platform for the President's box at the rear of the hall. The program was scheduled to end with the choir and audience singing "The Battle Hymn of the Republic." But first, to Bill's surprise, Vice-chairman Leonard H. Marks stepped to the microphone. Two of Bill's grandsons, Stephen and John, in their Eagle Scout uniforms, materialized from the wings. Attendants bore to the center of the stage, on a table, a white bisque porcelain statue of a pair of spirited horses in full gallop. It was called "Wild Mustangs" and had been fashioned by the Boehm Studio of Trenton, New Jersey.

"Our program tonight," said Marks, "hailed the heroes of yesteryear, patriots who had vision and determination to carry out the spirit of '76. But now I want to salute a patriot of 1976—a man who would have distinguished himself with the Founding Fathers had he been born 200 years earlier—a man in whom the fires of loyalty to country burn brightly—J. Willard Marriott, the founding chairman of the Honor America Committee."

Marks said that the members of the committee wanted publicly to recognize "his wise leadership and uncompromising zeal to achieve perfection," and so were presenting him with the Boehm porcelain. "Now, Steve and Johnnie," he said, "go find your grandpa." The boys carried the statue from the stage, and as the audience rose to its feet a spotlight played across the crowd and came to rest on Bill, standing in the President's box, next to the President and close to President Spencer W. Kimball of the Mormon Church. His simplicity, his modesty, the man he was, the good things he had done and stood for in Washington over the past fifty years, suddenly touched the hearts of the people there. Their warmth and love went out to him, and the applause went on and on, as though it would never stop.

At 10:30 the next morning, a beautifully sunny Fourth, Bill again stood by the President's side, this time on the broad speakers' platform outside Independence Hall in Philadelphia. The President, accompanied by his daughter, Susan, had flown by helicopter to Valley Forge for an earlier ceremony, then back to Philadelphia. Bill, because he wanted to fly up to New York first and see the Bicentennial parade of Tall Ships from the air, had chartered a Lear jet and had flown with Allie and White House staffer Warren Hendricks to Philadelphia International Airport. There they were met by a limousine and motorcycle escort provided by Mayor Frank L. Rizzo, to see that they made it to Independence Hall on time.

Master of ceremonies Charlton Heston, the movie star, and Governor Milton J. Schapp, Mayor Rizzo, Marian Anderson, the singer, and scores of other dignitaries were there on the platform. As bands played and a vast expectant hubbub swelled about them, they looked out across Independence Mall on an incredible sight— flags waving and a red, white, and blue dazzle of bunting and banners, and on the Mall itself an exuberant Fourth of July throng of 500,000 with thousands more on rooftops, bus roofs, stone walls, and jamming the streets leading to the Mall and Independence Square.

On the dot of the scheduled starting time of 10:30, the U.S. Armed Forces Bicentennial Bank Chorus launched into "The Star-Spangled Banner," and the program that the New York *Times* called "the centerpiece of the Bicentennial observance" was under way. There were prayers, a pageant of flags, a solemn, half-million throated Pledge of Allegiance from the great assemblage. Mayor Rizzo and Governor Schapp spoke, and Marian Anderson read excerpts from the Declaration of Independence, ratified in the red brick hall behind her, 200 years ago to the day.

Bill was one of three Americans chosen to speak on the subject "What America Means to Me." The others were General Daniel James, Jr., USAF, commander-in-chief of the North American Air Defense Command and the nation's highest ranking black military officer, and Miss Lenne Jo Hallgren, America's Junior Miss, 1976.

Bill, in dark suit and tie and white shirt, spoke first. Reserves of inner strength, ingrained courage, and iron-willed discipline rode roughshod over the effects of the punishing ills of the last year, and his voice came confident and firm from the loudspeakers of the Mall. He could never identify or measure the feelings that swept over him as he read from the six-by-nine typescript on the lectern before him, the mixture of pride and humility, the religious gratitude, the love of country, and love of family and life itself. "Sometimes," he said later, "it was hard to keep going."

His speech was only five minutes long. Network television cameras and microphones moved in to catch every gesture, every inflection. In swift review he mentioned his pioneer grandparents crossing the plains to Utah, his boyhood years in Marriott Settlement, peddling woolen goods in the lumber camps of the Northwest, his marriage to Allie and their model-T honeymoon to Washington, and how they opened the little root beer stand that now was a billion-dollar-a-year business employing 60,000 Americans, serving millions of meals a day, catering to airlines all over the world, operating hotels, cruise ships, and now Marriott's Great America theme parks in Illinois and California.

314

"America didn't give me a dole when I was broke, but she did give me some valuable assets—freedom and the opportunity to work and the right to worship God in my own way."

He read them the poem "Trees" because it captured and expressed "the philosophy which has characterized my life: 'Good timber does not grow in ease./The stronger the wind, the tougher the trees.' "

The finest things in life, he said, were the Golden Rule, work, and one's religion. They build character and good habits and a good family life, "without which there is little happiness or real success in this rich and blessed land of ours.

"I was a poor boy, as Mr. Heston reminded us," he concluded, "but America offered me freedom—an opportunity to work and the right to pray. And that, Mr. President"—he turned momentarily to President Ford, then back to the throng—"is why I love America."

When the program at Independence Hall was over, there was a luncheon for the President's party, the Governor, the Mayor, and other dignitaries at the Bellevue-Stratford Hotel. Bill and Allie arrived there in their limousine, with the Presidential motorcade.

Bill told the driver to wait, and followed Allie inside. They were not staying for the luncheon, but wanted to pay parting respects to the President and their hosts. Afterward, they made their way back through the noisy and crowded lobby to their car. Bill glanced at his watch. Twelve-fourteen. The Lear jet would be ready to leave.

The chauffeur stood beside the open door of the limousine. Bill helped Allie in, and slid beside her.

"Where to, sir?"

"The airport, please."

They would take a short flight up to New York, a swing around the harbor to look down on the carrier *Forrestal* and the Bicentennial procession of Tall Ships sailing up the Hudson, then back down to Washington to say good-bye to the Mormon Tabernacle Choir. Then to Garfield Street for a nap, and finally to the Key Bridge Marriott to watch, from a suite they'd reserved on the tenth floor, the Bicentennial fireworks the city was shooting off, after dark, over the Washington Monument. With a schedule like this, there was no time to lose.

In the car Bill reached for Allie's hand and found it. He looked out the windows at the holiday crowd and all the cars. He sat erect and alert, eager to get moving to his waiting jet.

"And don't get held up in this traffic," he said. "We've got a lot to do before the day is over."

Epilogue
"Reminiscing"

In the late afternoon of a day in February 1976, in the paneled living room of Jackrabbit Casa, where Bill and Allie stayed when they were at Camelback Inn in Scottsdale, Bill sat back in an overstuffed reclining chair to one side of the fireplace. From there he could look out the big picture window to the sloping back lawn, where doves and wrens fluttered about the feeder, and half a dozen quail and cottontails criss-crossed the slope in their endless quest for a late snack. Allie sat near Bill, fingers busy on a needlepoint piano-bench cover for Nancy. At their backs, another larger picture window framed looming Camelback, distant Phoenix, and the even more distant Salt River Mountains.

Certain things—endings, some of them; others beginnings—stood out against the months and years just past. For instance, Bill had received one of the annual Horatio Alger awards of the American Schools and Colleges Association, and Allie had become one of the first women in the University of Utah's history to receive an honorary degree, that of Doctor of Humane Letters—public recognition not only well deserved but long overdue in the judgment of those who knew her as a mother, as a friend, as a church and community leader, as co-founder of the Hot Shoppes, and as Bill's loyal and loving partner, in every sense of the word.

The new, $16-million, white marble Washington Temple, rising on a wooded hillside near Kensington, Maryland, above the Capitol Beltway, was finally finished and dedicated. In the six weeks between completion and dedication ceremonies, more than 750,000 visitors toured the six-spired edifice, inspecting its sealing and ordinance rooms, its great assembly rooms, the massive baptismal font supported by twelve cast-iron oxen, the tall, narrow windows of richly colored glass, the immense mural of the Second Coming of Christ in the broad, ground-floor reception hall. Bill, who had contributed the mural to the temple, in addition to a sizable gift to the temple building fund, had suggested that the artist paint the new temple into the mural's background. Sure enough, it was there. "Are you implying that the millennium will begin in Washington?" a visitor asked him. Bill had smiled. "Why not? What better place is there?"

But in all those months what stood out the most began happening on Monday, August 25, 1975, in New Hampshire. While walking in the woods Bill felt the warning chest pains, light at first, flickering through his chest like lightning before a storm. He took a nitroglycerine pill and they went away. But they came back worse the next day. Three nitroglycerines, one after the other, had no effect. Allie called the ambulance which drove him to Huggins Hospital in Wolfboro. The previous year, Bill had contributed an intensive care room to the hospital's new addition. Ironically, it had never been used as one because the hospital couldn't afford the seven extra nurses it took to staff it.

In the next two-and-a-half months, Bill had three more attacks, plus a near-fatal reaction to heavy medication prescribed for his heart condition. He traveled in succession by ambulance to Massachusetts General Hospital in Boston; by ambulance plane to Georgetown Hospital in Washington; and again by ambulance plane to Mayo Clinic in Minnesota. No doctor who treated him believed he'd ever see another Christmas.

Yet, miraculously, he had. And here he was, on a perfect afternoon of the next February, in 1976. He was in a relaxed and reminiscent mood. He felt like talking about things that had happened, not in any particular order, but as they drifted across his mind—things he was proud of, good times, exciting times, his feelings about work and religion and the full life he looked forward to.

About his survival

I am certain that the power of prayer made it possible for me to come through these heart attacks alive. Many friends and church members were praying for me all the time, especially the Council of the Twelve Apostles in the temple at Salt Lake City. President Kimball called Allie twice to see how I was getting along, and the last time, when all the doctors had just about given up hope, he said, "We had a prayer circle for Bill. Tell him that he is going to live and fill out his mission on earth."

I never worried after that. I knew he was a prophet of God and was speaking with authority. I also felt I had constructive things to do with the rest of my life—to give guidance to my sons and their great staff with its 60,000 employes; to see them and their families mature as respectable, worthwhile individuals capable of bringing to the affairs of their community and nation a renewal of the kind of spiritual character that made this country great.

About the Marriott Activities Center at BYU

Dr. Ernest Wilkinson, Ben Lewis, and Ken Garff, among my closest friends, mentioned the cultural center BYU was building on its campus and said that the university would be most grateful if I would help them build the largest indoor activity center on any campus in America.

Well, I thought this would be a great investment for the future, because it would provide so many on-going services for BYU, which I consider the greatest university in America for developing morality and religion in the lives of its students. So I made a substantial contribution, and the university generously named it the Marriott Center.

One of life's biggest satisfactions for me was the dedication of this beautiful building by my close friend for many years, Harold B. Lee, President of the Church. And one of the great thrills I still get is when I go out there to a basketball game or any other function, and they announce that I'm there, and the whole student body, 24,000 strong, stands up and cheers for several minutes.

It's most unfortunate that more young men and women can't attend BYU. More than any other school I know of, it not only educates; it builds character.

About the restaurant and hotel business
The service business is very rewarding. It makes a big contribution to society. A good meal away from home, a good bed, friendly treatment from those who come in contact with our customers—these are all so important. It's important to make people away from home feel at home and feel that they're among friends and are really wanted. When they come to our restaurants and hotels, we try to treat them well enough that they'll come back, and I think most of them do.

About the three most important things in life
One is being born right. I mean by that with goodly parents, in a good land, where there is freedom of worship, freedom to do the things one wants to do; where work and effort will earn a young man or woman an opportunity for an education, an opportunity to develop his or her talents and make a completely successful life, in whatever area he or she desires.

Number two is being married right, marrying someone who is congenial and has character and integrity, and

320

who desires a family life. Building a strong family life is one of our most difficult obligations. But nothing will bring more happiness or success.

Third, good habits, and protecting our health the best we know how. This will not only lengthen our lives; it will prepare us for death. Life after death? I'm certain that there is one—just as certain as I am that I'm alive at this moment.

About Allie

My wife, Allie, is undoubtedly the most important asset in my life. She has had the same faith and ideals that I've had. I must give her credit for rearing my two sons. I've had such a busy life in business and civic work and church affairs that I had little time for our family. But she's taken care of our home admirably—always with the boys when they were at home, teaching them, helping them with their lessons, encouraging them, helping them build the kind of character she has herself.

About the 1973 inauguration

There was a tremendous crowd in front of the Capitol, hundreds of newsmen and cameramen in front of us during the swearing-in-ceremony. After the ceremony the President invited Allie and me and his family and relatives and the Vice President and leaders of Congress to a luncheon in the Capitol.

When we emerged from the Capitol the chief of police rode in the first car, Allie and I rode in the second car, and the President and his party followed us. We started at the Capitol and went down Constitution Avenue into Pennsylvania Avenue and to the White House. Thousands of people lined the street, and all the windows of the buildings were filled with people. There were a lot of troublemakers, rioters, and hippies along the sidelines

*throwing bottles, rotten apples, and rocks. One rock
landed in Allie's lap, but it didn't hurt either one of us.
Police stood arm in arm all the way down the avenue
with the National Guard in case any riots or violence
disturbed the parade.*

*The parade was really fabulous. It was so well
coordinated and planned that there was no space
between any of the bands or the floats or other units. The
complete parade, passing a given point, was supposed to
last not more than 45 minutes, and it actually took only
43 minutes to pass the reviewing stand and the President.*

*Later on, I visited with President Ford and talked with
him about the inauguration. He asked me if I'd like to
stay on for the next one, if he was elected. I told him I
thought two inaugurations were enough for one man. He
asked if I'd help out with the preparations and I said "Of
course, Mr. President." I had had my office working with
the General Services Administration since May, planning
and remodeling a building to house 4,000 volunteers, so
the space was all furnished and would be ready for the
next inaugural.*

By now the fire was burning low. Bill poked it up,
sending showers of sparks snapping into the chimney. The
sun had gone down. One at a time, the quail and the rabbits were leaving the back lawn. Allie turned on a bridge
lamp, so she could continue her needlepoint.

Bill said one of the things he missed the most since being laid up was horseback riding. Ironic, wasn't it, he said,
that here he was in Arizona, in the great open spaces, and
he couldn't ride a horse because the doctor told him not
to. The doctor didn't think his heart could take it—not
now, anyway. He used to go on hunting and fishing trips
almost every year, either in Utah or the Jackson Hole
country, he and Hugh Colton, with Roland Parry or Ken
Garff.

About pack trips, broken ribs, and mountain trout

Yes, we had great old times in those days. One summer Hugh Colton arranged a pack trip through the Uintas, in the northern corner of Utah. We had thoroughbred pack horses and good riding horses and a guide, a wrangler and cook who'd been living with the Paiutes for 30 years.

We rode through tremendous snowbanks and saw some beautiful scenery and the deer would be close to our camps. One thing I'll never forget was when we forded a stream once and the guide said, "Do you want some trout?" I said, "Yes," and he waded to a stone in the middle of the creek, reached under the stone with his hand, and pulled out a big rainbow that must have weighed three pounds. He said, "Do you want some more?" and I said, "Sure do," and he went to another rock and did the same thing two more times. He caught three beautiful rainbows—with his hands. I'd never seen anything like it. "How'd you do that?" I asked. He said, "I tickle their bellies."

We had some great times that trip—great fishing, wonderful meals cooked over a campfire, good horses, beautiful scenery. Roland Parry was with us. He'd brought his ukulele, and we all sang together as we rode through the timber, and at night we sat around the campfire singing "There's a Long Long Trail," "Sleepy Time Gal," "With Someone Like You"—songs like that. We called our group the Hum-Drummers, and even had our own little song book printed for ourselves and our friends.

It was a great trip. I've always intended to go back to the Uintas. But it's been a busy life. So I never have.

A day or so later, at about the same time of day, maybe a little earlier, Bill and I went for a walk. We walked down Mummy Mountain Road to Desert Fairways Drive and then cut through somebody's yard, scattering quail as we went. It was chilly, in the high fifties. Bill wore a turtleneck, a heavy shirt, and a sweater over that. I asked him if he'd started out with the idea or the ambition to make a million dollars or build an empire:

No, not at all. I just had three general ideas in mind, all equally important. One was to render friendly service to our guests. The second was to provide quality food at a fair price. The third was to work as hard as I could, day and night, to make a profit.

When we added more Hot Shoppes, it wasn't just to get bigger, to spread out over the city and countryside. It was to build up a pool of capable, dependable employes who knew our ways of doing business and liked to work for us. Then, when we added the In-Flite service and the hotels and the specialty restaurants, it was a natural and logical extension of what we were already doing and knew how to do.

Also, I wanted to grow for other reasons. I wanted to reap the rewards of growth: jobs for more employes, money to take care of my family and to contribute to good causes. On top of that, we needed to diversify, and for this we needed different kinds of food service to satisfy a larger segment of society. There's a lot to be said for diversification. "Don't put all your eggs in one basket," they say. There's wisdom in that. If business slumps in one division, there are other divisions to carry it through. All businesses fluctuate. Diversification takes care of it.

You might not think so, but there are just as many opportunities for a young fellow starting out in life today as there were back in the '20s when I started out. Not on a little, one-man basis, but in big companies. Big companies today need executives badly. He ought to look at some of the big companies and pick a good one and learn the business from the ground up—get into an established business where he doesn't go through the hell

324

you go through when you start your own company, with all the worry and anxiety and the failure. He'd have security and a chance for big money, if he pays attention to his work. Nothing is so disturbing in life as insecurity.

Where would I head for? Well, there are opportunities in the restaurant business, the franchise business—but the field is crowded. Same with hotels. I'd look at something big, with a future. Energy, perhaps. There's a great need there.

But I don't know, if it were me, maybe I'd be a rancher. I like the cattle and sheep business. It's not too profitable, but if you take care of it, you can do pretty well. And it's a good life—round-ups and the winter range, visiting with the sheepherders, eating Mulligan stew around the campfire, time for a little hunting and fishing, moving on every week or so, after the sheep have grazed the area.

Whatever I did, I'd figure on doing a first-class job. I'd work day and night. I don't have much use for anyone getting by on a 40-hour week, as I've said before. The man who wants to build and make a contribution in the business world mustn't neglect his family or his church, but he can't lead a "vacation life."

I'm not saying that you shouldn't have any recreation or time off, but it should be respected and used properly— not wasted on cocktail parties and other things that are unproductive. Some men work in the house or in the garden, or spend time with the family—sure, that's good. But the other way—what's that saying? "Free time is the devil's workshop"? That's the way it goes. Kids who don't use their time properly take to hanging around the drugstore or the filling station. First thing you know, they're in trouble.

What am I going to do in the next ten or fifteen years? Well, I'll be 76 in September, and I'm temporarily kind of laid up, but I can tell you one thing: I don't expect to sit

*around and keep on getting old and have nothing to do.
The worst thing in the world is to retire at 65, then sit
around and do nothing. You see men like that, and
women, too, at resorts—eating too much, drinking too
much, playing cards, wasting away the rest of their lives.*

*That's not the way I'm going to do it. I'm going to use
my time constructively, doing something worthwhile.
Fortunately, I'm in an interesting business, and my
position is only as strenuous as I want to make it. I'm
going to advise our management. I'll visit our restaurants
and hotels and see that they're run properly. I'll keep
active in my church. I'm going to ride with cattle again.
I'm going to the mountains again, back to the Jackson
Hole country, if the doctors and Allie will let me.*

*A man should keep on being constructive, and do
constructive things, until it's time to die. He should take
part in the things that go on in this wonderful world. He
should be someone to be reckoned with. He should live
life and make every day count, to the very end. It takes
push and discipline. Sometimes it's tough. But that's
what I'm going to do.*

Index

Brown, Phyllis (Mrs. Russell
  Marriott), 189
Buick, children scratched
  initials in, 58
"Building for Strength," Weber
  College commencement
  address, 240
Burlington, Vermont, 75-77
Bushnell, George and Laura, 75,
  87, 171-72
Buxbaum, Martin, 136

Cafeterias: industrial, 198-99,
  213, 225; hotel, 208; public,
  208; at National Airport, 220
Cafritz, Mr. and Mrs. Morris,
  230
Camelback Inn, 292, 311, 317
Campbell, Glen, 300
Candland, Harold A., 164, 185,
  199
Cannon, Jack, 128-29
Cannon, Judith (Mrs. Woodrow
  Marriott), 181-82, 185
Carthage, Illinois, 20-21
Casper, Billy, 298
Chaplains, Mormon, 208, 272
Cherry Creek, Nevada, 99
Chesapeake and Potomac
  Telephone Company, 136,
  234, 250
China, Allie Marriott's
  collection of, 215
Chinatown, 66
Christensen, Joseph A., 120
Christian, George, 284-85
Church of Jesus Christ of
  Latter-day Saints: founding
  of, 16-21; Bill Marriott's work
  in, 72-93, 205, 208, 250; Word
  of Wisdom of, 208-9;
  Washington Temple of,
  317-18
Clark, J. Reuben, Jr. 208
Clay, General Lucius, 274
Cleveland, Governor's
  Conference in, 259

Colechester, Vermont, 81
Colton, Don B., 86, 111
Colton, Hugh, 111-12, 132-33,
  209, 251, 253, 322-23
Commencement exercises,
  Weber College, 239-40;
  Brigham Young University,
  241-42; University of Utah,
  273
Commissary, Upshur Street,
  194, 206
Connecticut Avenue Hot
  Shoppe, 140
Cowley, Matthew, 208
Cronkite, Walter, 257
Cushing, George, 107-8
Cushwa, Betty, 269
Custis, George Washington
  Parke, 227

Dallas Marriott, 245
Daly, Richard J., 273
Daniels, John S., 156, 165, 224
Davis, Nelson, 246
Dean, Max, 254
Denton, Mervel, 13
Deseret, Utah Territory called,
  39
DeVries, Dr. Walter, 278
Dewey, Thomas E., 274
Dirksen, Senator Everett, 274
Dixon, Henry Aldous, 237-38
Doctor's Hospital, 216, 280
Doud, Mrs. John, 232
Durbin, Jim, 261-62, 263, 308

Eisenhower, Dwight D., 13, 274;
  election of, 220-21; at
  Fairfield Farm, 231-32;
  thanks Bill for hat, 232; Bill
  visits, in White House, 248;
  Bill visits, in hospital, 283
Eisenhower, Mamie, 232, 248
Election returns, watching, 157,
  251
Emerson, Ralph Waldo: on
  Mormon Church, 80-81;

329

from memoirs of, 41;
reminiscences of, 43-45; death
of, 289
Marriott, Elizabeth Stewart,
22, 25-26
Marriott, Esther Amelia, 29
Marriott, Eva (Mrs. Harold A.
Candland), 34, 44, 45, 47, 92,
95, 164, 185
Marriott, Helen, 34, 43, 45, 47,
120
Marriott, Hyrum Willard,
14-15, 29, 35-36, 44-51, 58,
89-90, 98, 185-89
Marriott, John, 15, 22, 25-30
Marriott, J. Willard (Bill):
addresses Los Angeles
Marriott employees, 8-11;
office of, 12-13; learns to ride
a horse, 30; has typhoid fever,
32; birth of, 43; fire in
childhood home of, 46;
organizes Marriott children
to thin beets, harvest lettuce,
47-49; helps herd sheep,
51-52; kills rattlesnake, 53;
kills bears, 54-57; drives
family car, 58-59; goes to San
Francisco exposition, 63-69;
takes sheep to Omaha, 69-71;
as Mormon missionary, 72-
88; heals injured girl, 78-80;
driven out of church by mob
while on mission, 82-84; visits
Washington, D.C., after
mission, 87-88; preaches
following mission, 92-93; at
Weber College, 93-94; sells
woolen goods, 96-98, 105;
herds sheep in Nevada, 98-
104; at University of Utah,
105-6; meets Alice (Allie)
Sheets, 107-9; works at
Weber College, 109; decides
to open A&W stand in
Washington, 109-11; opens

first A&W stand, 114-16; tries
to collect from woolen mill,
117-18; turned down on loan
by bank, 118-19; marries, 119-
20; honeymoon trip of, 120-
21; opens second A&W stand,
124; adds hot foods in stores,
127-30; buys out Hugh
Colton, 133; loses law suit,
151; has Hodgkins disease,
160; healed through blessing
of elders of Church, 161-62;
moves to Senator Smoot's
mansion, 163; Salt Lake
Tribune article about, 176,
209-10; Madison (Maine)
Bulletin article about, 177-78;
trip of, to Mexico, 201, 204;
called to stake position in
church, 205, 208; featured in
Look, 211; has hepatitis, 216;
buys farm in Virginia, 217-20;
awards of, 226; entertains
President Eisenhower, 231-
32; works for Eisenhower
inaugural, 233; vacations in
Puerto Rico, 234-35; speaks
at Weber College
commencement, 239-41;
receives honorary doctorates,
241-42, 273; has lung disease,
246-47; visits Eisenhower at
White House, 248; travels
around the world, 253; writes
letter to Bill Jr., 268-69; as
George Romney's fund-
raising chairman, 258, 274,
276; quoted on George
Romney's qualifications, 279;
has heart attacks,
279-80, 318; gives receptions
for George Romney, 282; has
burst blood vessel in brain,
289; 1969 inaugural
chairman, 293; gives money
for University of Utah

library, 295; heads Fourth of
July Honor America
program, 297-301; 1973
inaugural chairman, 302-5;
gives money to BYU for
activities center, 305-7; at
Great America park opening,
309-10; heads Bicentennial
program, 310-16; speaks at
Independence Hall, 314-15;
receives Horatio Alger award,
317; gives mural to
Washington Temple, 317-18;
reminiscences of, 317-26
Marriott, John Willard III, 312
Marriott, Julie Anne, 281
Marriott, Kathryn (Kay) (Mrs.
Ferdinand Kaufholz), 34, 44,
47, 95, 164, 215
Marriott Library at University
of Utah, 295-96
Marriott, Margaret, 29
Marriott, Mary Alice, 298
Marriott, Nancy. *See* Peery,
Nancy
Marriott, Paul, 34, 44, 47, 72, 92,
95, 106, 159, 185, 197, 216, 224,
268; involvement of, with
in-flight catering, 184, 189,
200, 225; becomes executive
vice-president of Marriott
corporation, 205
Marriott, Rebecca, 215
Marriott, Richard. *See*
Marriott, Dick
Marriott, Russell, 34, 47, 72,
174, 185, 189-90, 197, 216
Marriott, Sandra, 281
Marriott Settlement, 14-15
Marriott, Sherman, 110
Marriott, Stephen, 245, 281, 312
Marriott, Susanna, 26
Marriott, Trezer, 29
Marriott, Woodrow, 34, 44, 72,
174, 181-82, 185, 189, 197, 216,
268

Marshall, James, 217
Mather, Richard, 78
Mather, Ruth, 78-80
Mayo Clinic, 238-39, 246, 318
McCune, George W., 74, 86
McIntosh, Robert J., 276, 278
McKay, David O., 221
Meany, George, 298
Merrill, Dina, 246
Mexico, 201, 203-4
Miami, Florida, 236, 280
Mighty Mo fast-foods business,
225
Miller, William P., 239
Miner, Gil, 177-78
Missionary, Bill Marriott's
experiences as a, 72-93
Mitchell, Don G., 263, 304
Moore, Colonel and Mrs.
Gordon, 232
Moosehead Lake, Maine, 161
Mormon Church. *See* Church of
Jesus of Latter-day Saints
Mormon Tabernacle Choir, 294,
296, 311, 316
Morris, Ellen. *See* Marriott,
Ellen Morris
Morris, Elizabeth Hamblin,
37-39
Morris, Harriett, 37
Morris, Kate, 41
Morris, Russell, 24-25, 33
Morris, William, 22, 37, 39
Mugs, breaking of, in hot water,
131

National Restaurant
Association, 205, 208
National Symphony, 230
Nauvoo, Illinois, 20, 302
Nauvoo Restoration project, 272
Nelson, Ed, 96
Nevada, herding sheep in,
98-104
New Christy Minstrels, 300
New Hampshire, 281, 282, 318

Rosslyn project, 235, 236. *See also* Key Bridge motor hotel
Rowlett, Louise, 176-77
Roy Rogers restaurants, 292
Running boys, symbol of Hot Shoppes, 135-36
Russell, Ellen Blackwood, 37
Russell, John, 37-38
Russia, trip to, 233

Salt Lake Theatre, 108
Salt Lake *Tribune,* 176, 209
Sams, Earl, 171-73, 192-94, 214
Sams, Lula, 214
San Francisco, California, 60, 66-69, 259
Sanborn, Mabel Young, 216
Saturday Evening Post, 211, 257
Savage, Mrs. Ethel, 168, 197
Schapp, Milton, 313
Schlusemeier, William E., 230
Scott, Hugh, 278
Scranton, William W., 258-59, 278
Shaller, Brigadier General H. H., 262
Sheen, Bishop Fulton J., 300
Sheepherding, Bill Marriott's experiences with, 52-54, 99-104
Sheets, Alice (Mrs. J. Willard Marriott). *See* Marriott, Alice Sheets
Sheets, Alice Taylor (Mrs. Reed Smoot), 12, 223, 232, 253; marriage of, to Senator Reed Smoot, 143-44; honeymoons at White House, 144-46; death of, 254-55
Sheets, Walter, 195
Shettler, Mary, 108
Shore, Dinah, 300
Shotgun, Bill's gift of, to President Eisenhower, 247, 248

Siedman, William, 278
Sirloin and Saddle restaurants, 245, 254
Skelton, Red, 300
Slaterville, Utah, 23, 30-31
Smith, George Albert, 216
Smith, Joseph, story of, 16-21
Smith, Kate, 299
Smoot, Alice Sheets. *See* Sheets, Alice Taylor
Smoot, Senator Reed, 87, 142, 148-49; marriage of, to Alice Taylor Sheets, 143-44; honeymoons at White House, 144-46; loses election, 157-58; death of, 195-96
Soda pop, Bill pays brothers and sisters in, 47-49
Speed reading, 249-50
St. Alban's, 215
St. Thomas, Virgin Isles, 235
Stamford, Connecticut, 85
Standart, Mr., 117-18
Stanger, Glenn, 30-31
Statler, E.M., quotation from, 139
Statue of Brigham Young in Capitol Rotunda, 215-16
Stephens, Tom, 248
Stevenson, Adlai, 220
Stewart, Isaac and June, 148, 157, 221
Stock, Marriott corporation: goes public, 223; rise of, 225; splits two-for-one, 251, 292
Stockholders' meetings, 268-69, 283
Stunz, Mr. (Park Savings Bank), 133, 152-53
Survival, reminiscing about, 319
Symphony, National, 230

Tanner, T.W., 75-84
Taylor, John, 21
Theme parks, 304, 309-10
Thomas, Elbert D., 158

Three most important things in
life, 320-21
Time magazine, 257, 277
Titus, Dr. E.W., 157
Toronto, Canada, 246
Tracy, Aaron W., 93-94, 95, 109,
239
Train, taking sheep on, 63-66,
69-71
Trees, poem about, 11, 315
Truman, Harry S., 207, 298
Twin Bridges motor hotel,
226-30

University of Utah, 98, 256; Bill
Marriott's graduation from,
106; Allie's graduation from,
116; Dick and Nancy
Marriott graduate from, 256;
Marriott Library at, 295-96
Upshur Street commissary, 194,
206
U.S. Armed Forces
Bicentennial Bank Chorus,
313
U.S. News & World Report, 275
Utah Territory, 40, 43

Vandenburg, Arthur S., 146
Van Dusen, Richard, 278
Vietnam, 283, 284-86
Vinson, Fred M., 220-21
Virginia, looking for ranch land
in, 217
Volpe, John, 304

Walter Reed Hospital, 283
Ward, Bud, 7, 11
Wasatch Mountains, 12, 22, 251
Washington, D.C., 87, 120, 148,
207
Washington Monument, 300
Washington Post, 273, 279, 284
Washington Restaurant
Association, 181

Washington Stake, 205, 208, 250
Washington *Star,* 226-27
Washington Temple, 317-18
Watergate, 307
Watkins, Senator Arthur, 230
Wayne, John, 8
Weber Canyon, 22-23
Weber College, 93-95, 109, 238;
commencement address at,
239-40; honorary degree from,
298
Wesley Heights. *See* Garfield
Street home
Westmoreland, General, 286
"What America Means to Me"
speech, 314-15
White House, honeymoon at,
144-47
White House Caterers, 106
Whiteford, Roger, 151, 154-55,
168, 221, 223, 224
Whitehurst, Captain H.C., 229
Widtsoe, Dr. John A., 205
Wilbur, Dr. Ray Lyman,
quotation from, 240
Wilcox, Sid, 224
"Wild Mustangs," statue, 312
Wilkins, Roy, 298
Wilkinson, Ernest L., 205, 238,
241, 319
Willey, Robert, 139-40
Wolfboro, New Hampshire, 318
Wood, Evelyn, 249-50
Woods, Bill, 199-200
Woolen goods, experiences in
selling, 95-98
World's Fair, San Francisco, 61,
67-68

Young, Brigham: quotation
from, defining Zion, 15;
quotation from, concerning
Salt Lake Valley, 16; statue
of, in Capital rotunda, 215-16
Young, Mahonri, 216